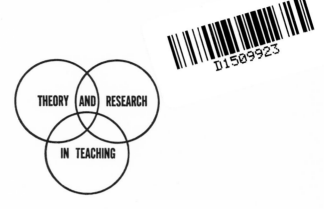

Teachers College, Columbia University
Arno A. Bellack, editor

Recent years have witnessed a resurgence of interest on the part of educational researchers in the teaching process. Volumes in the *Theory and Research in Teaching* series report significant studies of instructional procedures in a variety of educational settings, at various organizational levels in the schools, and in many of the subjects included in the curriculum. These studies present fresh perspectives on teaching both to educational researchers and to practitioners in the schools.

Research into Classroom Processes

Recent Developments and Next Steps

Ian Westbury & Arno A. Bellack

Editors

TEACHERS COLLEGE PRESS

Teachers College, Columbia University

New York, 1971

Preface

This book grew out of a seminar conducted by the Department of Curriculum of the Ontario Institute for Studies in Education in Toronto during May, 1967. The seminar, which we called "Next Steps in Research into the Teaching Process," was a response to our feeling that there was little communication between researchers who were interested in teaching and teacher behavior. We felt that we knew less than we should about the varieties of theoretical orientation being brought to the asking of questions about the phenomenon of teaching, and we hoped that interaction between schools and workers could be improved by getting the questions onto the table in a free discussion. Only later did we connect our intentions with the work that one of us had done in 1962 in sponsoring the two Teachers College conferences that produced *Theory and Research in Teaching*. It is our hope now that by reporting in book form the papers and discussion at our 1967 conference we can show where research in teaching has been and suggest some of the directions in which it might go.

The papers by McClellan, Travers, and Adams were prepared for the seminar. Biddle presented a review of the research to 1967 to the seminar, but this has been published elsewhere (1967) and we did not feel justified in reprinting this now well-known paper. The remaining papers in this book had their beginnings as responses to the question "What are you doing?" that was asked again and again at the seminar. These additional papers were prepared during 1967–69. The discussion that is included in Part I is a version of a day and a half of questions and concerns: it is included here both as a way of highlighting the issues raised in the theoretical papers and as an illustration of the difficulty of some of these issues.

Inevitably the papers collected here show a considerable variety of problems and methods. They are drawn together by a common concern with teaching, but at times the links seem more tenuous than real. This heterogeneity is a reflection of the varieties of the research into classroom processes; we feel that this diversity is enriching. We are more concerned that we were not able to show the practical significance of even the taxonomic research we are reporting. We would, for example, have added, had we known of his work, a paper reporting the work of Dahllöf (1969).

Many people made this book possible. The contributors to the seminar (and all who attended contributed) made the seminar a success; the seminar inspired this book. Those who thought they were coming to Toronto to listen and were then persuaded to write are our chief creditors.

These writers mention, too, the financial support of a number of funding agencies. The seminar itself and much of the editorial work on the initial manuscripts were supported by the Department of Curriculum of the Ontario Institute for Studies in Education. Teachers College, Columbia University, gave us that extra moral and financial support that made it possible to finally bring off an idea.

We are particularly grateful to Marion D. Jenkinson, formerly chairman of the Department of Curriculum, O.I.S.E., for her real and sustaining help and encouragement, and to Arthur W. Foshay of Teachers College, whose help when we were planning what we might do was invaluable. Roald F. Campbell of the Department of Education, University of Chicago, helped one of us get through the horrors of the bibliography. Irene Anderson carried us through the unpleasant last phases of the enterprise. Mrs. Olga Dimitri brought a fine and rare skill to the manuscript; her editorial and organizational talents kept us to our duties after we had tired.

I. D. W.
A. A. B.

Contributors

RAYMOND S. ADAMS, Massey University, Palmerston North, New Zealand

MARIA BELGARD, Stanford Center for Research and Development in Teaching, Stanford University

ARNO A. BELLACK, Teachers College, Columbia University

BRUCE J. BIDDLE, University of Missouri

T. A. BIRKIN, James Cook University of North Queensland, Australia

JOHN B. CARROLL, Educational Testing Service

DARYL DELL, Stanford Research Institute

NED A. FLANDERS, University of Michigan

N. L. GAGE, Stanford Center for Research and Development in Teaching, Stanford University

JOHN R. GINTHER, The University of Chicago

ROBERT GLASER, Learning Research and Development Center, University of Pittsburgh

PAUL V. GUMP, University of Kansas

JACK H. HILLER, Night Vision Laboratory, United States Army

J. W. GEORGE IVANY, Teachers College, Columbia University

JAMES E. McCLELLAN, Temple University

BARAK ROSENSHINE, University of Illinois, Urbana

LOUIS M. SMITH, Washington University

EDMUND V. SULLIVAN, Ontario Institute for Studies in Education

ROBERT M. W. TRAVERS, Western Michigan University

W. R. UNRUH, University of Calgary

IAN WESTBURY, The University of Chicago

Contents

Part IV CONCLUSION

Fundamental Questions

ONE

Classroom-Teaching Research: A Philosophical Critique

JAMES E. McCLELLAN

I could make a better job of this critique if I knew a bit more about what's going on in classroom-teaching research itself, or if I had a clearer idea of what a philosophical critique should be, or if I were a better person. The last is relevant in a particular way to this project (as well as in a general way to any project), as I shall try to show at the end of my remarks.

Basic Conceptions

What is classroom-teaching research (CR)? How does it differ from other sorts of research? I should like to present a very simple-minded conception, the model for which was contained in a paper by Lewis Eigen (1963) which defined "programming" for a group not familiar with the word. Eigen's achievement was twofold: to establish the categories which (taken together) determine what programming literally *is*, while avoiding any substantive claims *about* programming. Thus one can use such "programming" terms as "frame," "cue," or "lag time" to speak metaphorically about anything. But if one uses these terms as variables for which values can be supplied, then one is talking literally, and the subject of one's discourse is the programming of something. It is strictly an empirical question whether, say, the motions of planets can be described literally in the language of programming.

I should know even less than I do about CR had I not received assistance from my colleagues at Temple University, particularly B. Paul Komisar, Barak Rosenshine, and Edmund Amidon. I am especially grateful to them for the references that appear in this chapter.

Although the conception of programming is derived from a certain psychological–pedagogical activity, the conception itself is perfectly general; whether it fits anything outside the activity from which it is derived can be decided only by trying.

What, comparably, are the elements (variables-for-which-values-must-be-supplied) in classroom-teaching research (CR)? Apparently, one must have teachers and pupils if one is to conduct CR, for we all know the extraordinary lengths to which researchers will go to get at teachers and pupils. But it won't do to get at them singly, or in their sleep, or in the supermarket where, by chance, a lot of them just happen to congregate. We begin with the truism that CR takes place in a classroom, that is, within *certain* space-and-time limits. A classroom, C, is spatially bounded even when it is not (though of course it usually is) physically enclosed. A session, S, is a temporal duration, an interval from some t_1 to t_2. CR ordinarily takes place at a particular kind of socially designated space-and-time intersection, (C, S), viz. a scheduled class meeting; thus the space-and-time limits of any (C, S) investigated by CR closely approximate those of ordinary class meetings, for example, occurring in rooms of a size such that any speaker should be audible from any point, held for a time interval such that attention can be focused on something other than moving in and out of the room, and so on. All this is obvious, in a way, yet one must not forget that CR is conceived by its practitioners as a way of finding out what happens in classrooms and that it carries that strength and limitation with it, wherever it goes.[1] *

Thus far, we've been looking at CR *sub specie aeternitatis;* before returning to a more conventional perspective we should note the following two points:

1. In CR there is no action-at-a-distance, as there is, typically, in the clinical study of human behavior. Anything *going on* in (C, S) is going on *right* there and then.[2] But even at the descriptive level nothing can be described in the language of CR (despite all the differences in dialect amongst different research teams engaged in CR) except what happens in some particular (C, S). This is not a criticism, for all advances in science can be taken, in part, as limitations on natural language. It is just to note a common feature—in my view, *one* defining feature—in many quite different versions of CR.

2. In CR, simultaneity can be predicated only of two events within the same (C, S); there are no transformation formulas by which what occurs in one (C, S) can be equated in time with what occurred in a

---

* Superscript numbers refer to the Notes gathered on pages 253–257.

different (C, S). In experimental psychology, of course, one has a wide choice of transformation formulas: two events occur at the same time if they both happen n minutes after testing commences, or on the nth trial, or when rate reaches n responses per unit of time, and so forth. Any such equivalence in time is relative, of course, but we no longer believe in an absolute time anyway (Grunbaum, 1963, ch. 10 and pp. 342–368).[3]

These two points arise when one poses to CR certain standard questions from the philosophy of science. It seems quite predictable that an experimental psychologist should complain of CR that it does *not* provide for simultaneity (Cronbach, 1966, p. 84); it is equally predictable that a clinical psychologist will criticize (or, unknown to me, has already criticized) CR for not recognizing the potency of factors distant from the (C, S), at least factors such as the past histories and future aspirations of the persons within the (C, S). Such criticisms and complaints may or may not be justified, depending on the further claims made for CR. But more important for our purpose is the simple fact that CR may be distinguished from clinical studies and from experimental studies by its different answers to these standard questions. This simple fact yields a formal (hence fairly useless) definition of CR: CR is the study of (C, S)'s under the restrictions that nothing not strictly within a (C, S) may be mentioned, and two events may be called simultaneous only if they occur within the same (C, S). The results of CR, then, would be comparisons of (C, S)'s in terms of the number of different kinds of events, the order of kinds of events, or the "pattern," which involves both order and frequency.

This definition of CR by time and space boundaries does not deny, nor should it, that CR can be a part of much larger kinds of research. The conclusions of any CR can be dependent or independent variables in studies of student learning, school organization, teacher personality, supervisory procedures, or anything else one happens to think of. *That*'s not the question: our focus is on CR, whether it occurs by itself or as a part of some large design.

But what is one to look at when engaging in CR? That's a slightly different question from "What is one to look for?" The latter suggests the primacy of criterion measures, and there have been many anguished cries raised about criteria. But if CR is concerned with a process (as the title of this symposium suggests), and if, as I shall argue, a process is not the sort of thing that can be looked at, we have to decide what we are to look *at* before deciding what to look *for*.

Why does one hesitate to use the word "process" as the label for what goes on in a (C, S)? Let's look at a paradigm case: The opening of a day lily is a process; it's something that happens. One can look *at* the lily and look *for* movement. Sometimes, with luck, one can actually see a lily opening. At other times one must infer the movement: it *was* closed and now it's open. One must look *at* the hands of the clock if one is to look *for* their usually indiscernible but always inexorable motion.

So what is one to look at when doing CR? It won't do to name a process, as we don't ordinarily call anything we *see* (or hear, or touch) a process. We see the lily's movement; we invoke some process to explain, not to name, what we see. We don't quite see the hands of the clock move, but the process which causes its movement is clear (or opaque) to us, whether or not we actually sense the motion. Process language, we may say, belongs in the context of explanation or justification rather than in the context of immediate, concrete description.

Saying, Doing, Making

So what are we to look at? Well, the teacher and pupils. Do we really mean that, or do we mean the physical, chemical, organic entities, or transcendental souls bearing the labels "pupil" and "teacher"? Of course we really mean the teacher and pupils, human beings in certain quite specific social roles. And thereby hangs the moral of this tale: There is no simple way to look at human beings so as to see this particular system of roles. Every significant action by a participant in the classroom has three different aspects. I borrow from Aristotle's distinctions as elaborated quite recently in the work of Buchler (1955). Any pedagogically significant action will typically take the mode of a linguistic utterance; i.e., somebody will *say* something. But the saying itself is, as we noted, an action; in other words, somebody *does* something. But the saying and doing are expected to have a product beyond themselves, which is to say, somebody *is making* something. The same significant motion (Buchler, strangely, calls it a "judgment") is at once a *saying*, a *doing*, and a *making*. Now that's the triple-aspected interaction which CR has to *describe* before it can even begin to explain or account for what happens in a (C, S).

These distinctions go deeper than the surface. Not only are there three aspects, but in each aspect quite different criteria apply: to the *saying* aspect, logical criteria; to the *doing* aspect, moral criteria; and to the *making* aspect, aesthetic criteria. About *what* someone says, we may ask: Is it true or false? Is it well supported and reasoned, or is it not? Is it relevant or irrelevant? Is it consistent? In itself? To other things said by the same speaker? These questions illustrate but do not exhaust logical criteria.

About the *act* of saying we may ask, typically, questions of morals or manners. It takes a crisis and a prophet to make use see the deeper moral questions in a (C, S). But issues of manners are easily visible: Does the teacher talk too much? Does he respect the feelings and opinions of his students? Does he listen carefully to what his students say? Does he encourage students to bring up matters of interest to *them*? These questions are quite the same as one would ask about a dinner partner. It's a revealing feature of moral progress that we have to make such a big deal over simple, decent *civility* for students in the classroom.

What is functionally equivalent to a new religion, viz. Interaction Analysis, has made an appearance, carrying the message, according to its chief prophet, Flanders (in Amidon & Hough, 1964, p. 206), that "the most successful teachers undoubtedly develop a sensitivity to the ideas and feelings of students that is quite similar to the sensitivities of a therapist." Since students lack political and economic power to force teachers to treat them with good manners, it is of positive social value that many teachers come to want to behave more decently toward students: Interaction Analysis often serves as a kind of conversion experience to bring about that new desire and, perhaps even more important, to provide the new convert with skills and techniques of good classroom manners.

Other prophets proclaim more directly the moral aspects of what a teacher does in the classroom. A teacher may act justly or unjustly; Paul Goodman and Edgar Friedenberg remind us that injustice may be a great deal more subtle than we had realized. Anyone can recognize the injustice of a teacher's failing a student because of personal dislike; it takes more sensitivity (but now a political as well as psychological sensitivity) to recognize injustice in a teacher's constantly favoring, say, neatness over boldness or form over content. In principle, of course, any deliberate act of a human being is subject to moral judgment; we *can* ask about any act: Is it just? Is it morally right? Is it in accord with the ethical obligations inhering in the life conditions of the agent? and so on. The problem is to see the relevance of these grand moral questions applied to simple, everyday doings in a classroom. The economy of institutional life demands that fundamental moral questions be kept decently hidden while one is performing one's institutional role. But one can always ask the moral questions of the institution itself: Does *it* promote justice and moral rectitude? When we substitute "the usual public school classroom" for "it" in that question, we initiate the external criticism of CR, a matter I'll turn to at the end of the paper.

More difficult to grasp than saying or doing is the teacher's making. Several common forms of speech, however, give a clue to what is meant. A teacher told me recently of his work with the new social studies material from ESI; he summarized his experience by saying, "We had to guard against making too great an impact with the baboon unit; if we weren't careful the students would see mankind as only a degenerate species of apes." Even more common is a statement like "Right now I'm trying to make them learn the Declaration of Independence," or "The purpose of our social studies curriculum is to make good citizens" (or, if one happens to be a citizen of the U.S.A., ". . . to make militaristic nationalists").

Putting these three common idioms together, we can say that teachers make an impression on students in or by making them do something in order to make them *into* something they wouldn't have been otherwise. There's nothing more to be said here about the second of these usages, "making students do something," since the points made about moral criteria apply paradigmatically to a case of a person with greater power and knowledge making those who are inferior in these terms *do* what they would not otherwise do.[4]

My concern here is with the first and third idioms, "making an impression" and "making students into something they would not be otherwise." For both these "makings," aesthetic criteria apply. About a teacher's impression on the student, we may ask: "Is it made crudely or subtly?" "Is it made boldly or timidly?" "Is it profound and lasting, or shallow and evanescent?" "Is it pleasant or unpleasant? Does its quality change—improve or degenerate—in retrospect?" These are precisely the questions we would ask about the effect made by any artist *in* his medium. His brush strokes, his monologues, his crescendoes, or his alliterations—whatever his medium, his style and its effect can be described and criticized along these lines. We rightly hesitate to regard criteria of this sort as canons of commendation as we did with moral and logical criteria. For us, criteria of aesthetic production constitute leading questions to promote comprehension rather than standards for invidious judgment. But we know that such questions are always relevant when a person is making an impression on another in or through some medium of interchange.

But the more important aesthetic questions are asked about what's made *by* the artist, what product emerges—shaped, formed, in some degree determined by the efforts of a maker. While the first set of aesthetic questions is concerned with style, the second set touches directly the work achieved and forces us to confront questions of beauty. An inescapable feature of the present spiritual scene is our immediate, unthought tendency to collapse the distinction between personal and aesthetic predication. Said by anyone over thirty, the statement "He is a beautiful person" is fairly offensive: one regards it as either arch or archaic. But more particular aesthetic predicates (adjectives) constitute our ordinary descriptions of persons: He is well (or poorly) integrated. He is vigorous and dynamic. Or he isn't so. He is spontaneous and open. Or he is constrained and closed. He is colorful or dull, flamboyant or pale. Like Jacob, he's rough-textured or smooth. He is whole or self-divided. He is authentic, or else in varying degrees he's a fake to self and others.

One can say that such predicates are anthropomorphic when applied to art objects. Or that their use means that persons are being treated and judged as things. Or, as I should prefer, one can hold that persons, in some very important sense, *are* works of art as well as being *like* works of art. The use of aesthetic criteria in judging persons is, on this last view, entirely valid. It does not follow that it's valid to apply more clearly personal predicates, such as "autonomous" or "self-accepting," to works of art; but fortunately this paper does not have to resolve *that* question (Aiken, 1965).

The conclusion to be drawn from this truncated treatment of aesthetic criteria should be clearly visible by now, but I wish to add three disclaimers before I state it explicitly. First, no particular view of character traits or personality theory is implied by the notion that teaching is, in part, a matter of making persons—causing persons to be somewhat different, as well as to behave somewhat differently, from what they would have been in the absence of teaching. Exactly what mechanisms are involved in that kind of making, or whether the term "mechanism" makes any sense when talking about a person's becoming what he is, are questions I do not have to answer.

Nor am I required to resolve the perennial question of the relative weight of nature and art in making persons what they are. It is in this context, I believe, that one should place the observation that the language of aesthetics (as well as the language of personal descriptions) has been penetrated by terms from therapy. Aristotle took therapy as rather the paradigm case of art and nature cooperating. Saint Thomas held that the teacher was like the doctor in that his efforts were successful only when they acted to further the natural tendencies within the learner. For Aquinas, of course, "natural tendencies" meant those tendencies that are part of a universal human nature. I've not been able to locate an origin of the concept of *individual* nature and its corollary that teaching is the art of actualizing the unique potentialities of each child.[5] In any event, that doctrine had been anticipated by the Renaissance view of the artist as constrained by the peculiar, unique properties of the object immediately before him. Thus it is quite appropriate that forms of speech most typical in therapy also find use in art and in teaching. The artist, therapist, and teacher have a common *form* of endeavor. Each works with some particular nature in the interest of wholeness, harmony, and integrity. The greater his success, the less separable is his making from nature's.

Nor, finally, am I obligated to clear up once and for all the relation of teaching style—*how* a teacher makes an impression—to the ultimate teaching product—what kind of person a teacher helps to make. In part, of course, this relation is an empirical one and, to some degree, may be pursued by CR. Getzels and Jackson (1963, p. 533) recommend that we "shift from studying the personal qualities of teachers as if there were an ideal teacher to an analysis of the interaction between personalities of students and teachers." An important way to look at *their* subsequent research is as a contribution to the analysis of that interaction. And yet there is another sense in which this relation goes beyond empirical research. For the kind of person we want to make through teaching is one who can learn from, or learn to decide *not* to learn from, many different styles of teaching. This criterion measure *might* be built into a research design; there's no law of logic to prevent it; but at the present rate of expansion of our educational technology, that design is unlikely to appear in our lifetime.

Criteria and Categories

This last remark returns us to the problem of criterion measures from which we began. We have discerned three major categories of criteria and recognized two subdivisions in two of them, as follows:

Logical	*Moral*	*Aesthetic*
Truth	1. Justice	1. Teaching
Relevance	&	style
Consistency	Freedom	2. Personhood
Evidential	2. Manners	
quality		
(Et cetera)		

I submit that we have made a fairly good start toward studying classroom manners. Perhaps the correlation between a teacher's indirectness and student achievement may be considered strictly a matter of manners: if a teacher is decently civil to students, they are more likely to perform decently when forced to take a test. The non-facetious point is that student performance on the kinds of tests we ordinarily use for these purposes cannot be considered an adequate criterion test for anything, certainly not for a teacher's actions.

Once we get beyond manners we have very little to look at. Certain studies started off to analyze a teacher's *sayings*, but for different reasons got pulled back into studying manners. I do not know the details of the Smith and Meux *Logic of Teaching*, but I've been told that the failure to demonstrate significant correlations between student achievement and desirable logic in teacher talk discouraged further study of logical variables. If I rightly understand what happened, I'm amazed (*a*) that Smith should have ever anticipated such correlations and (*b*) that he should have been put off when such correlations failed to appear.

The significant point here is quite technical, and I can't do justice to it. But, just to indicate what the point is, suppose we started on the other track: Say we chose one group of teachers who always made true statements instead of false, avoided self-contradiction, spoke relevantly at all times, assigned the proper evidential weight to particular statements vis-à-vis generalizations, *and* recognized and reinforced those logical virtues in students. Suppose also we chose another group entirely lacking those logical virtues but otherwise equally attractive and competent teachers. We should feel that if we had two such groups, our research staff was terribly delinquent if it could not find *some* instruments which would show *some* difference between the students of the two groups of teachers. But, of course, we do *not* have two such groups. In fact, we cannot even give any concrete meaning to the expression "attractive and competent teachers" who lack the capacity to distinguish truth from falsehood, consistency from contradiction, and so on. Thus we have to come back to relative frequencies (of truthful statements, logically consistent arguments, and so on) as ways of distinguishing groups of teachers for research purposes. The trouble with relative frequencies is that cognitive rationality in teaching (to use a single expression for all the virtues mentioned above) is a matter of *form*, not frequency. As far as I can tell, we simply do not have the techniques for separating out the logical *form* in teaching from all the personal and content variables which account for a large proportion of the measurable variance in student performance. In fact, of course, we are only coming to see what *is* the logical form of a teaching act (as contrasted with all sorts of other things teachers do in a classroom) so that we can perfect techniques for observing that form.[6]

The reasons why Bellack and his associates did not study logic but rather manners is a little easier to determine. They were misled by a seductive theory, one that has pulled most of English language philosophy down a primrose path. (As might have been predicted, the primrose path proved rather more fertile than the straight and narrow.) Wittgenstein's later philosophical works arose from a most critical, complex, and polemical situation in philosophy. He invented the notion of language games as a reaction against the unitary, logical-construction theory of language which he himself had helped to invent. Following his metaphor of the language game, Bellack was enticed into asking for the teaching *moves* made by teachers and pupils; and these moves, as we might have expected, turn out to be the sorts of things we would evaluate by criteria of manners, not logic (Bellack *et al.*, 1966, ch. 1).[7]

There is a great deal that I should like to know about the influence of certain philosophical movements on education research. (I don't even *mention* the pernicious influence of behaviorism and operationism, doctrines which enjoyed a brilliant but brief career as liberating ideas in philosophy and now survive as tenets of dogmatic orthodoxy in the Holy Office of the AERA.) But it seems perfectly clear that English language philosophy in this century has been dominated by an effort to understand *meaning* as *not* a purely linguistic phenomenon. The death of idealism (in its technical, philosophic sense) left meaning as the prime philosophical problem; American pragmatism and British linguistic analysis had at least that much in common (White, 1956). But the pragmatic doctrine of meaning had little utility for CR; if one holds that the *meaning* of an idea is the difference it makes in the actions of the person who believes it true, then one has to deal with certain variables like "believes it true" which do not seem to lend themselves easily to empirical research. The British analysis seems more profitable. From G. E. Moore through Wittgenstein ("The meaning of a word is its use in the language") to the late J. L. Austin's analyses of the illocutionary and perlocutionary "force" of utterances, we seem to be reaching something very researchable: if you want to know what a linguistic utterance *means,* find out what the person (who says it) is *doing* in or by saying it. The apparent utility of this philosophical doctrine has tempted at least one educational research effort to formulate a language system in which the *sayings* in a (C, S) may be described as *doings* (Westbury, 1968). Not at all surprisingly in hindsight it turns out that the new, "illocutionary force," way of describing the doings of a (C, S) adds little to what is already described in the small but useful vocabulary of Interaction Analysis (in this case the Amidon-Hunter dialect). Of course, if the researcher opens the door for *everything* a student might be doing in or by saying "I don't know," then one has admitted the whole of the so-called "language of action," which means that there is possibly an infinite number of *true* descriptions of this event ("He's admitting ignorance," "He's exhaling," *ad infinitum*), and that doesn't make the research effort any easier.

I should feel more like criticizing the practitioners of CR, particularly the sophisticated ones like Bellack and his colleagues, for failing to do justice to *saying* as having its own distinctive criteria, quite apart from rules governing what the sayer is *doing* ("soliciting," "responding," "structuring," and the like), if I were able to offer any helpful advice on how saying could be studied in a (C, S) and criteria applied to the results of that study.

One last point on *saying:* Rosenshine's discovery that the use of certain logical words by teachers is an excellent predictor of student performance is obviously suggestive (Chapter 9). In reading some of the protocols I was struck by the fact that none of the teachers seemed to use these words very well; but those who used them more often than others did seem, as we would expect from operant conditioning, to use them better—more apparently, more logically. Can we train teachers to be critical of their own and pupils' use of logical words and increase the frequency of that use? And obey the code of manners called indirect?

The problems of aesthetic criteria are so terribly complex that one hesitates even to begin. In the first place, CR's restrictions against simultaneity and action-at-a-distance are difficult to reconcile with the making of persons. What is going on, so far as personal becoming is concerned, involves a great deal beyond the borders of a (C, S). To the classroom student, simultaneous with his participation in a (mostly meaningless) language game are the real events of life. If the teacher's makings are to be considered relevant, CR must escape the limitations that its methods have imposed on it. I do not know how this is possible.

Another problem is how the personhood of students is related to the moral and logical goals set for a classroom. John Dewey, as you know, set up this problem as a matter of being "compelled to make a choice between these personal attitudes (open-mindedness, wholeheartedness, and responsibility) and knowledge about the principles of logical reasoning." In that case, he said, "we should decide for the former." But then when he has the problem set up, Dewey cops out: ". . . there is no opposition between personal attitudes and logical processes. . . . What is needed is to weave them into unity" (Dewey, 1933, p. 34). Perhaps Dewey spent too much time playing occupations on the looms of his Chicago school.

No one else, so far as I know, has even considered this relation, and I see no reason *a priori* for holding any particular view on the matter. There seems to be, I'll admit, some correlation between decent manners and logical reasoning. But this common variance from the mean seems easily accounted for by general factors and does not imply causal connection. Nor is there any logical connection in the strict sense. One does not violate the laws of logic by being ill-mannered, unjust, or (the interesting case) extremely paranoid. The vicious inhumanity of the United States Government against the people of Vietnam is neither illogical nor irrational; it's just vicious.

And so through all the other criteria mentioned: I see no reason to believe that they are related in any particular way. I can imagine no results of CR which could convince me that what I should regard as desirable traits on one criterion have more than a chance relation (let us say, fortuitous relation, for I don't mean "chance" in the statistical sense) with desirable traits on other criteria. A most mannerly teaching act may be a lie and a stroke toward producing a monstrosity of a person. Or a truth may be quite uncivil and yet shape a beautiful soul. Or any other combination of desirable and undesirable features seems equally plausible—so plausible that any result deviating from random probably represents a stacking of the deck.

The fact that I can see only randomness among these criteria may represent only my own randomness, disjointedness of soul. If I were better—more integrated and authentic a person—I might *see* that truth and logical consistency are related to civility in manners, to openness in style, to attractiveness in personality. I might or I might not. But lacking those qualities, I cannot see how CR can claim to be studying teaching behavior and not be working like anything to integrate all these criteria into one design. For we cannot tell in any total sense what the teacher is doing unless we recognize and account for the fact that the same move is *at once* a saying, a doing, and a making. All must be given their due else none is given its due.

Conclusion

But what about justice and freedom? I close with the passing thought that the (C, S) studied by CR is typically a place of injustice and repression, that we are learning how to study the classroom just as the classroom is finally becoming obsolete—inefficient technologically and repulsive to our newly refined moral sensibilities. If that is so, what is our strategy? We can just go ahead in the conviction that knowledge is always a good; we can take solace in Hegel's view that the owl of Minerva takes his flight when twilight descends. Or we can try to take a more spirited role: to learn something about the achievement of educational values in the (C, S) which can still be known and applied when present limitations of the (C, S) are forgotten. This line of thought, which cannot be pursued further here, tempts me back to the threefold set of criteria for describing and judging what goes on in a (C, S). If we can advance toward integrating those criteria, the next generation of educators, hopefully better as well as more skillful than we, will be happy to stand on our shoulders.

Postscript

Since preparing this paper for the 1967 seminar, I have read two other papers which bear directly on the problems treated here. Paton (1967) used precisely this "saying–making–doing" scheme of categories in his "Teaching People to Think—Unresolved Dilemma and Instructional Challenge." He used this trichotomy, however, as a way of classifying educational objectives or *student* activities, rather than as ways of talking about what happens in a (C, S). Some of his entries seem to me misplaced (see p. 27), but surely he's on the right track in proposing a complex, rather than simple, *system* of objectives. The reason he's on the right track is that otherwise education, like its military and industrial benefactors, is involved in a most vicious reduction of human action to something less than human (see also Bernard, Ottenberg & Redl, 1965).

SEMINAR DISCUSSION OF McCLELLAN PAPER

Editor's Note

Despite agreement about broad principles and questions within a research tradition, a vigorous debate (that in its resolution can transform what actually happens in a research field) can still arise between two contrasting points of view: one that demands that the specific terms of a research tradition reflect the presumed complexity and richness of the phenomena being studied and another that, while granting the need for meaningful reflection of phenomena, puts stress on the problems of operationalizing, in unambiguous ways, the terms that are used in scientific discussions. The tensions between these demands became the major issue explored in the discussion in Toronto. This concern is reflected in the discussions reported here of the McClellan and Travers papers. The totally different concerns of Travers and McClellan generated a need for a middle ground; the search for this ground unified the themes that the discussants raised.—I. W.

The Discussion

Intent

BIDDLE: It seems to me that McClellan is doing something that was done, particularly in sociology, more than a generation ago but has more or less disappeared as a result of the impact of functionalism. McClellan is confusing the intent of the actor with the observed effect of the actor's actions. Whatever the teacher may accomplish in the classroom with an activity is something that can be observed directly. The intent of the teacher's actions may be observed only inferentially; you may ask the teacher what his intention was in a situation, but you cannot jump to the conclusion that he had intended to accomplish whatever he succeeded in accomplishing. I believe that many inadvertent things are accomplished within social systems. If we go back and seriously consider McClellan's three aspects of 'saying', 'doing', and 'making', it seems that when you talk about *making*, you are talking about the *intent* of the actor in the situation. Often we do not have intent information in our observation of individuals in classrooms; we can, if we have really sophisticated systems, observe the *apparent effects* in terms of continued probabilities of the events following other

16

events. But there is no possibility, whatsoever, of building a coding system for judging intent of actors in a given system. This is a psychological phenomenon, and, furthermore, it is quite likely that many of the events achieved in the classroom were not intended at all.

McCLELLAN: You are quite right in inferring from what I said that I believe the intent of an agent cannot be ignored. However, you are overly sanguine to think that functionalism in sociology clears up this problem. Let us take an example right here and now. You could ask what am I doing. If one of the things I am doing is digesting the kipper I had for breakfast, then all kinds of chemical processes are involved.

BIDDLE: We can't observe you digesting the kipper. But I want to go back to your basic premises. You placed yourself firmly in the position of one who observes overt events in a particular context; consequently your digestion of the kipper has nothing to do with classroom research. The pains or pleasure you may be feeling as an individual are, in fact, not fit for discussion here. If you were to attempt to make photographs, as I have, then I can assure you that you cannot observe these phenomena.

IVANY: The point is that Biddle's coding system doesn't have a space in it to indicate that the kipper is being digested. The fact that the information is available has nothing to do with the coding instrument you choose.

BIDDLE: If that information were available, the coder should not make the judgment. The digestive process cannot be judged—it is not an overt act taking place within the classroom environment.

McCLELLAN: If all philosophical problems about what constitutes an act were cleared up, then we could proceed on the happy assumption that there are some sorts of things which are acts, and other sorts of things which are internal events. The classic study of this problem is dealt with by Anscombe (1957). She offers an example of a father moving a pump handle up and down and asks, "What is he doing?" He doesn't know it, but it turns out that he is pumping poison out of this well and he will kill his children. He is engaged in an overt act, the outcome of which is to poison his children. If we ask, "What is he doing?" is it reasonable to say that he is poisoning his children? He is getting water for his children. The difference between these two acts is not just in the overt events; rather, it lies in the 'intention'.

BIDDLE: In the classroom you can observe a small child doubling up his fist and shaking it at a bigger child. The action may be categorized in overt terms and defined in very molecular units as an 'actone'. You can say that the fingers doubled up to make a fist, and that certain kinds of muscle motions are involved. On the other hand you could describe this in molar terminology, and say aggression was displayed. If we could get inside the minds of the individuals involved, we might discover that the motive of the smaller child was hostility, but the effect of the behavior upon the bigger child is amusement. Neither the hostility nor the amusement but rather the overt characteristics of the action are all that can be judged reliably. A system which deals with classroom processes can only reflect the overt, judgeable qualities of the action which takes place.

McCLELLAN: Suppose a trained kinesiologist were describing the situation. He might say that the smaller child was flexing his muscles, or tensing certain tensors. Or suppose a trained cardiologist were watching and were to say that certain capillaries were distended at a certain rate, would these be observations of overt acts? To judge overt action, we choose certain sets of descriptions from the infinite number of true descriptions of any overt situation. My suggestion is to ask about what the teacher 'says', what the students 'say', and then to ask what the teacher and students are 'doing' by 'saying' what they say. These typically are what we do pay attention to as 'saying'. And then we ask why a particular 'saying' is also a 'doing', for example accepting students' feelings or not accepting students' feelings. I certainly agree with Biddle that if we ask about what a person 'says' and what he is 'doing' in that particular 'saying', we are asking questions which cannot be separated from his intention. There isn't a typical language by which we describe our own or other people's hunches. If you are asked, "What are you doing in this conference now?" you wouldn't give a description of such difficult-to-observe events as heartbeats or digestion, nor even of such easily observed events as drumming fingers on table or wrinkling eyebrows. You would give a description such as "I am participating in a conference, listening to or responding to a certain paper." An inexperienced person might have to infer a great deal to make sense of this perfectly obvious description of the interaction. The same principle applies more generally with the assertion that any description is theory-laden.

'Saying', 'Doing', and 'Making'

BIDDLE: Are you using the word 'doing' to mean the person's intentions, and the word 'making' to mean that which is accomplished by the action? You could, in fact, discover what a person is 'doing' by interviewing him and what a person 'made' by observing the effects of his actions.

McCLELLAN: We have many intentions that we don't act on and some actions which unfortunately follow from other intentions. I certainly support your second proposition.

BIDDLE: In the case of the man pumping water: he thought that he was getting water for his family, while in fact he was poisoning them. That is what he was 'making'. If this is correct, then the description is legitimate. It follows that 'doing' has no place in classroom research because, to use your terminology, we don't interview people. We can observe what they 'do'—that is, what they say and what they make— by watching the response of the action over a period of time.

McCLELLAN: It is only in the exceptional case that one has to interview a person in order to know what he is 'doing'. This is the most important insight to come from behaviorism as a philosophical movement. There aren't two events—one internal, mental, unobservable and the other external, physical, observable. Rather, there is one event —a person acting. And when we describe a person's action, the most ordinary, natural way to do it is often by reference to what he intends to accomplish.

GAGE: I feel a need for further clarification of your distinctions between 'saying', 'doing', and 'making'.

McCLELLAN: Let's take your last utterance. This is a 'saying' and there are certain logical criteria that we can apply to it: Was it consistent? Did you contradict yourself? At the same time, what was it 'doing'? Was it asking a question? Was it making a request? Was it what Arno Bellack (1966) would call *structuring*? We can then ask certain other questions: Was it socially appropriate? You can ask whether a saying is consistent. (Deontic logic has finally led us to talk about true questions and false questions. It is a true question if it admits to a true answer.) You can ask such logical questions, but you can also ask other kinds of questions about a 'doing'. It is appropriate in this context to ask what is a 'just' question, if we mean 'just' in the moral sense. And finally there was a 'making'. You were 'making' an impression upon us which could be described aesthetically: How did you make an impression upon us?

GAGE: I only see arbitrariness in your linking up of 'saying' with logic, of 'doing' with morals and manners, and of 'making' with beauty or aesthetics. Why can't the 'making' have moral attributes and the 'doing' have logical aspects?

McCLELLAN: There are moral aspects to everything. Suppose you make a very true statement. We can always ask a moral question: Should he have made that statement? Or was it an appropriate thing to do? Very often some part of manners is not telling all the truth. And so we can always ask questions of morals and manners about anything. But we can surely distinguish the aesthetic qualities of your statement—its style—from whether it was morally right. Remember that 'doing' is primary, and this led Wittgenstein and Bellack down the primrose path in the theory of language. Because all saying is a doing doesn't mean that you can successfully analyze all 'saying' *simply* as a 'doing'. What a teacher is 'doing' is a question that involves all three aspects.

SMITH: What do you do with a 'saying' when you've got it?

McCLELLAN: We can ask logical questions about 'saying': Is it true or false? Is it consistent or non-consistent? It would be important to apply these logical criteria to 'sayings'.

BIDDLE: Let us assume, for a moment, when you are working with a record of classroom events, that you have a series of events that come in a sequence: event A, event B, and event C, and so on. You have a record of all these events as they occurred in the classroom, and it is possible to devise a code categorizing the events. Let us further assume that these are all verbal events, as many events in the classroom are, and that they have properties which can be coded. They can be coded as 'saying' syntactically, and presumably semantically; also they are 'doings' because one of the primitive characteristics of action is that it is a 'doing'. Is it necessary to devise a code for 'makings' at all, since each event *per se* is produced by or effected by events which have preceded it in time?

McCLELLAN: You do not have to have a 'making' code. You recall B. O. Smith's episodes: What he really wanted was to get a large enough set of these sequences so that he could apply a set of criteria to them. You can't go to any one exchange, like "Shut the door," and apply an aesthetic criterion to it.

John Dewey said that a situation was determined by its quality. The question is how much of a teacher's action, how large a micro-teaching unit, would you have to have before you could start talking sensibly about a teacher's style?

BIDDLE: I am not sure that I understand the answer you have given to the question I asked. Is it necessary to have a code for 'making' if, in fact, you have a good sequence, if you have each one of the items within a classroom sequence coded?

McCLELLAN: You don't have to have a 'making' code.

BIDDLE: Does it add anything to have such a code?

FLANDERS: Yes, because if you put all the events together it can be judged in terms of what its product is.

BIDDLE: But that, then, comes out of your sequential analysis. When you put one of your matrices together and discover that a particular teacher is responsive or non-responsive to pupil questions, *this* is something new. *This* was not originally judged as part of the primitive system. You judged a set of events in sequence, and were able, by analytical reconstruction, to discover that certain kinds of processes were taking place in the classroom.

It is perfectly possible to code, in a primitive sense, the styles and the manner of delivery. It is possible to say, of a given act, "Was this delivered harshly? With vigor? Quietly? Whispered? Or smilingly?" These are, in fact, the 'doing' elements of the teacher. Now I am asking a question: If you have a good sequential record, is it necessary to devise primitive codes for 'makings'? I think not. I think the 'makings' can be judged from an analysis of the sequence of events. If you recognize that the first two categories are bases for devising a coding system and that the last is not an analytical basis but rather something you discover by analyzing the sequence of events in the classroom, then this does not mean that you have exhausted the bases for an analytical coding system.

McCLELLAN: There is more going on in a classroom than any particular person's or combination of persons' 'doing'. You can ask two kinds of questions: "What is going on in the classroom?" and "What are teachers and pupils doing?" Obviously there are other things going on in the classroom which cannot be analyzed as the sequence of 'doings' of the individuals. We really are, and should be, concerned with the kinds of persons we produce, and if a coding system does not take that into account then we need to expand it.

SULLIVAN: How can you analyze the moral dimension?

McCLELLAN: I distinguish between morals and manners, and if there is a morality about good manners, the Flanders Interaction Analysis gives us a clear picture whether the teacher is mannered, or ill-mannered.

Some Further Reflections on the Nature of a Theory of Instruction

ROBERT M. W. TRAVERS

In a previous paper (1966) I attempted to describe the general characteristics of a theory of instruction developed in terms of scientific tradition. I pointed out that such a theory would have to be derived from empirical statements that represented the end products of research and that the statements of the theory would have to have clear-cut relationships to the empirically derived statements on which the theory was based. Undocumented statements representing personal views on the nature of good teaching would not fall within this definition of a theory of instruction, however attractive and inspirational such statements might be. The development of a theory of instruction, thus conceived, would cease to be the happy, carefree, do-it-yourself activity it has been in the past, and would become a painstaking, meticulous, and empirically oriented activity that would have to enlist the efforts of high-level scientists. What was proposed is not likely to be particularly popular, partly because talent for scientific theorizing has always been rare, and partly because it shows up, in proper perspective, the happy breed of educational reformer who can concoct a brand-new, rabble-rousing theory of educational reform while waiting for the water to fill the bathtub.

Here I want to explore further some of the problems faced by the systematic theorizer in the educational field; but before proceeding I would like to acknowledge that much of what I have to say had its roots in discussions held by the Commission on Theory of Instruction of the Association for Supervision and Curriculum Development

(ASCD). After several years of working with this group, I sometimes find it difficult to distinguish my own ideas from those that have originated in the group.

Models of Instruction and Theories of Instruction

A major problem encountered by the ASCD Commission on Theory of Instruction was that of distinguishing a theory of instruction developed in the pragmatic and scientific tradition from other kinds of sets of statements that are also referred to as theories of instruction. Many of the most influential of the latter statements represent beliefs concerning the nature of man. Froebel's concept of education reflects his deep religious convictions concerning the unity of the soul. Combs' (1965) recent treatise on education reflects, in my estimation, the modern humanist's conception of man, colored by existentialism. Although the Combs book does have a title that appears to link it to the psychology of perception, I can see no such link in the book itself; but I do see that the central argument for the educational program proposed follows from philosophical assumptions about the nature of man. At this time I do not see any way of testing the validity of Combs' assumptions related to his position or to other positions that may be taken concerning the extent to which man is an agent controlling his own destiny.

Combs' book provides a philosophical framework for planning education, but the framework is so inclusive in the educational events to which judgments of good and bad, worthy or unworthy, can be applied, that it leaves virtually no room for the application of scientific knowledge. It is somewhat like a set of dietary principles that a religious sect might draw up in terms of their religious beliefs covering every phase of man's consumption of food. Once such a comprehensive set of dietary rules is accepted as the only "right" one, then scientific knowledge has nothing to offer in the planning of diet. Empirically based theories have something to offer only to those whose moral rules do not prescribe behavior in every phase of activity.

A framework of values within which an educational program is to be developed establishes the limits that must be recognized by those who wish to apply scientific knowledge to the solution of learning problems. The system of values also determines the kinds of positive applications that are made. A scientific and comprehensive theory of educational phenomena might include statements concerning the conditions under which punishment is an effective modifier of behavior, but the values that provide the foundation for an educational program might exclude the use of punishment. Indeed, if the teacher, as a humanist, is morally opposed to punishment, then any statements regarding punishment in an educational theory can have no relevance for the planning of any of the teacher's activities.

Scientific theories can provide statements which tell one how to perform acts that are morally and inexcusably wrong, as they have in the case of the atomic bomb. Empirically based theories of instruction may do the same, and we must be constantly on guard lest our use of scientific theories lead to the development of atomic bombs for the classroom. Whatever is utilized from a scientific theory of instruction must be compatible with the values that we hold. In our enthusiasm for the development of empirically derived theories of instruction, we have sometimes tended to forget that in the planning of education, the moral issues are the ones of incontestably supreme importance and that all scientific knowledge plays a role that is both secondary and subordinate.

Prescriptions for teaching that represent plans for achieving particular goals through the application of scientific knowledge summarized in theory of instruction are here referred to as *models*. Thus a *model of teaching* represents a prescription that is consistent with both the value system within which education takes place and the available instructional theory that scientists have developed. Such a model is obviously necessary for any design of teacher training, but it can be no better than the theory of instruction on which it is based.

I would like to emphasize, at this point, that the development of a model of instruction should not be regarded as a carefree activity which any dilettante has a license to pursue. On the contrary, it should be regarded as an extension of the painstaking and meticulous work from which theories of instruction will emerge. A reputable model of instruction should certainly be documented so that the theory of instruction, together with the research on which such a theory has been based, can be properly identified. A model must show all the marks of scholarship.

The representation of teaching that Marie Hughes (1959) has drawn up comes very close to a model of teaching. Her work is nearer to providing a model, in the sense in which the term is used here, than any contemporary work I have been able to locate. One can point in the distant past to the work of Madame Montessori as representing, in her time, a conception of teaching based both on the limited knowledge available to her and on an identifiable set of values. The Montessori representation of teaching would certainly be classed here as a model, but, in contrast, the Froebel conception would not. I think that one would have to regard Froebel's prescription as a philosophical position that would, in practice, leave little latitude for the application of empirical knowledge. Froebel's application and implementation of what he calls the "law of divine unity" is a complete plan for education far and remote from empirical knowledge. One can hardly blame Froebel for failing to make provision for the use of empirical knowledge in the design of educational programs, for so little knowledge was available to him. One can, however, take him to task for doing what some of our colleagues in education still do today, namely, inventing knowledge that did not exist. Thus, Froebel does not present a model of education in the sense in which the term model is used here, and neither do most of our contemporary writers who have prescriptions for the reform of education.

Some Problems in the Development of a Theory of Instruction

Despite the fact that we need desperately to have sound models of instruction, scholarly effort must still be directed toward the development of a *theory of instruction.* A recent attempt to develop a theory of instruction on the basis of the conclusions of empirical classroom research has been particularly valuable because it provides considerable insight into the difficulties that the development of a theory of instruction will encounter. The project I am referring to is a joint enterprise of the School District of Norwalk (Connecticut) and New York University, and is sponsored by the Ford Foundation. It has been developed with the leadership of Dr. Esin Kaya (1967) who has functioned as principal investigator. One of the very important products of this venture is the bringing together of the results of numerous empirical studies that attempt to relate some condition in the classroom to some educational outcome. In addition, a survey has also been made of the relationships that different professional persons have judged to exist between conditions to which pupils are exposed and various outcomes. Although one may well question the value of any theory of instruction based on opinion, however enlightened it may seem to be, it is nevertheless interesting to find out whether the judgments of the bold do lead to a theory of instruction that contains propositions similar to those that might be included in a theory of instruction based on research.

This project permits us to take stock of our position with respect to the data available for constructing a theory of instruction. Such an appraisal of available information enables us to make decisions concerning what the next steps should be, and also to identify some of the inherent limitations of present data.

Pseudo-operational Definitions
and Their Genuine Counterparts

A primary difficulty that is encountered at every stage in the
Norwalk venture is the problem of the operational definition of terms.
In order to collate and organize the findings of what appear to be
similar researches, one must have some assurance that they involve
similar variables. Since much of the work involves rating scales, sim-
ilarity of variables is not assured. Most studies do go through the kind
of ritual that Ralph Tyler (1934) introduced many years ago of attempting to define both outcomes and teaching events in terms of
what are called "specific behaviors," but this ritual accomplishes no
more today than it did in the past.

Most of our difficulties arose originally because Tyler attempted
to adapt Bridgman's operationism to the problem of defining some of
the empirical terms used in evaluative statements related to education.
Tyler's work in the mid-thirties was undertaken at the height of the
influence of the logical positivists on the behavioral sciences and during a time when the belief was commonly held that all scientific communications should be stated with operationally defined terms. At that
stage, little recognition was given to the fact that scientific discourse
always involves primitive terms and, at the more advanced levels,
requires the introduction of theoretical terms. As Bridgman so elo-
quently and forcefully pointed out, one can define a term with great
precision by operations which involve pointing to well-identified events
of the kind that occur in laboratories. When Tyler attempted to adapt
Bridgman's operationism to events in the world of education, he misled
most of us in education into thinking that clear-cut operational definitions could be achieved by pointing to "specific" events involving
teachers and pupils. The formula looked like one that might save us
from drowning in a deluge of meaningless terms, but it was in reality
based on a false analogy. There are no specific events in classrooms to
point to in the formulation of definitions, as there are specific events
in the laboratory.

Let us consider this point further. In the laboratory we can ask
a subject to press a button every time a light shows a small and
momentary increment in brightness. The behavior is quite specific
and defines a variable, though, as Hull (1943, p. 422) pointed out,
it may vary in vigor, in speed, and in other attributes. Behaviors of
teachers and pupils cannot generally be identified with such precision
because they do not show the same invariant properties as laboratory
behavior. In contrast to a laboratory-derived statement, a proposition
such as "The variable X refers to the frequency with which the teacher

engages in rewarding behavior" refers to a broad category of behavior with only vaguely identified boundaries. We can try to be more specific and say that the rewarding behavior of a teacher includes such items as "tells the pupil that his work is good," or "permits the pupil to engage in some activity of his choice." Yet these amplifications of what is meant by "rewarding behavior" do not solve the problem, for they again only refer to ill-defined and quite broad categories of behavior. Classroom events are such that we can rarely define our variables in terms of specific behaviors by some kind of pointing operation. It is time that we stopped deluding ourselves that we can. I think we would be better off if we stopped using such glib phrases as "defining outcomes in terms of specific behaviors."

There are, of course, certain kinds of classroom events, generally of a trivial character in themselves, to which one can point unambiguously for the purpose of defining terms. For example, one can identify such events as "teacher writes with chalk on board," or "teacher speaks" (in the sense that he emits some modulated sound with the help of the vocal cords), or "pupil speaks" (with a parallel definition). One can also identify, unambiguously, such sequences as "teacher speaks and then pupil speaks," or "pupil speaks and then teacher speaks." However, the utilization of the occurrence of such unequivocal events by research workers has not led to any particular understanding of how intellectual development is produced in the school, though it has provided some rather vaguely understood relationships between teacher–pupil interactions and the extent to which the pupil expresses a liking for school. In short, the Tyler approach is typically applicable in school situations to events that other sources of knowledge would lead us to judge as rather trivial in character.

I must make it clear at this point that I am concerned, in this part of the paper, with those terms that can be operationally defined, as directly contrasted with what are commonly referred to as "theoretical terms." The distinction is an important one to emphasize here, particularly because Ennis (1964) does not appear to make the distinction and therefore has great difficulty in developing the concept of an operational definition. The definition of theoretical terms would require a separate treatment and cannot be developed here.

The "lists of specific behaviors" approach presents other problems that have not been commonly recognized. Generally, the behaviors listed do not provide a comprehensive list, but are supposed to represent some kind of sample from a universe of behaviors. An investigator interested in studying the effect of "rewarding behaviors" of teachers might begin by listing some rewarding behaviors. He obviously cannot list all possible rewarding behaviors, but must attempt to present a sample of some universe. Usually, however, no effort is made to specify the boundaries of the universe sampled or the method by which the sample was derived. Yet unless these are specified, we are dealing only with a nebulous and unidentified something-or-other—even though we may have a list of what we euphemistically call "specific behaviors." Much of what we have been doing for the last thirty years conjures up the illusion that our terms are being operationally defined; but this is only an illusion, and one which has greatly retarded educational progress. I would not want to belittle the contribution that Tyler made in the mid-thirties, but we should have been moving on from where he left off thirty years ago, rather than being fixated on an obsolete formula that leaves us with very large bodies of virtually useless data. In the widespread usage associated with that formula, the term "specific behavior" refers to a very broad and general category of behavior. Once we recognize the fact that we have been using "specific" as a synonym for "general," we will at least have recognized one source of confusion in our thinking that has blocked the road to systematic theorizing about instruction.

Operational definition of independent variables. The problem of operational definition is particularly acute in the area of the independent variables of a theory of instruction, the variables that refer to the events to which the learner was exposed. It is in this area that we have a long tradition of using very sloppy and hazy variables such as "traditional *vs.* progressive," or "pupil-centered *vs.* teacher-centered" or "democratic *vs.* authoritarian." All these have been "defined" in terms of general categories of behavior, but since the limits of the categories are never specified, the concepts involved remain obscure. Not until these, or other concepts, have been defined in terms of measuring instruments other than rating scales can one consider that the definitions involved have even begun to become approximations of operational definitions. The kinds of instruments for measuring characteristics of learning environments that were developed back in the thirties by McCall and others (1937) represented a movement in the direction of operational definition, but the fact is that the recent trend has been in the opposite direction. The National Assessment Program, which might have helped clarify the manipulable independent variables in educational research, has moved in the opposite direction and ignored their existence entirely. The result will be that this program will be able to spot deficiencies in the achievements of pupils with perhaps greater accuracy than ever before but is designed to keep us in complete ignorance of the manipulable conditions that led to these deficiencies. The data from the assessment program will undoubtedly have great political utility, much as the results of the Eight Year Study had political utility, but as a source of information that might be of worth in improving education, the National Assessment Program must be viewed as useless and, indeed, as a step in the wrong direction. Data that are to be of value in the improvement of education must have strong independent variables representing manipulable conditions that are clearly defined and unambiguously identified.

Even if the day arrives when the independent variables of a theory of instruction can be measured in terms that provide effective operational definitions, we will still not move ahead very rapidly unless the measurements are derived from situations in which a degree of control is exercised over some of the obvious and important conditions related to learning. The most important of these other neglected variables, beyond any question, is that of *time*. The Norwalk review of available studies too often shows that some particular teaching condition produced more learning than another teaching condition, but one cannot tell from the report of the study whether the results simply reflected differences in the amount of the pupil's time occupied by the two conditions. Many independent variables are likely to appear to be related to amount of pupil learning because the methods involve the use of a greater and lesser amount of time. The results of older studies of the type comparing two obscure conglomerations of teaching conditions were not too seriously contaminated by a lack of control over the time factor, since they generally dealt with large and equal chunks of time, such as a semester or a school year; but the results of newer studies are often rendered meaningless by a lack of control over time. Even such simple studies as those based on the use of a programmed text in comparison with a conventional text rarely report the time spent under each condition. Whatever differences may appear to be produced, they may be only reflecting differences in time spent with the materials. A very large fraction of the data that one might consider using as a basis for aspects of a theory of instruction cannot be used because of the possibility that the independent variable may be only a time variable.

Operational definitions of basic terms. If we abandon the myth that the basic terms of educational theory can be operationally defined by pursuing the deceptive ritual of listing "specific" behaviors that are not specific at all, then other procedures must be enlisted for providing genuine operational definitions. The behavioral sciences provide a number of alternatives that need to be examined in turn.

The definition of variables in terms of tests and test performance under standardized conditions provides one approach that psychologists have long used. In most areas of educational endeavor, I would prefer to see the achievements or skills to be acquired defined in terms of performance on particular tasks organized into measuring instruments, rather than in terms of lists of behaviors. The measuring instruments, then, define the outcomes to be achieved. The definition of teacher characteristics through reference to objective measuring devices has, at this time, limited possibilities only. One limitation is the narrow range of instruments available, but there are other problems too. Suppose, for example, that an authoritarian teacher is defined as one who scores high on the California F-Scale. On the surface this seems like a satisfactory operational definition, but it really is not; for a crucial factor that has to be specified is the set of conditions under which the F-Scale was administered. There is probably no way of making the conditions of administration of any personality test uniform, though much greater uniformity can be achieved in the administration of tests of intellectual performance.

Measuring instruments that provide operational definitions of variables are crucial for the development of a theory of instruction. I also believe that, in the early stages of the development of such instruments, the old "specific behavior" formula may have to be used to locate very crudely and roughly the territory to be covered. However, in doing this one must recognize that the practice of preparing lists of so-called "specific behaviors" is about as scientific as the practice of the mariner recognizing the presence of land beyond the horizon by a faint smell in the breeze. In developing measuring instruments we need the vague cues carried by the wind, but the properties of the measuring instrument itself will tell us whether we have identified a variable that *may* play some part in a theory of instruction.

The definition of terms with reference to performance on tests very clearly limits the language in terms of which a theory of instruction can be constructed. Another promising approach to the problem of defining terms comes from what has long been done in the established experimental sciences, namely defining the basic terms through references to laboratory events. The chemist defines elements through experiments which involve their laboratory properties. The psychologist defines reinforcement in terms of specific laboratory events that have particular consequences. The laboratory as a source of language for discussing problems of learning and instruction has obviously much to offer. Indeed, physics and chemistry have developed their entire vocabularies in laboratory settings and have then gone on to use them successfully for discussing naturally occurring phenomena. One can refer to similar successes, though less striking, in the behavioral sciences. Most of the knowledge derived from research that has had applications to education has come from the laboratory—a fact that is clearly seen when one views the work of such giants as Ebbinghaus, Thorndike, Hebb, Skinner, Piaget, and Gesell. Insofar as we have any technical language in education involving clearly defined terms, that language has been derived from laboratory experimentation. Laboratory settings provide unequivocal opportunities for defining terms through operations. Such opportunities are not provided by the ever-changing and ever-varying scene of the classroom.

Those engaged in the practice of education have shown little appreciation for the usefulness of the Galilean laboratory model for the development of knowledge, and can be hardly expected to look to the laboratory as a source of a suitable technical language in the terms of which the problems of education can be unambiguously discussed. Moreover, there continues to be a distrust of laboratory-derived knowledge, and the money available for educational research continues to flow into avenues involving direct attacks on educational problems— avenues that have been extraordinarily unproductive in the past and that have not even led to the development of a language in which the findings can be clearly and unambiguously reported.

Although I am saying that much of the language of educational research has to be derived from laboratory situations, I am *not* saying that all research has to be undertaken in laboratories. Just as the language of chemistry permits one to describe and discuss naturally occurring phenomena of great complexity, such as the formation of coal, so too can a laboratory-derived language in the behavioral sciences provide the foundation for the study of naturally occurring phenomena. My hope would be that a program of educational research would combine both laboratory and field studies and that the two sets of studies would move ahead hand in hand. What I am concerned with is the present tremendous expansion of field studies that have absolutely no foundation in the on-going systematic research of the behavioral sciences and which do not attempt to utilize the vocabulary of empirical terms that experimentalists have slowly and carefully evolved.

Limitations of Available Data from Classroom Research

Classroom research of the past has not led to protocol statements, summarizing the findings, that represent clear statements that are correct beyond dispute. A summary appraisal of such data as the Norwalk study provides, for example, generally leads to rather vague generalizations of extremely limited utility. If one were to spend a great amount of time working over the data, one might come up with perhaps four or five statements such as "Teacher behavior variously described as authoritarian, structured, autocratic, controlling, direct, and so forth, is less favorable for the achievement of academic skills than is teacher behavior with the opposite characteristics." This is a very weak kind of empirical finding, and the few others that could be stated are no stronger. The interpretation of such a statement is highly dependent upon the intuitive belief that the given adjectives describing teacher behavior pertain to a common dimension. Such a statement is far from the clear empirical finding upon which scientific theories are built. I do not think that we have to be satisfied with knowledge at this crude level; and so long as this is what we have available, we must be on our guard against deriving complicated sets of propositions from it.

Our basic difficulty in utilizing the knowledge derived from classroom research is to put together the findings from different studies. Each investigator tends to use his own favorite language in naming variables, and no synthesis of different studies is possible without engaging in a guess-what-this-means game. At present, there seems to be no end to the creative task of inventing new names for vague something-or-others that happen to intrigue a particular investigator; but the result is not organized knowledge, only chaos. The extraordinarily poor yield of useful generalizations from classroom research, despite massive financial support in recent years, reflects the fact that something is wrong. Perhaps the lack of productivity of the area is not, as those who pursue pure classroom research in naturally occurring situations suggest, that the problems are very difficult. Perhaps it is the approach that is fundamentally unsound.

The generalizations that derive from classroom research also appear to have little to do with the controllable variables that are known to have an effect upon learning. The kind of research that has been undertaken in the past, including much that is currently in fashion such as Interaction Analysis, would never have discovered such important facts related to teaching and learning as those discovered in the laboratory about the effect of an early enriched perceptual environment, the conditions of teaching under which transfer will or will not take place, the function of language in organizing the perceptual world, the perceptual processes performed by the beginning reader, the effect of stimulus complexity on attention, and the numerous other findings—actual and still to be realized—which represent the body of knowledge that must be taken into account in educational planning and teacher education in the future.

Let us consider further the difficulties that are encountered in using the Norwalk study data for constructing a theory of instruction. The difficulties presented by a lack of operational definitions of basic terms are just the beginning of our problems. The data also reflect other serious limitations.

An examination of the typical teacher behavior variables found in the Norwalk review of research indicates that research workers have tended to emphasize in their studies those characteristics that are believed to have generality and to permeate behavior. Such characteristics as turbulence, hostility, warmth, and permissiveness, appear much more frequently than more limited and situation-tied characteristics such as "assigns child remedial exercise" or "helps pupil to identify errors in work." In terms of the development of a theory of instruction with a potential utility, the emphasis on traits that have generality should be recognized as an emphasis on those aspects of the teacher's behavior structure that are deeply ingrained, rather than those that are readily modified and trained. In other words, the teacher characteristics emphasized are those that teacher training is least likely to be able to control. The training of the young adult has generally been more successful when it has been directed toward the modification of relatively specific aspects of behavior rather than of highly generalized traits. Studies of the relationships of highly generalized teacher traits to achievement of pupils provides data of interest to those selecting candidates for teacher training rather than data that might be of value in a teacher training program.

There is another factor that has inclined investigators to turn to general behavior characteristics of teachers rather than to more specific aspects of skill. When observation is undertaken under classroom conditions, a general trait, because of its ubiquitousness, provides many opportunities for observing manifestations of it. The very frequency of relevant instances makes for reliability of observation, much as having many items in a test is likely to make it easier to produce a reliable measure. On the other hand, the more limited the aspect of behavior studied, the fewer are the naturally occurring instances in which it can be observed; hence there is great difficulty in accumulating a sufficient number of observations to yield a reliable measure unless very long and very frequent periods of observation are involved.

The focus of classroom research on the study of personality traits that permeate the activity of the teacher in the classroom has tended to draw attention away from the study of relatively narrow teaching skills—skills that are, perhaps, both limited in scope and highly trainable. If teaching is believed to involve identifiable and quite specific skills, and if the manifestation of these component skills is an important condition for pupil achievement, then one important task of the research worker is to discover whether relationships do exist between pupil achievement and the extent to which these relatively specific skills are manifested. However, as a practical matter, such a relationship may not be demonstrable in a naturally occurring classroom situation, since a sufficient number of instances of each skill could perhaps be observed only after months or years of observation.

But important teacher behaviors do not have to be commonly occurring teacher behaviors. A single interaction between a pupil and a teacher—an interaction lasting only a few minutes—may be the most critical event in the entire school year for a particular pupil, since it may solve an overwhelming difficulty that the pupil has had in some aspect of his work. Events of that kind are not found either by typical observation procedures or by interaction-analysis data collection devices that make no distinction between important and unimportant events in the instructional channel. I do not think that this problem is going to be resolved by the detailed analyses of classroom data collected on video tapes that some are now undertaking, for the fault is in the data-collection procedures themselves in that they do not permit the careful study of particular classes of teaching events.

The impression gained from the Norwalk summary of available data is that those aspects of a theory of instruction dealing with specific teaching skills will have to be derived from laboratory data: that is to say, data collected in highly controlled and artificial situations. The kinds of laboratories in which such data are to be collected don't necessarily have to be the aseptic white coat variety. Indeed, they may involve situations set up within schools. Nevertheless, they have to be situations in which a high degree of control is exercised over the independent variables related to learning and in which the incidence of particular classes of teaching events is sufficiently high to permit the observer to establish the degree of effect. In such situations one can collect information about the contribution of a particular teaching skill to the learning of the pupil. Such data can be collected because one can arrange the teaching situation so that specific teaching behaviors do actually occur and so that the skill is clearly manifested. In the laboratory, we can arrange for the occurrence of particular sequences of teacher behaviors, though in the classroom setting we can only hope that behaviors belonging in a general broad category will occur. Thus does the laboratory permit us not only to begin our research with genuine operational definitions of our terms, rather than with the pseudo-operational definitions that have been cluttering up our thinking for the last thirty years; in the laboratory, we can also arrange for a sufficiently high incidence of particular teacher behaviors so that any effect produced will be clearly evident in pupil achievement. In the classroom, any effect that certain behaviors may have is so diluted with the effect of other events that the consequences in which one is interested cannot be discerned.

Another way of looking at this problem is to say that our major difficulty in deriving discoveries from classroom research is that of reducing the size of the error term in our statistical analyses. In studies of relationships between teaching conditions and the acquisition of intellectual skills, numerous uncontrolled factors combine to influence acquisition, producing very large error terms in the analysis of the data. So long as there are these inflated error terms, nothing can be learned about factors that have genuine influences on behavior. Suitable experimental controls result in the reduction of the size of these error terms in relation to the size of the main effects. Experimental controls handle this very practical and important problem.

I am quite convinced that the kind of data needed for the development of a theory of instruction will have to be produced from laboratory research. This research may involve classroom-like situations, but these situations will have to be under much closer control by the experimenter than have been those situations involved in classroom research of the past.

I must also point out that when I say that research on teaching needs to be pursued through laboratory experiments, many of which may involve classroom-like situations, I am not suggesting a return to the old type of pseudo-experiment in which one vague conglomeration of procedures referred to as the "experimental method" was compared with another vague conglomeration described as the "traditional method." Such studies do not represent scientific experimentation in any sense of the term.

The Hierarchical Structure of a Theory of Instruction

After looking at the various classes of data from which a theory of instruction might be derived, one begins to arrive at a clearer view of what a theory of instruction will look like when one is developed. I would envisage that it would present a hierarchy of propositions. At the top of the hierarchy would be propositions stating relationships between pupil acquisition variables and general permeating characteristics of the educational environment. These would include measures of those characteristics of teachers having widespread impact on events in the classroom. At the base of the hierarchy would be statements pertaining to environmental events tied to much more specific aspects of learning.

Let me illustrate further the nature of this hierarchy. The kinds of statements found at the top of the hierarchy would summarize, for example, the numerous studies that have related a permissive–authoritarian dimension to pupil achievement. This is one of the few independent variables tied to measuring instruments that could be referred to in such statements at the present time. In my judgment, the research shows a trend of findings indicating that the more authoritarian the teacher the less the achievement of the pupils; and the relationship does not seem to be tied to any particular achievements. The effect is a very small one but, I think, genuine. A statement of this relationship would have a legitimate place in a theory of instruction, though I doubt whether it would have much value either for helping the teacher to manage the classroom more effectively or for developing programs of teacher education. Again, if it had any practical implications at all, it would be for the selection of teacher training candidates.

At the lower end of the hierarchy would be those statements that summarize findings relating quite specific conditions of learning to such events as the acquisition of some aspect of spelling skill, the learning of vocabulary in a certain foreign language, the acquisition of a particular motor skill, and so forth. These statements would include many that referred to teaching techniques in particular situations and to the design of special materials for the achievement of narrow objectives. The terms of these statements would be most frequently defined in terms of events in experimentally controlled laboratory situations. These statements would be those to which one would turn to find guidelines for the design of programs of teacher education, the development of instructional materials including audio-visual materials, and the planning of particular classroom events. These are also the statements that are seen least frequently in current educational literature on curriculum, method, and related areas. These statments will have to be derived mainly from laboratory experimentation. We can already begin to assemble some statements thus derived. The literature on learning and perception can yield far more statements at this level of theory construction than contemporary educational literature would lead one to expect.

Such a set of propositions will probably have to be developed first without too much attempt being made to give them the unity that characterizes high-level theorizing. This unity is ultimately brought about through the emergence of a system of empirical and theoretical terms that provide unity within the system of propositions. Perhaps the best place to start might be with a system of empirical propositions, that is to say, a set of propositions closely tied to data. A review of such propositions might permit us to begin to introduce the necessary theoretical terms that would give both unity and conciseness to the system. It is then, particularly, that we will have to be on our guard, for it is the improper introduction and use of theoretical terms that has so often produced theorizing which is nothing short of nonsense. If we continue to disregard what is known about the development of theoretical terms, we are likely to end up with nothing more than a new version of the old pedagogical moonshine that made us euphoric but accomplished nothing else. The new theories of education are not going to include meaningless clichés such as "The whole is greater than the sum of its parts" or the more modern pieces of philosophical nonsense that continue to clutter elementary education textbooks.

The Introduction of Theoretical Terms in the Interpretation of Classroom Research

Any study of the products of research conducted in naturally occurring classroom situations clearly reveals that, at the most, it has produced only a few rather vague generalizations of very limited utility. The data do not lead to a theory of instruction; and data collected under similar circumstances in the future probably can do no better, however clever the data collecting and coding techniques may become. While we should not cast aside the little that has been learned by these procedures, we must also be on our guard lest we use the meager products to elaborate a theory of instruction that introduces theoretical terms. The problems connected with the introduction of theoretical terms have already been mentioned, and it is sufficient here to state that there is widespread agreement among empirical scientists that the introduction of theoretical terms is justified only after there has been considerable accumulation of substantive empirical knowledge. Such a state of knowledge has not been reached in the area of classroom research; indeed, we are still at the stage of exploring problems of technique.

The matter of the introduction of theoretical terms is mentioned here because of the facility manifested by persons in education for introducing theoretical terms long before the data warrant such an introduction. Such terms are justified only when the empirical knowledge derived from research comes from replicable findings, when it is represented by protocol statements about which there is little or no dispute, and when the basic terms can be defined through well-identified operations. Classroom research has clearly not yet reached that stage, and there are even questions whether laboratory research can ever be that far developed. The basic problem we have to face, then, is that of designing studies that will yield protocol statements representing clear empirical findings. This is probably a much more difficult task than we have assumed it to be.

Summary

This paper is an extension of a previous paper (Travers, 1966) that described the major characteristics of an empirically based theory of instruction. A serious stumbling block in the development of such a theory stems from the fact that most educational research does not result in empirical propositions involving operationally defined terms. This unfortunate state of affairs stems largely from the fact that research on instruction has been founded on a simple formula developed more than a quarter of a century ago which postulated that terms relating to behavior could be operationally defined by listing specific behaviors. However, the lists of so-called specific terms turn out to be nothing more than lists of very general categories of behavior. The results of classroom research generally produce statements in which few of the terms, if any, are adequately defined. The result is a state of confusion in which the findings of one study cannot be compared with or consolidated with the findings of other studies. Consolidation is possible when the basic empirical terms involve similar operational definitions.

Useful knowledge about the conditions that are related to learning is not likely to be derived from the observation of naturally occurring teaching situations. A much more profitable approach is to construct genuine laboratory experiments involving classroom-like situations, but with a much higher degree of control over experimental conditions than was found in some of the older forms of educational experiment that compared method A with method B. Experimental situations developed in classroom-like situations can present all the rigor of classical laboratory experimentation.

Once the study of teaching has developed techniques that approximate those of an experimental science, the difficulties at present associated with the widespread usage of ill-defined terms ceases to exist; for an experimental approach inevitably permits the definition of terms through laboratory operations. Two major sources of operational definitions are available. One of these involves the use of testing instruments that have appropriate characteristics. The other involves the use of laboratory situations in which terms are defined through identifiable laboratory operations.

Serious difficulties exist in determining, through observation of classroom events, the extent to which quite specific teaching skills are effective in producing learning. The more specific the skill involved, the more one is likely to have to depend on laboratory data and on a Galilean model of developing knowledge about instruction. This latter model involves the hazard of having to make inferences from data collected in simplified situations. To some degree these hazards can be reduced by constructing the laboratory situations so that they include as many as possible of the features of the classroom.

In my previous paper, the suggestion was made that, as a first step towards the formulation of a theory of instruction, an attempt be made to formulate and list propositions that present established relationships between the independent and dependent variables of such a theory. Such propositions could probably be ordered into a hierarchy: from those that involve conditions that tend to permeate the many learning situations to which the learner is exposed, to those that state relationships between specific teaching procedures or conditions and the acquisition of particular skills. Later, as theoretical terms emerge that are properly tied to systems of operationally defined empirical terms, the propositions can have woven into them the unity that a theory must ultimately possess.

SEMINAR DISCUSSION OF TRAVERS PAPER

The Language of Classroom Research

BIDDLE: Could you explain, with examples, those few terms which have come out of the laboratory and have been the most useful, so far, for the studies of teaching?

TRAVERS: *Reinforcement* comes from the laboratory, and *transfer of training* is certainly derived from the laboratory; I think a great deal of the language of the laboratory has infiltrated talk within education.

ROSENSHINE: In your first paper (1966) on this theme, you argued that the production of theory by metaphorical extension of laboratory studies is a dangerously misleading activity.

TRAVERS: It can be, and I used the term "metaphorical extension" to emphasize the difference from scientific generalization.

GUMP: Everybody could agree on your saying that you can get un-equivocal content for terms by using the laboratory; but to say the laboratory situations have contributed a great deal to an understanding of the educational factors is a value statement.

TRAVERS: They aid in, and are central in, the operational definition of terms. You cannot get along without operationally defined terms in any language, but you must settle for certain terms in your language which have only a very rough approximation to operational definition. My proposition is that you cannot take all of this classroom research and derive any kind of theoretical term that has any meaning. A scientific theory that is worth anything must have protocol statements with operationally defined terms.

ROSENSHINE: Do we understand that you don't know what the terms of classroom research mean?

TRAVERS: Knowing what they mean doesn't mean that you have the phenomenon there to which they refer.

41

SULLIVAN: One must make distinction between kinds of operational definition. In the one case the reference is to an operational definition which clearly grows out of some observable conditions; the second meaning refers to whether or not a concept is useful. If usefulness is the criterion, a theory does not need to be empirically derived. I wonder whether a theory of instruction could proceed independently from your model of teaching, or are some of the terms of a theory of teaching actually derived from a model that will be based on a set of axioms?

TRAVERS: I wouldn't think that anybody is going to get anywhere by an axiomatic derivation of theory. My conception of a theory of instruction is that it would be some kind of summarization of what we know about learning events in a classroom, and some of the data will be derived from observation of classroom situations. A theory of instruction will be a putting together of empirically verifiable findings. The model will simply take some of these that are within the limits prescribed by the value system.

BIDDLE: You specified grounds for discriminating good and bad classroom research and, unfortunately, if we use these criteria most of the research seems to be bad. If one were to take these criteria and apply them to the studies that Kaya (1967) has in fact summarized, one would discover that ninety per cent of those studies constitute bad research. However, to say that classroom research is, therefore, bad and that we should not do any more of it, that rather we should go to the laboratory to look for variables for our theory of instruction, does not follow.

TRAVERS: I am talking about the language in terms of which we might discuss a theory of instruction. Most of such a language has to be derived from the laboratory.

ROSENSHINE: Let me quote from your 1966 paper: "The evolution of a language for starting a theory of instruction would appear to require the medium of empirical research. Components of such a language appear to be evolving in such varied work as that of Bellack (1966), Hughes (1963), Atkinson (1960), Skinner (1950), Taba (1964b), Smith and others (1963b)." These people have looked to the classroom for their terms.

TRAVERS: Yes, but as I look at the recent data, I am skeptical about whether you can get a set of terms out of this work. You merely have a dictionary of relationships. When I was involved in classroom research and tried to pull it together, I found that I could not match terms across the different studies.

GAGE: Suppose we take a term from laboratory work—like *reinforcement*. Skinner, to take one example, defines this operationally in terms of pellets or seeds, something that increases the likelihood of the recurrence of a certain kind of behavior. We might become metaphorical and suggest that, in the classroom, it won't be a pellet of food, but words like "good," "that's fine," or "nice work," and they would be tallied by Flanders (1965) in Category 2. Cogan (1958) adopted a different approach and asked the pupils how often their teachers said nice things to them. Ryans (1960) used rating scales and summarized the ratings. Suppose we persuaded Flanders to observe in the same classrooms as those in which Cogan got the pupils to report and Ryans had his observers rate. And suppose we then found high positive correlations between these three operational definitions of reinforcing behavior. Then we would find that we could empirically equate these three operational definitions of the degree to which a teacher provides reinforcement, and we might call them indices of "warmth."

TRAVERS: Yes, but nobody does this empirical operationalization. You start in this case with a body of laboratory information which shows that you have a great range of reinforcing events. You have a population and there is some possibility of generalizing from laboratory events. Empirically, if you can show similar kinds of events in the classroom producing the same kinds of results, then you would have a classification which you might use.

GAGE: Do you mean that you get a concept like reinforcement out of the laboratory and search for its analogues in, or its translations into, terms of classroom behavior?

SMITH: Can you go backwards and take a concept like "warmth," as it were, and try to reduce it to a laboratory phenomenon?

TRAVERS: All the studies of handling and fondling of rats would fall into this category, but in general, when you go backwards you end up with muddy kinds of constructs.

SMITH: Another example would be reducing many of the clinical, Freudian terms to make them experimentally verifiable and then trying to work out a theory of psychodynamics which is laboratory-based.

The real richness of the concepts came out of patients and seems more potent than conceptual outcomes derived from the laboratory and utilized in the classroom. I think of the Dollard and Miller (1950) attempt to make sense of "displacement" as an example of this.

ROSENSHINE: Yet, the correlational research of Bellack (1966), Soar (1966), Spaulding (1963), and Wallen (1966) proceeds differently. These investigators have used adjusted achievement scores as one criterion and have gone into the classroom in order to find specific behaviors which correlate with student achievement. I think that the results of this type of research may be quite different from the development of effective variables in a laboratory setting. The work of Kounin (with Friesen & Norton, 1966) is the best case in point. Using student attention to task as his criterion, and teacher behaviors as the correlates, his naturalistic research has yielded variables which he named "indirectness," "jerkiness," "thrusts," and "dangles"—variables which are quite different from those developed in a laboratory.

It is also very difficult to apply variables developed in laboratory research to a classroom setting. Repetition, for example, is a variable which can be studied easily in a laboratory situation. But it is quite another thing to identify instances of repetition in an on-going classroom.

I am not suggesting that naturalistic studies should be the only approach, but significant correlates of school achievement might come out of this work, and such research might be one of the sources which will contribute to the development of a theory of instruction.

Control of Classroom Studies

TRAVERS: I agree, and I want to be very eclectic without going through all that has been done before. I think this method of classroom research offers the possibility of a very important control of teaching and one which hasn't been used in the past. As we go on, we shall include more control and we will get more reproducible data. One of the most important needs is to get a reproduction in two different places of the same study. Most classroom studies cannot be reproduced. Reproduction should not be by those who did the original work. Often in laboratory studies you will find that the people who designed the study can replicate and get the same results, but other people do not get these results. In other words, the original work and designs were simply not reproducible.

GAGE: The positive thing Travers is suggesting, about the way in which research ought to proceed, is this: delimiting much more sharply the range of phenomena that we look at in the classroom and controlling much more thoroughly. Bellack controlled the curriculum for a week. Microteaching cuts down the phenomenon of teaching into even more manageable bits, but it has been useful as both a training and a research device.

TRAVERS: We want greater control of what we are studying, and less observation in naturally occurring situations, for this has been a very unproductive method of research.

Research Strategies

BIDDLE: It seems to me that there is a variety of research strategies within modern social science. I would like to refer you to L. M. Smith and Geoffrey's (1968) participant observation studies in schools. Their hypotheses are not necessarily all correct or useful. I suspect that a large proportion of the ideas that have been suggested by them are wrong; participant observation leads only to the proposal of ideas, and does not test them. If you were to take some of these ideas and operationalize them in field studies in the classroom you might find that, in some cases, you cannot get the observers to agree on the presence of any particular phenomenon. On those grounds alone, you would throw out any particular idea.

However, let us assume that in a field study you can, in fact, operationalize several classes of events: as you observe events of Class A vary in some way, you have events of Class B that are also varying, and also Class C; you suspect a predictive relationship between events of Classes A, B, and C. You are ready at that point to manipulate variables. You might want to manipulate the classroom in a field experiment or, alternatively, recreate some aspect of class activity in the laboratory. You want to manipulate a variable A to see whether it does produce a change in B and C or to find that B and C are covarying with A because of some other factor that you didn't think of. It is unreasonable to argue that laboratory experiments are useful for getting conceptual insight. Laboratory experiments are almost by definition sterile; they are designed with the exclusive purpose of giving an unambiguous assesssment of the relationship between variables A and B or A, B, and C. They are uniquely useful and irreplaceable for this purpose. But they cannot tell you what you should think about, and they certainly cannot tell you whether the variables you are experimenting with are operational.

TRAVERS: I think the key to our knowledge about the way visual information is handled—and this includes the kind of perception you get in early reading behavior—comes from study of the optic nerve of very simple organisms. This is the key which has cracked the whole code of visual analysis and has enormous implications for what the visual reading process involves and how this process is to be facilitated. I am not saying that Interaction Analysis isn't going to yield anything; but we need to look for richer concepts, and I would define a rich concept as one which ultimately will fit into a complex system of sentences which we call a theory. I don't know how you can find such concepts.

GUMP: We will never have concepts that can handle the classroom if we retreat to the laboratory and narrow the situation. My proposition is that psychologists are not well trained to investigate classrooms.

TRAVERS: I have two recent papers published describing teaching the principles of refraction to sixth and seventh graders by various means, including realistic and non-realistic situations, like line drawings and so on (Overing & Travers, 1966, 1967). The physiology of visual analysis was the stimulus for these studies in a classroom setting. Ideas come from many places, and I don't believe that we have to look into a classroom to understand what is going on there.

GUMP: There are certain larger problems which are inescapable. If we agree that the context must be respected and that it restrains and limits phenomena, then the classroom context will have to be respected. It cannot be respected using four students instead of thirty or by going into a laboratory. Context variables have to be labeled and studied in a classroom.

BIDDLE: I wonder why it is that so many of us are using the criterion of achievement as the way of exploring the effects of classroom processes. There are many things happening in classrooms today which may disappear or be changed radically if we changed the classroom itself. Along with the cognitive learnings that go on in the classroom, students must be learning adult roles (by observing the teacher as a model) and child roles (by observing what other pupils in the class-room situation are doing). Willy-nilly they learn creativity, or lack of creativity, and a great many other things.

BELLACK: I think it has been an error in all the research that no atten-tion has been given to the unanticipated consequences of school situa-tions. In our study we naively started out postulating what we thought students ought to learn and were not sensitive to the importance of the many things that are unanticipated and unrelated to conventional outcomes.

BIDDLE: We might be about to dismantle the classroom, but I suspect we'll be disturbing a great deal more than simply the rate of knowledge acquisition. I think that what is learned unintentionally is perhaps much more important than that which is intentionally taught and learned.

BELLACK: Merton (1957) claims that in sociology the most important insights have come from the study of latent functions, and I suspect that very much the same thing is true of education.

GAGE: There are two sets of variables to be matched against one another. On one side would be a test of designs for education or instruction, such as the conventional classroom, programmed instruction, the lecture hall, TV, small discussion groups—that is, a whole array of possible approaches to teaching or the education of children. On the other side would be a list of kinds of outcomes, such as knowledge of paired associates, ability to listen to disagreeable arguments of a fellow participant in a discussion, comprehension of career models— that is, all the things that we want children to learn. The grand strategy, of course, is to draw lines making the optimal connections between the two lists—types of outcomes and designs for teaching. So far we've only dealt with the conventional classroom, of the kind that Flanders, Bellack, Smith, and the others have studied. Isn't this a problem?

Research to Date

THREE

Teaching Behaviors Related to Pupil Achievement: A Review of Research

BARAK ROSENSHINE

Introduction

Fifteen years ago, two reviews were written about the relationships of teacher characteristics and behaviors with measures of pupil achievement (Morsh & Wilder, 1954; Ackerman, 1954). In 24 out of the 25 studies reported by these reviewers, the teacher characteristics included presage variables such as age, intelligence, experience, and scores on personality tests; the teacher behaviors were assessed by rating scales marked by pupils, supervisors, or the investigator. The reviewers concluded that the results of the studies were contradictory and inconsistent, and recommended the use of systematic observation techniques in future studies of teacher behaviors which may be related to pupil achievement:

> Because the actual behavior of the teacher in the classroom is such an important factor, it is necessary to devise means of observing and recording this behavior. Methods must be used in which only a minimum of inference is allowed. . . . Such a process does suggest a potentially wider range of investigation which it is hoped will provide more reliable information in the

The author expresses his appreciation to Barbara Rosenshine, Norma Furst, and Ned Flanders for their insightful comments concerning this paper. The review was supported in part by a Temple University Summer Faculty Research Award.

areas of teacher effectiveness and pupil change (Ackerman, 1954, pp. 286–287).

Proposals of this kind were well received in the educational community, and many workers developed objective, reliable observational systems which did not rate, but *counted* the frequencies of specified teacher behaviors. Twenty-six different systems of observation have been collected in *Mirrors for Behavior* (Simon & Boyer, 1967); at least twenty more were not included in these volumes, and probably others could be uncovered with little effort.

It is relatively easy to develop observational systems and obtain high inter-rater agreements. However, at some point we must ask which of the hundreds of behaviors that can be objectively and reliably counted are related to pupil growth. Many of these behaviors *ought* to have significant correlations with pupil growth; but, as Gage has noted, "We have been fooled before in educational research and I, for one, shall rest uneasy until the evidence on these plausible but undemonstrated connections is in" (Gage, 1966, p. 35).

Some evidence is in. This review focuses upon nineteen investigations which have used category systems in an attempt to determine specific relationships between what a teacher does and what pupils learn. It is offered as a sympathetic review.

In order to sharpen our focus, several excellent studies have been excluded and only parts of other studies have been included in this review. Reports on correlations between *rated* teaching behavior and pupil achievement (e.g., Wallen & Wodtke, 1963; Solomon *et al.*, 1964a, 1964b; Chall & Feldmann, 1966; Fortune, 1967) are not included because it is difficult to translate dimensions such as pupil interest ratings or type of pupil questions; the strength and consistency of the correlations of these measures and adjusted class achievement scores has not been adequately established. Results on the relationships between teacher behaviors and pupil scores on tests of creativity were also excluded, because this area merits a separate review.

The studies discussed in this review are those in which investigators used the natural setting of the classroom to find relationships between specific teaching behaviors and pupil achievement. All of the studies are labeled correlational, although a number of investigators used an *F* or a *t* test to determine the significance of their findings.

A number of methodological problems make it difficult to compare these studies, assess the results, and use the findings in teacher education (cf. Biddle, 1967; Meux, 1967). Some of the difficulties most relevant to this review will be elaborated below.

Problems in Comparing Studies and Using Results

Research relating classroom behavior and pupil achievement usually includes four steps: (1) the development of an instrument which can be used systematically to record the frequency of certain specified teaching behaviors; (2) use of the instrument to record classroom behaviors of teachers and their pupils; (3) a ranking of the classrooms according to a measure of pupil achievement adjusted for initial difference among the classes; and (4) a determination of the behaviors whose frequency of occurrence is related to adjusted class achievement scores.

The observational instruments described in this review contain sets of non-evaluative, relatively objective categories to describe what goes on in the classroom. In the process of developing inter-rater agreement, each investigator had to develop many ground rules to clarify distinctions between such items as "questions that stimulate thinking" (Perkins, 1964) and "praise and encouragement" and "use of pupil ideas" (Flanders, 1965). Some reports included detailed descriptions of the coding protocols (e.g., Bellack *et al.*, 1966; Spaulding, 1965), but others provided only the names or short definitions of the observed behaviors. The reports that did not include detailed protocols require the reader to infer what might be meant by a category in interpreting the results of the studies. For example, of the eight investigators who employed the Interaction Analysis system (Flanders, 1965), only one (Snider, 1966) specified the ground rules used to distinguish between different categories. This ambiguity has another consequence: although the investigators all reported high inter-rater reliability, the degree of inter-investigation reliability remains uncertain. We do not know whether raters trained by Flanders (1965), Soar (1966), or Furst (1967) would have agreed in their scoring of behaviors if they had all viewed the same classroom.

The adjustment of the measures of pupil achievement for the initial differences among the classes also creates problems in interpreting the results, even when all the investigators used regression procedures to make the adjustments. Three issues seem important. First, investigators used different covariates—some used a subject area pretest, some a measure of verbal and/or non-verbal intelligence, and some both. Second, investigators differed in their statistical treatment of these covariates—some used the within-class regression coefficient, and others used the between-classes regression coefficient (cf. Coats, 1966; Wallen & Wodtke, 1963). Third, different test instruments yield different results. When Snider (1966) used both the New York State Regents Examination and the Cooperative Physics Test as his criterion instruments, teacher behaviors significantly related to adjusted pupil achievement on one instrument were not significantly related on the other. Chall and Feldmann (1966) found that teacher ratings significantly related to pupil achievement in reading on the Stanford Achievement Test were not significantly related to scores on the Fry Reading Test or the Gates Reading Test.

Finally, many of the statistical procedures used to relate teacher behaviors to pupil achievement may be questioned. Because intact classrooms were used as the primary unit and many teacher behaviors were investigated, the number of variables tended to become too large for the number of teachers or classrooms measured. In one study, 114 variables were studied in 27 classrooms (Spaulding, 1965). As Meux (1967) and Gage (1968) have pointed out, the low ratio of variables to subjects tends to invalidate the assumptions of multicorrelational and factor-analytic procedures. Even in studies in which 100 bivariate correlations were run and 12 correlations were statistically significant, we have no way of knowing which variables to eliminate as occurring by chance.

Several investigators used analysis of variance or other inferential, experimental designs to test the statistical significance of their findings. In such studies, the sample was divided into high–low or high–middle–low classes on the basis of either the independent or the dependent variable; in some studies only the extremely high and extremely low classes were analyzed. These procedures create problems in interpretation, because we cannot conclude that a significant F ratio also indicates a significant correlation between the incidence of a variable and the level of the adjusted achievement scores. For example, neither Soar (1966) nor Furst (1967) found significant linear correlations between i/d ratio and the adjusted class mean achievement score(s); but both investigators found a significant F ratio when extreme classes were compared. Generally, investigators have found it easier to obtain significant results using an inferential design.

The most appropriate design depends upon the purposes of the research. Correlational designs are necessary in order to develop statements about lawful relationships between specified teaching behaviors and pupil outcomes. But if our purpose is to identify those behaviors associated with the most successful and the least successful teachers, so that this information can be applied in a teacher education program or serve as a hypothesis for future research, then inferential designs seem appropriate.

Interaction Analysis

Nine of the studies discussed here have used Interaction Analysis (IA) to describe teacher and pupil behavior; two of the others used modifications of the IA categories. This systematic observation procedure, developed by Flanders (1965) (cf. Amidon and Flanders, 1967), is well known and does not need to be discussed here in detail. There are, however, a number of labeling problems associated with the procedure which do affect interpretation of the kind being undertaken in this review.

Figure 3.1 shows a summary matrix and some of the variables resulting from combinations of cells that have been identified as

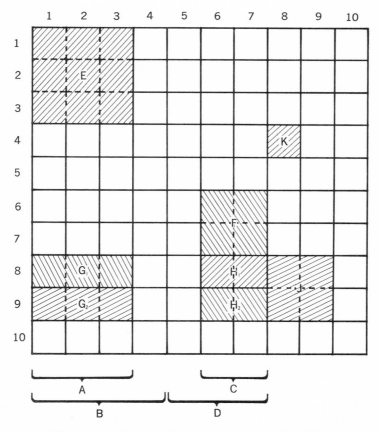

Figure 3.1 Selected Interaction Analysis Variables

phenomenally significant. Coats (1966) described 27 such variables, and 20 more have been developed by others. This large number of variables has resulted in some confusion when different investigators apply the same label to what are different combinations of cells, or label the same combinations with different titles; thus, the terms "i/d" and "Revised I/D" have been used to refer to identical combinations of cells. The operational definitions of some of the common IA variables to be discussed in this review are set out in Table 3.1.

TABLE 3.1
DEFINITIONS OF THE INDEPENDENT VARIABLES

Name	Definition
I/D ratio	Ratio of the number of tallies in columns 1–4 to the number of tallies in columns 5–7 (ratio of area B to area D in Figure 3.1).
i/d ratio	Ratio of the number of tallies in columns 1–3 to the number of tallies in columns 6 and 7 (ratio of area A to area C in Figure 3.1).
i/d 8	The i/d ratio for row 8 only (ratio of area G_1 to area H_1).
i/d 9	The i/d ratio for row 9 only (ratio of area G_2 to area H_2).
i/d 8-9	The i/d ratio for rows 8 and 9 (ratio of area $G_1 + G_2$ to area $H_1 + H_2$).
extended indirect (xi)	Percentage of tallies in the following cells: 1-1, 1-2, 1-3, 2-1, 2-2, 2-3, 3-1, 3-2, 3-3 (area E).
extended direct (xd)	Percentage of tallies in the following cells: 6-6, 6-7, 7-6, 7-7 (area F).
extended i/d ratio (xi/xd)	Ratio of the number of extended indirect tallies to the number of extended direct tallies (ratio of area E to area F).

Overview of Studies

The nineteen studies summarized below are similar in that each investigator used a systematic observational system to tally the frequencies of certain teacher behaviors in the classroom, and then attempted to determine relationships between the frequencies of the behaviors and measures of adjusted pupil achievement. The investigations differed in the behaviors observed, the procedures used to determine the existence of significant relationships, the grade level, and the instructional period. In almost all studies the class was used as the statistical unit.

Nursery School to Grade 3

Fortune (1966) studied the teaching behavior of 30 Operation Headstart teacher-trainees who taught special lessons lasting from five to seven minutes on social studies concepts such as policemen, community worker, ships, and trains. The video tapes of the performances of the most effective and least effective teachers, as determined by adjusted pupil test scores, were studied using a guide containing 13 items related to concept formation practices and types of affective interactions. The final report did not give specific definitions of the observed teaching behaviors. Three of these behaviors were called the "strongest discriminating" behaviors—the more able teachers were scored as using the following behaviors more frequently: (1) allowing pupils to physically explore and manipulate the objects, (2) introducing and leading pupil verbal practice, and (3) praise and repetition of pupils' correct answers.

Conners and Eisenberg (1966) studied the behavior of 38 experienced preschool teachers during a six-week summer program in Operation Headstart. Each series of teacher–pupil interactions was classified into one of seven "episodes." These included development of self-concept, intellectual growth, personal responsibility for property and materials, and creativity and stimulation of personality. The observational system was based upon the earlier work by Reichenberg-Hackett (1962), although again neither report contained clear, operational definitions of these behaviors. Teachers were classified as high, middle, or low according to their classes' mean growth on the Peabody Picture Vocabulary Test. The high-achieving teachers participated in significantly more episodes which focused on intellectual growth and in significantly fewer episodes which focused on personal responsibility for property and materials.

Wallen (1966) studied the classroom behavior of 36 teachers in grade 1 and 40 teachers in grade 3 during a school year. The criterion measures were the class scores in vocabulary, reading comprehension, and arithmetic computation, all adjusted for initial standing in reading vocabulary. One of the observational instruments was developed from IA and contained eleven categories of teacher behavior. Zero-order correlations were computed between the frequency and percentage of each behavior and the adjusted class mean score. Separate analyses were computed for each grade. The more able teachers spent more time asking questions and giving "minimal reinforcement"—positive feedback (e.g., "Right," "Okay"), which is less strong than "praise and encouragement." Praise and encouragement itself was not a significant correlate of pupil achievement. The more able teachers spent less time on "personal control"—directing the pupils to perform or stop certain acts related to personal rather than academic behavior. Academic control, moralizing, and hostility were not significant correlates of achievement. The significant results differed in the strength of their correlation across different criterion measures and different grades. These correlations are presented in Table 3.2.

TABLE 3.2

SIGNIFICANT CORRELATIONS BETWEEN TEACHING BEHAVIORS
AND ADJUSTED CLASS ACHIEVEMENT IN THE
INVESTIGATION BY WALLEN (1966)

	Reading Vocab.		Reading Comp.		Arithmetic	
	Grade 1	Grade 3	Grade 1	Grade 3	Grade 1	Grade 3
Minimal Reinforcement (frequency)	.278	.092	.386 °	.061	.423 °	.090
Minimal Reinforcement (percentage)	.110	−.069	.138	−.040	.372 °	.141
Asking Questions (frequency)	.439 °	.132	.528 °	.117	.248	.277
Asking Questions (percentage)	.401 °	.072	.317	.120	.200	.361 °
Personal Control (frequency)	−.239	−.153	−.088	−.144	−.137	−.085
Personal Control (percentage)	−.379 °	−.226	−.136	−.219	−.220	−.144

° $p < .05$ (2-tailed)

Harris and his associates (1966, 1968) used a special instrument, OScAR–R (Medley, Impellitterri, & Smith, n.d.), to observe the teaching behaviors of the first- and second-grade teachers for the same group of pupils. Forty-eight classrooms participated in grade 1, 38 in grade 2. The criterion measures were the class scores on standard tests in reading and language arts, adjusted for initial standing.

For the first year (Harris & Serwer, 1966) the variable labeled "total interchanges" had significant positive correlations with three of the five criterion measures (word reading, spelling, and word study); the variable labeled "control" had significant negative correlations with four criterion measures (word reading, paragraph reading, vocabulary, and word study).

At the end of the second grade, all pupils took the Metropolitan Achievement Test, and these scores were adjusted using previous scores on the Stanford Achievement Test as the covariate (Harris *et al.*, 1968). The results on total interchanges were not replicated. The correlations between control and achievement remained negative, but none of them was significant at the .05 level. The single significant finding was between negative motivation and reading achievement. Although the scoring key for those specific behaviors which formed the variables "control" and "negative motivation" was not given in any of the reports, some behaviors such as criticism of pupils were counted in developing both variables (Medley, personal communication). In the second year, the amount of time teachers spent telling stories to their classes had significant negative correlations with all criterion measures.

It should be noted that when teachers were classified according to the reading approach to which they were assigned (e.g., language experience, basal) the sizes of the correlations varied.

Grades 3 through 6

Powell (1968) studied the relationships between selected teaching behaviors and the achievement of 168 pupils in grade 3 and again in grade 4. Only pupils who had one teacher for the first three years and a second teacher in the fourth year were included in the sample. The 9 third-grade teachers and the 17 fourth-year teachers were classified as "indirect" or "direct" on the basis of a composite of the standard scores on six variables derived from their IA matrix. Pupils taught by indirect teachers for their first three years had significantly higher achievement scores in arithmetic, but not in reading. There were no significant differences at the end of the fourth year, even for pupils who had only indirect or only direct teachers for all four years.

Soar (1966) studied process and product measures in 55 classrooms during one school year. All classes of grades 3 through 6 in four elementary schools were observed using IA, the Hostility–Affection Schedule (Fowler, 1962), and selected items from OScAR (Medley & Mitzel, 1958, 1959). The 39 observational measures were reduced to nine factors, and the teachers' factor scores were correlated with pupil true-gain scores on each of four subtests on the Iowa Tests of Educational Development: vocabulary, reading, arithmetic concepts, and arithmetic problems. Four of the factors had a significant correlation with at least one of the achievement measures (Table 3.3): teacher criticism; extended discourse *vs.* rapid teacher-pupil interchange; teacher support and pupil interest; and one unnamed factor. The factor containing a number of i/d ratios was not significantly correlated with any of the achievement measures.

In addition, Soar performed separate three-way analyses of variance selecting the four classes at each grade level which best represented the extremes of four conditions: high-direct and high-hostility; high-direct and low-hostility; low-direct and high-hostility; low-direct and low hostility. Two analyses were formed, one using pupil residual

TABLE 3.3
CORRELATIONS OF FACTOR SCORES AND MEAN PUPIL RESIDUAL
TRUE GAIN SCORES IN THE INVESTIGATION BY SOAR (1966)

| Factor | Iowa Tests of Basic Skills | | | | |
| | | | Arithmetic | | |
	Vocabulary	Reading	Concepts	Problems	Total
1. Teacher Criticsim	—.160	—.128	—.294 °	—.337 °	—.362 °°
3. Disc. *vs.* Rapid Inter.	.288 °	.273 °	.438 °	.091	.242
6. P.Host *vs.* P.Int.	—.299 °	—.060	—.290 °	—.277 °	—.290 °
9. Unnamed	.179	.139	.289 °	.202	.245

° $p < .05$ °° $p < .01$

	Loading
Factor 1. Teacher Criticism	
Pupil initiation following teacher criticism	.74
Teacher verbal hostility	.76
Steady-state teacher criticism	.83
Factor 3. Extended Discourse *vs.* Rapid Teacher–Pupil Interchange	
Steady-state lecture	.80
Inquiry/drill ratio	.60
Drill	—.81
Student talk following teacher talk	—.93
Ratio of teacher activity to student activity	.42
Factor 6. Pupil Hostility *vs.* Teacher Support and Pupil Interest	
Pupil non-verbal hostility	.79
Pupil verbal hostility	.66
Teacher non-verbal affection	—.56
Pupil interest–attention rating	—.65
Factor 9. Unnamed	
Pupil verbal affection	.75
Teacher encouragement, interpretation, generalization, solution	.61
Pupil central	.56

true-gain scores in vocabulary as the cell entries, the other using reading scores. One main effect was significant across both analyses—classrooms with indirect teachers were superior to those with direct teachers.

Medley and Mitzel (1959) studied the classroom behaviors of 49 first-year teachers in grades 3 through 6. All pupils were given standard tests in reading at the beginning and end of the school year. Classroom behavior was measured using the 2V version of OScAR (Medley & Mitzel, 1958). Specific behaviors were combined into 20 keys *a priori*, and these keys were reduced to three factors by centroid factor analysis: emotional climate (which included teacher or pupil behaviors indicating warmth or hostility); verbal emphasis (which indicated the proportion of verbal activities); and social organization (which indicated the social grouping and pupil autonomy in the class). None of these factors was significantly correlated with the mean adjusted class reading score.

Thompson and Bowers (1968) studied the teaching style of 15 fourth-grade teachers by asking all teachers to present a thirty-minute lesson to their classes based on identical material dealing with geography and map skills. An observation schedule, modified from versions of the OScAR, was used to classify teachers in terms of their "supportiveness," "verbosity," and the "convergent or divergent" content of their questions. Six $3 \times 2 \times 2$ analyses of variance were performed, with the teachers grouped as high, middle, or low according to their observed behaviors on each of the three measures, and with the pupils grouped according to two levels of intelligence and two levels of creativity. In three of the analyses, pupil end-of-course scores on word meaning were used in the cells; in three, the criterion measure was scores on a standard social studies test.

There was only one main effect for teacher behavior. Teachers who were classified as moderate in their use of convergent–divergent questions had pupils with significantly superior scores on the Stanford Word Meaning Test. "Verbosity" interacted with IQ so that teachers who were medium or high in "verbosity" were more effective in word meaning with pupils of high intelligence. There was a highly significant main effect for intelligence in all comparisons.

Fortune (1967) studied the teaching behavior of 42 teacher-trainees in English, mathematics, and social studies. Each teacher taught four lessons of ten to fifteen minutes each, using specially prepared material. Pupil scores were adjusted according to the pupils' performance on tests following their reading of specially prepared programmed material. Video tapes of the three highest- and three lowest-scoring teachers in each content area, as measured by the adjusted class mean scores, were viewed by two judges. Each judge counted the frequencies of behavior using an observational guide containing items related to lesson development and discussion skills.

There was no behavior which discriminated between the most effective and least effective teachers in all three content areas; but five behaviors did discriminate significantly in two of the content areas. The most effective teachers were scored as using the following behaviors more frequently: (1) introductions using instructional set, (2) review and repetition within the lesson, (3) reinforcement of student responses, (4) patience to wait for student response, and (5) integrates student response within the lesson.

Spaulding (1965) studied 21 teachers in grades 4 through 6 during a school year. The criterion measures were class mean adjusted achievement scores on the STEP tests in reading and mathematics. The observational instrument contained 144 items based upon four major teaching categories: disapproval; approval; instruction; and listening. Within each category, behaviors were also classified four ways: source of teacher's authority; tone of voice; means or methods; and topic. The observational measures were reduced to 17 components by factor analysis, and three of these components had a significant or nearly significantly correlation with reading achievement; none correlated significantly with mathematics achievement (see Table 3.4). Strong

TABLE 3.4

THE CORRELATIONS OF SEVENTEEN COMPONENTS OF TEACHER–PUPIL TRANSACTIONS WITH THE EIGHT TARGET PUPIL VARIABLES IN THE INVESTIGATION BY SPAULDING (1965)

Component	Target Pupil Variables	
	Reading	Math
2. Dominative–threatening	.49 *	.10
6. Businesslike–orderly	.44 *	.39
10. Formal group instruction, using shame	.42	.08

* $p < .05$

	Loading
Component 2. Dominative–threatening	
Total disapproving behavior	−.42
Disapproval by veiled or explicit threat to do harm	−.44
Approval regarding personal interpretations, ideas, judgments	.52
Component 6. Businesslike–orderly	
Disapproval by commanding conformance	.41
Disapproval by eliciting clarification in a non-threatening way	.36
Disapproval regarding lack of knowledge or skill	
(directed to boys)	−.65
Instruction directed to boys	−.42
Instruction in a normal tone of voice	.41
Instruction in accepting, pleasant, warm voice	−.56
Instruction by eliciting a verbal response in an open-ended way	−.70
Instruction regarding children's interests, interpretations,	
and ideas	−.59
Component 10. Formal group instruction, using shame	
Total listening behavior	.47
Approval, using teacher-centered "I"	−.66
Approval, using appeal to convention or constituted authority	.73
Approval regarding planning or organization	.44
Disapproval by social shaming or sarcasm	−.55
Disapproval by anonymous or impersonal warnings	−.45

disapproval behaviors, approval using teacher-centered "I," and eliciting verbal response in an open-ended way appeared most disruptive of learning. Positive behaviors included approval using appeal to convention or constituted authority, approval regarding pupils' planning or personal ideas, and disapproval by commanding conformance.

Perkins (1965) observed 27 teachers of grade 4 using ten items of teacher behavior modified from IA and five items of teacher role behavior created by the investigator. Criterion measures were class mean end-of-year scores on language arts, reading, social studies, and arithmetic subtests of the California Achievement Tests adjusted for scores on previous standard tests.

The observational data were reduced to four factors, with the achievement scores expressed as loadings on the factors (see Table 3.5). The strongest results were the loadings on Factor 2—Teacher

TABLE 3.5

COMMON FACTORS FROM ANALYSES OF RELATIONSHIPS OF
LEARNING-ACTIVITY, TEACHER-BEHAVIOR, AND TEACHER-
ROLE VARIABLES AND PUPIL-ACHIEVEMENT VARIABLES
IN THE INVESTIGATION BY PERKINS (1965)

	Loading
Factor 1. Quiet Study	
Seatwork	.37
Reading or writing	.93
No class discussion	.83
Total-class increase in grade-point average	.89
Factor 2. Teacher Lecturer–Criticizer	
Recitation	.36
Teacher does not listen or support	.42
Teacher lectures	.55
Teacher criticizes	.97
Teacher socialization role	.97
Total-class gain in "Reading Vocabulary" score	.46
Total-class loss in "Reading Comprehension" score	.63
Total-class loss in "Mechanics of English" score	.68
Factor 3. Teacher Leading Recitation	
Recitation	.76
Teacher leader role	.87
Teacher uses student's idea	.49
Teacher does not accept student's answer	.47
Teacher not silent	—
Total-class gain in "Arithmetic Reasoning" score	.41
Factor 4. Student Individual Work	
Individual work	.79
Teacher does not accept student's answer	.49
Teacher in resource role	—
Total-class gain in "Spelling" score	.92

Lecturer-Criticizer. Teachers who were rated high in lecturing, criticizing, and not supporting students tended to have classes whose scores were low in reading comprehension and mechanics of English.

Using IA, Morrison (1966) observed 30 sixth-grade teachers for one school year. The Metropolitan Achievement Tests were administered in the fall and spring, and seven subtests were selected as criterion measures: language usage; parts of speech; punctuation and capitalization; language study; arithmetic computation; problem-solving skills; and social studies. Teachers were grouped as high, middle, or low according to three behaviors: praise and encouragement (2–2 cell); use of pupil ideas (3–3 cell); and criticism (column 7). Different teachers were studied for each behavior. Teachers in the first four stanines on each behavior were classified as "direct," those in the last four as "indirect"; teachers in the fifth stanine were not included in the analyses.

A special test was used to classify pupils as "external" or "internal" according to their belief in the source of responsibility for their actions, and the pupils in the highest and lowest thirds on the external–internal continuum were selected for analysis. Twenty-one two-way analyses of covariance (using pupil pretest scores as the covariate) were run for each of the teaching behaviors and criterion measures. Almost all main effects for teaching behaviors were significant in favor of teachers who ranked high in the use of praise, high in the use of pupil ideas, and low in the use of criticism.

Grades 7 through 12

The first investigation of the relationships between IA measures and pupil achievement was conducted by Flanders (1965) in 1958. Two separate investigations were conducted, one involving 15 seventh-grade social studies teachers, the other involving 16 eighth-grade mathematics teachers. Each teacher taught a two-week, specially developed unit in his subject area. Class posttest scores were adjusted by analysis of covariance using pretest scores in the subject area as the covariate. Teachers in both studies were classified as "indirect" or "direct" according to their i/d ratios, and no teacher classified one way in one study would have been classified differently in the other. In both studies, the teachers with the higher i/d ratios (the more "indirect" teachers) had classes with significantly higher adjusted posttest scores.

LaShier (1966) used IA to record the performance of 10 student teachers who taught a six-week block from the BSCS curriculum to their eighth-grade pupils. Median difference scores for each class between pretest and posttest were computed, and these scores were correlated with the teacher's i/d ratio using the Kendall partial rank correlation coefficient with the ranked scores on a reading test as the third variable. The resulting correlation coefficient was positive and significant.

Furst (1967) used both IA and measures developed by Bellack *et al.* (1966) to relate classroom behavior to pupil achievement. In the original study by Bellack, 15 teachers taught four lessons on foreign trade to their tenth- or twelfth-grade classes. All lessons were based upon identical material. The criterion measure was the class mean posttest score adjusted for pupil intelligence and class size.

Furst formed two composites, representing affective and cognitive behaviors. The affective composite was extended i/d, i/d 8–9, and extended pupil talk. The cognitive composite, developed from data supplied in the study by Bellack, was based on the hypothesis that high-achieving teachers would be moderate in the use of structuring statements, moderate in number of teacher–pupil interchanges per minute, and high in the use of a variety of types of cognitive processes. Teachers were classified as high, middle, or low on the basis of their classes' mean adjusted achievement score, and two analyses of variance were computed using the teachers' scores on the two composites. In both analyses, the three high-achieving teachers had composite scores significantly superior to those of the remaining twelve teachers.

Snider (1966) used a variation of IA to categorize the teaching behaviors of 17 high school teachers during one year's instruction in the New York State Physics Course. The three criterion measures were adjusted class mean scores on the Regents Physics Examination, the Cooperative Physics Test, and the Test on Understanding Science. An elaborate regression procedure was used to adjust all scores for pupils' previous achievement. The observational measures used included a number of i/d ratios and measures of teacher variation in i/d ratios across different teaching activities such as lecturing, leading a discussion, and conducting laboratory periods. No behavior was consistently related to pupil achievement across all three criterion tests. Significant results tended to favor teachers who were more direct during lectures and had smaller variation in their I/I+D scores across different activities.

College

Solomon, Bezdek, and Rosenberg (1963) used a specially developed protocol for the systematic observation and rating of the behaviors of 24 teachers of adult evening classes in introductory American government. All pupils took a factual test on the American Constitution and a comprehension test on a passage from a book on political theory at the beginning and at the end of the one-semester course. The investigators chose difference scores between pretest and posttest as the criterion measures.

Sixty-one measures were developed from the systematic coding of the tape recordings of two class sessions. Statements and questions were coded into eight cognitive categories such as "organizing," "hypothetical," "opinion," "factual," and "interpretation." Teacher feedback to pupils was also coded in terms of the information given about the correctness of the pupil's statement ànd in terms of the type of reinforcement, if any. These 61 measures, together with an additional 100 measures based upon observer and pupil ratings, were reduced to eight factors through factor analysis. Teacher scores on Factors 2, 4, and 6 had significant linear correlations with one of the two gain scores (Table 3.6). A chi-square analysis indicated that teachers at the middle level of Factor 1—Permissiveness *vs.* Control—achieved significantly higher comprehension gain scores than teachers at either extreme.

In most cases, the ratings had higher loadings on these factors than the tabulated measures, and therefore the factor titles reflect these ratings. In terms of the tabulated behaviors themselves, Factor 1 appears to represent a moderate amount of questioning; Factor 2, emphasis upon *both* interpretative and factual questions; Factor 4, unclear teacher presentations; and Factor 6, emphasis upon hypothetical questions and personal references.

Summary of Results on Affective Variables

Almost every investigator discussed above included an affective variable such as approval or disapproval in his study of correlates of cognitive achievement. This choice is well founded in experimental research and would seem to reflect the concern of generations of psychologists with effects of positive and negative reinforcement upon learning. Investigators specializing in behavior modification have begun to apply variables derived from this tradition to the natural classroom (Orme & Purnell, 1968; Wasik *et al.*, 1968; O'Leary & Becker, 1967); yet classroom researchers working within the tradition being discussed here seldom cite this experimental research as the justification for their concern with the effects of praise or blame. Instead, as Wallen and Travers (1963) and McDonald (1963) have noted, the usual reference is to a philosophical tradition or to the line of research beginning with Anderson (1939) or with Levin, Lippitt and White (1939). A reconciliation between these traditions would seem to be in order.

This section contains a synthesis of the results on the relationships between affective teaching behaviors and pupil achievement. Affective variables are divided into five types: non-verbal affect; praise and encouragement; use of pupil ideas; criticism; and variables described as a ratio of approving and disapproving behaviors. Each table includes data only for those studies which appeared to include variables in one of the five types, and each table presents the results across all achievement criterion measures used in each investigation. These divi-

TABLE 3.6

SIGNIFICANT CORRELATIONS BETWEEN FACTORS AND PUPIL
ACHIEVEMENT MEASURES IN THE STUDY BY SOLOMON,
BEZDEK, AND ROSENBERG (1963, 1964a, 1964b)

Factor	Target Pupil Variables	
	Factual Gain	Comprehension Gain
2. Energy *vs.* Lethargy	.23	.44 °
4. Clarity *vs.* Obscurity	.58 °	.04
6. Flamboyance *vs.* Dryness	.08	.42 °

° $p < .05$

	Loading
Factor 1: Permissiveness *vs.* Control	
Proportion of teacher requests hypothetical of total teacher speech	.78
Proportion of teacher requests opinion of total teacher speech	.70
Proportion of teacher requests non-specific of total teacher speech	.67
Proportion of teacher requests organizing of total teacher speech	.66
Proportion of teacher requests non-reinforcement of total teacher speech	.62
Proportion of teacher requests interpretation of total teacher speech	.49
Proportion of non-informative teacher feedback of total teacher speech	.45
Proportion of teacher speech of total classroom speech	−.92
Proportion of teacher factual statements of total teacher speech	−.59
Factor 2: Energy *vs.* Lethargy	
Ratio of teacher requests interpretation to student requests	.76
Proportion of positive reinforcement coupled with no information of total teacher speech	.71
Proportion of non-informative feedback of total teacher speech	.70
Ratio of teacher requests opinion to student requests opinion	.63
Proportion of teacher requests interpretation of total teacher speech	.63
Proportion of feedback with no reinforcement and no information of total teacher feedback	.63
Ratio of teacher requests facts to student requests facts	.62
Proportion of teacher requests factual of total teacher speech	.49
Proportion of teacher factual of total teacher speech	−.53
Factor 4: Clarity *vs.* Obscurity	
Proportion of student requests for interpretation of total student speech	−.56
Proportion of student interpretation of total student speech	−.47
Proportion of teacher interpretation of total teacher speech	−.43
Proportion of high information coupled with negative reinforcement of total teacher speech	−.40
Factor 6: Flamboyance *vs.* Dryness	
Ratio of teacher personal references to student personal references	.51
Ratio of teacher interpretation to student interpretation	.45
Proportion of student personal references of student total speech	.45
Proportion of teacher hypothetical statements to total teacher speech	.41
Ratio of teacher requests hypothetical to student requests hypothetical	.41

sions are tentative, and should be revised as the results of future investigations are reported.

The tables on specific approval or disapproval behaviors are limited in that they include only those studies which provided information on the relationships between these variables and achievement. Some investigators who used IA or OScAR (Medley & Mitzel, 1959) as their observational instrument also counted instances of approval and disapproval, but their independent variables were some combination of these behaviors into an i/d ratio or a measure of "supportiveness." Reanalyzing the original data or IA matrices to isolate frequencies of specific approval and disapproval behaviors may clarify the relationships between those variables and achievement, and the results summarized below may well be changed by such analysis.

Non-verbal Affection

In three studies the investigators isolated variables labeled non-verbal affection and studied the relationships between them and achievement (Table 3.7); in two, there were no significant relation-

TABLE 3.7
SUMMARY OF RESULTS ON NON-VERBAL APPROVAL

Investigator and Variables Studied	Subject Areas of Achievement Measures	
	Arith.	Reading
Wallen (grade 1)		
0 non-verbal affection	0/1	0/2
Wallen (grade 3)		
0 non-verbal affection	0/1	0/2
Soar (grades 3, 4, 5, 6)		
+ Factor 6	2/2	1/2
+ teacher non-verbal affection		
− pupil non-verbal hostility		
+ pupil interest–attention rating		
− pupil verbal hostility		

NOTE: The numerators in the column entries indicate the number of achievement measures with which the variable on the left was significantly, *positively* correlated. The denominators indicate the number of achievement measures used.

ships. Soar (1966) found that instances of non-verbal affection loaded on a significant factor; curiously, however, this variable was the only teacher behavior to load on the factor—the other variables were pupil verbal and non-verbal hostility and a rating for pupil attention. Furthermore, teacher non-verbal affection did not have significant zero-order correlations with any of the achievement measures. That this factor was the strongest correlate of over-all achievement and yet was almost without other supporting teacher behaviors is a surprising and disappointing finding.

Praise and Encouragement

Table 3.8 presents the results obtained by nine investigators who specifically investigated the relationship of variables which appear to

TABLE 3.8
SUMMARY OF RESULTS ON TEACHER USE OF
PRAISE AND ENCOURAGEMENT

Investigator and Variables Studied	Subject Areas of Achievement Measures			
	Arith.	Lang. Arts	Reading	Soc. Studies
Fortune (preschool)				
+ praise				1/1
Harris & Serwer (grade 1)				
0 positive motivation		0/2	0/3	
Wallen (grade 1)				
+ minimum reinforcement	1/1		1/2	
0 praise and encouragement	0/1		0/2	
Harris & Serwer (grade 2)				
0 positive motivation		0/1	0/3	
Wallen (grade 3)				
0 recognizes pupil's raised hand	0/1		0/2	
0 minimum reinforcement	0/1		0/2	
0 praise and encouragement	0/1		0/2	
Fortune (grades 4, 5, 6)				
+ praise or repetition of pupil's answer	0/1	1/1		1/1
Morrison (grades 4, 5, 6)				
+ extended praise (cell 2–2)	2/2	3/4		1/1
Perkins (grades 4, 5, 6)				
0 praises and encourages	0/1	0/2	0/2	0/1
Spaulding (grades 4, 5, 6)				
+ Component 2 approval regarding pupil's interpretation	0/1		1/1	
+ Component 10 [a] — approval source: teacher centered "I" approval source: appeal to convention approval regarding pupil's planning	0/1		1/1	
0 Component 12 total approval	0/1		0/1	

NOTE. The numerators in the column entries indicate the number of achievement measures with which the variable on the left was significantly, *positively* correlated. The denominators indicate the number of achievement measures used.

[a] Negative loading on this factor.

represent praise and encouragement with achievement. Of the nine studies in Table 3.8, five indicated that some praise variable was positively associated with achievement. However, three of the five investigators (Fortune, 1966; Morrison, 1966; Fortune, 1967) studied only extreme groups of teachers, and in the two other studies (Wallen, 1966; Spaulding, 1965) praise *per se* was not the significant variable. To summarize these data in a different way, six long-term studies correlated total frequencies of praise with pupil achievement: those by Harris *et al.* (grades 1 and 2), Wallen (grades 1 and 3), Perkins, and Spaulding. In none of these six studies was praise a significant correlate.

Despite these non-significant results, the findings have interesting implications. For example, Wallen found that although praise was not a significant correlate for first-grade pupils, both minimum reinforcement and the frequency of the teacher's asking questions had positive correlations with the adjusted achievement scores. Minimum reinforcement was defined as positive reinforcement which is less strong than praise. (Examples: "Uh huh," "Right," "Okay.") This combination suggests that for the first grade, practice rather than encouragement is the significant variable. However, the observation system developed by Wallen did not include tallying of pupil behavior, and so this suggestion cannot be studied using his data.

The research of Spaulding (1965) suggests that the *topic* of praise may be more important than the frequency. In his investigation, total instances of approval did not load on a significant component (Table 3.8). However, there were positive loadings for two topics of approval: approval regarding pupil's interpretation; and approval regarding pupil's planning. Other topics of approval—personal qualities, accurate knowledge, attention to task, and personal interests—did not load on a significant component. Approval regarding pupil's interpretation and pupil's planning would appear to be critical for developing cognitive independence and appropriate for the above-average pupils whom Spaulding studied (the sample average was the 86th percentile on the School and College Ability Test). Different topics of approval may be important for pupils of low ability, and there may be interactions between the type of approval and the cognitive styles of the pupils. Such questions remain to be investigated.

The research by Spaulding also suggests that not all approval is related to achievement. Approval through "teacher-centered 'I,'" the use of a warm voice, and the selection of instructional topics related to the pupils' interests all appeared to be negatively related to achievement.

In sum, research of this type has not shown that there is a consistent linear relationship between achievement and the frequency of approval, although the possibility of curvilinear relationships remains open. However, the research does suggest that certain types and topics of approval may be positively related to achievement, and that some forms of approval may be negatively related to achievement.

Use of Pupils' Ideas

The concept of a separate category coded "Teacher accepts or uses ideas of pupils" is unique to the work of Flanders (1965). Behaviors in this category (Flanders, 1970) include the following:

1. *Acknowledges* the pupil's idea by repeating the nouns and logical connectives he has expressed.
2. *Modifying* the idea by rephrasing it or conceptualizing it in the teacher's own words.
3. *Applying* the idea by using it to reach an inference or to take the next step in a logical analysis of the problem.
4. *Comparing* the idea by drawing a relationship between it and ideas expressed earlier by a pupil or the teacher.
5. *Summarizing* what was said by an individual pupil or a group of pupils.

This is a fascinating category of behavior including both affective and cognitive components so intertwined as to be inseparable.

Thus the behaviors in Flanders' Category 3 would appear to be more powerful affective variables than praise for two reasons. First, the repetition and summary of, and the referral to, pupils' ideas would seem to be related to the greatest tributes of the academic world, publication and citation; secondly, the teacher must listen and engage in implicit practice in order to apply, compare, summarize, or even repeat an idea. Such *use* of ideas would seem, therefore, to be a more intensive form of praise than a perfunctory "Very good" given possibly at the end of a rambling statement which the teacher does not quite understand. At the same time, however, repetition and the like may have cognitive importance in providing further or reformulated exposure to a given idea.

Because of the importance of this variable on this intuitive basis it is unfortunate that we have so little specific information on the effects of using pupils' ideas. Most investigators who have used the IA matrix have included all or part of column 3 as part of an i/d ratio, but few have studied the effects of this variable alone. Of all the behaviors which might be taken to indicate approval of the pupil or what he said, the strongest results have been obtained for teacher behaviors labeled "use of pupil ideas" (Table 3.9). Four of the five studies investigating this variable report some positive findings; the exception

TABLE 3.9
SUMMARY OF RESULTS ON ACCEPTANCE, REPETITION,
AND USE OF PUPILS' IDEAS

Investigator and Variables Studied	Subject Areas of Achievement Measures			
	Arith.	Lang. Arts	Reading	Soc. Studies
Fortune (preschool)				
0 repeating				0/1
Soar (Grades 3, 4, 5, 6)				
0 Factor 8	0/2		0/2	
extended elaboration (cell 3–3) use of student idea (column 3)				
+ Factor 9	1/2		0/2	
teacher encourages pupil's interpretation				
Fortune (Grades 4, 5, 6)				
+ praise or repetition of pupil's idea	0/1	1/1		1/1
+ integrates pupil's idea into lesson	1/1	1/1		0/1
Morrison (Grades 4, 5, 6)				
+ use of pupil's ideas (cell 3–3)	2/2	4/4		1/1
Perkins (Grades 4, 5, 6)				
+ Factor 3	1/1	0/2	0/2	0/1
accepts or uses pupil's idea				

NOTE. The numerators in the column entries indicate the number of achievement measures with which the variable on the left was significantly, *positively* correlated. The denominators indicate the number of achievement measures used.

(Fortune, 1966) dealt with preschool children in only five- or seven-minute learning sessions. The variable "integrates student response into the lesson" in Fortune's study of grades 4, 5, and 6 (1967) appears to be a clear, higher-level use of Flanders' Category 3. The results obtained by Morrison (1966) using the frequency of tallies on extended use of pupil ideas (3–3 cell) as an indicator of this behavior were stronger than her results on teacher's use of extended praise. In the study by Perkins (1965), the use of pupils' ideas was positively related to only one of the six criterion tests (arithmetic), but this behavior was one of the strongest of the positive teacher actions. The other findings in this study primarily involved negative teacher behaviors.

In the study by Soar (1966), the frequencies in both column 3 and cell 3–3 had very low zero-order correlations with the achievement measures, and these behaviors did not load on a significant factor. A different behavior, recorded using a modification of OScAR—teacher encouragement of pupil's interpretation and generalization—did have a positive significant zero-order correlation with arithmetic achievement. Yet although these two kinds of behaviors both appear to involve teacher use of pupils' ideas, they were uncorrelated. This finding reinforces an impression that the concept of teacher use of pupils' ideas is a complex one, although certainly one deserving further research. We have some support for the positive effects of the teacher's use of pupil ideas, but not as strong or as clear as we might like.

Criticism and Control

For purposes of analysis, it would have been preferable to develop two tables, one on giving directions and the other on criticism. But many investigators have used variables which appear to include both directions and criticism. For example, the variable "personal control" (Wallen, 1966) included directions aimed at controlling pupils and criticism (Norman Wallen, personal communication). The vicious circle (or extended direct) variable used by Soar included instances of Categories 6 and 7. Harris and his associates (1966, 1968) did not operationally define their variables "negative motivation" and "control," but according to the coding instructions these variables appear to include both directions and criticism.

Of the nine investigators who studied criticism and/or disapproval as an independent variable, seven of them found criticism or disapproval to be a significant negative correlate of achievement in some specific academic area. Criticism may not have been a significant variable in the study by Fortune (1966) because the teachers of the preschool children taught short lessons. Of the seven long-term correlational studies (Fortune and Morrison excluded), six showed significant negative relationships between criticism and achievement.

It is unfortunate that in our search for teacher behaviors which predict pupil achievement the negative behaviors summarized in Table 3.10 yield the clearest results of all affective variables. Although not consistent across all subject areas, all grade levels, and all varieties of disapproval, the results were remarkably consistent when compared with the results presented in other tables.

Several investigators studied the effects of mild and strong forms of criticism. In no study did mild criticism have a significant negative relationship to achievement. Thus, Wallen did not find significant correlations between academic control and achievement; Perkins did not find that giving directions loaded on any of his factors; Spaulding did not find that disapproval by negative evaluation loaded on a significant factor; and Soar did not find significant results for the vicious circle, that is behaviors in the 6–6, 6–7, 7–6, and 7–7 cells combined.

TABLE 3.10
SUMMARY OF RESULTS ON CONTROL AND CRITICISM

| Investigator and Variables Studied | Subject Areas of Achievement Measures | | | |
	Arith.	Lang. Arts	Reading	Soc. Studies
Fortune (preschool)				
0 control				0/1
Harris & Serwer (grade 1)				
0 negative motivation		0/2	0/3	
— control		1/2	3/3	
Wallen (grade 1)				
— personal control	0/1		1/2	
0 academic control	0/1		0/2	
0 moralizing	0/1		0/2	
0 hostility	0/1		0/2	
Harris *et al.* (grade 2)				
— negative motivation		0/1	1/3	
0 control		0/1	0/3	
Wallen (grade 3)				
0 personal control	0/1		0/2	
0 academic control	0/1		0/2	
0 moralizing	0/1		0/2	
0 hostility	0/1		0/2	
Soar (grades 3, 4, 5, 6)				
— Factor 1	2/2		0/2	
teacher verbal hostility				
steady-state criticism				
(cell 7–7)				
0 Factor 5	0/2		0/2	
vicious circle				
Spaulding (grades 4, 6)				
— Component 2	0/1		1/1	
total disapproval				
disapproval by threat				
+ Component 6	0/1		1/1 (pos)[a]	
disapproval by commanding				
conformance				
disapproval by eliciting				
clarification in a				
non-threatening way				
— Component 10	0/1		1/1	
disapproval by shaming				
disapproval by warning				

TABLE 3.10 (continued)

| Investigator and Variables Studied | Subject Areas of Achievement Measures | | | |
	Arith.	Lang. Arts	Reading	Soc. Studies
Perkins (grade 5)				
—,+ Factor 2	1/1	1/2	1/2	0/1
teacher criticizes			(pos)[a]	
teacher does not support				
+ Factor 3	1/1	0/2	0/2	0/1
teacher does not accept	(pos)[a]			
student answer				
0 teacher gives directions,	0/1	0/2	0/2	0/1
commands				
Morrison (grade 6)				
— criticism	1/2	3/4		1/1

NOTE. The numerators in the column entries indicate the number of achievement measures with which the variable on the left was significantly, *negatively* correlated. The denominators indicate the number of achievement measures used.

[a] (pos) indicates that the variable on the left was significantly, *positively* correlated with pupil achievement measure(s) in the subject area.

In two studies, mild criticism was *positively* related to achievement. Perkins found that the behavior "teacher does not accept student's answer" loaded on the same factor as the total class gain in arithmetic, and Spaulding found that disapproval both by commanding conformance and by eliciting clarification in a non-threatening way loaded on a factor positively related to achievement in reading.

The four investigators who found that mild criticism was not related to achievement or was sometimes positively related to achievement also found that strong criticism had significant negative relationships with achievement. Wallen found significant results for personal control in Grade 1; Perkins found negative correlations between criticism and achievement; Spaulding found that total disapproval and disapproval by shaming or threat loaded on significant negative factors; and Soar found that teacher verbal hostility and the frequencies in the 7–7 cell loaded on a significant factor.

Strong disapproval or criticism was a significant correlate of achievement not only in studies of disadvantaged children (Harris & Serwer, 1966; Harris *et al.*, 1968) but also in studies involving upper-middle-class pupils (Perkins, 1965) and, in particular, upper-middle-class pupils with above average ability with teachers rated as superior (Spaulding, 1965; Soar, 1966). Soar (p. 189) developed a table to show that the teachers in his sample had higher i/d ratios than those in the samples studied by Flanders (1965) and Furst (1967); yet Soar found that teacher criticism was a significant correlate. In the study by Spaulding (1965), 10 per cent of the mean teacher's behavior was classified as overtly disapproving, compared with 12 per cent approving behavior; yet the disapproving behavior had the greatest effect. (The technique of disapproval appeared to be more important than the topic disapproved. Thus, disapproval by threat, shaming, and warning appeared negatively related to reading achievement, whereas disapproval by commanding conformance and disapproval by eliciting clarification in a non-threatening manner were positively related.)

One puzzling finding obtained by Perkins (1965) was that teacher criticism loaded on the same factor as total class *gain* in reading vocabulary. (The remaining results on this factor were as expected: teacher criticism was related to total class *loss* in reading comprehension and mechanics of English.) This finding is in the opposite direction from the trends and significant findings in all the other studies.

In summary, there is no evidence to support a claim that teachers should avoid telling a student that he is wrong, or should avoid giving him academic directions. However, teachers who use a good deal of strong criticism appear to consistently have classes which achieve less in most subject areas.

"Indirect"–"Direct" Ratios

In eight studies, achievement scores were used as the criteria, and i/d ratios were used to describe the teachers' verbal behaviors. These studies and their results are listed in Table 3.11. The most liberal interpretation of the results would be that six of the eight studies found some statistical procedure which indicated a significant relationship between high scores on an i/d ratio and pupil achievement as measured by at least one of the achievement tests.

One of the advantages of the IA system is that it yields a 10×10 matrix containing 30 cells taken to indicate warm, supportive, or "indirect" teacher behavior (columns 1, 2, and 3) and 20 cells taken to indicate critical, controlling, or "direct" teacher behavior (columns 6 and 7). Although the first i/d ratio (Flanders, 1965) was the ratio of the frequencies in these two sets of cells, investigators have formed other ratios using selected cells within the total array of indirect and direct behaviors. All eight studies summarized in Table 3.11 used at least one of three i/d ratios to describe teaching: the i/d, the i/d 8–9, and the extended i/d (see Table 3.1 and Figure 3.1).

The use of different i/d ratios makes comparison between these studies difficult. Because there has been little research on the correlation of these i/d ratios, it is possible that if the investigators had used different i/d ratios, they might have obtained different results. In four of the five studies which used more than one i/d ratio to describe teaching, the results apparently would have been the same using any one of them (Soar, 1966; Snider, 1966; Furst, 1967; Powell, 1968: fourth grade). In the fifth investigation, the study of third-grade teachers by Powell (1968), different teachers would have been classified as direct or indirect if only the i/d ratio or only the i/d 8–9 had been used in place of his composite score.

More specific results can be obtained by classifying the studies according to the statistical procedures used. Of the four investigators who used measures of linear correlation, only one (LaShier, 1965) obtained significant results. When inferential statistics were used, the results were stronger: five of the seven studies obtained significant results. (Three investigators used both correlational and inferential statistics.)

In summary, these results on the i/d ratios are moderately consistent; they are as good as we have come to expect from classroom research, but not as good as we should hope for. They indicate that the issues are more complex than we should like, and that there is a need for further study and quantification. An i/d ratio is a useful discriminator between high- and low-achieving teachers when inferential statistics are used to compare them, but the results do not demonstrate a direct relationship between the use of pupils' ideas and adjusted achievement scores.

Cognitive Aspects of Instruction

There has been much less systematic observation of the cognitive aspects of instruction than of affective aspects, and the observational measures developed by the different investigators are much more difficult to compare.

Reviewers of the research on classroom behaviors (Medley & Mitzel, 1963; Spaulding, 1963; Amidon & Simon, 1965; Gage, 1966; Flanders & Simon, 1969) have noted that most studies of teaching behaviors emphasize affective interactions; the cognitive aspects of teaching (e.g., the ability to explain new material, the effectiveness of various types of questions) have received comparatively little attention.

There are several possible reasons for this neglect. Research on child development, group dynamics, and experimental psychology can be used to discuss and code techniques of approval and disapproval; but as yet there exists no analogous discipline for developing observable cognitive variables.

Moreover, although there has been considerable experimental research on cognitive variables within educational psychology, few of

TABLE 3.11

SUMMARY OF INVESTIGATIONS USING INTERACTION ANALYSIS RATIOS

Investigator and Grade	No. of Class-rooms	Type of Ratio	Statistical Procedures			Significant Product Measures	Non-significant Product Measures
			Corre-lational	Inferential			
				Extremes	High vs. Low		
Powell (3)	9	i/d xi/xd i/d 8–9	—	—	yes	arithmetic	reading
Powell (4)	17	i/d i/d 8–9 xi/xd	—	—	no	none	reading, arithmetic
Soar (3–6)	55	i/d, i/d 8–9	no	yes	—	(reading, vocabulary) [a]	(reading, vocabulary, arith. concepts, arith. problems) [b]
Flanders (7)	15	i/d	—	?	yes	social studies	none
Flanders (8)	16	i/d	—	?	yes	mathematics	none
LaShier (8)	10	i/d	yes	—	—	biology	none
Snider (12)	17	i/d, i/d 8–9	no	no	—	none	physics
Furst (10, 12)	15	i/d 8–9, xi/xd	no	yes	—	social studies	none

NOTE. In the entries under *Statistical Procedures*: "yes" means significant differences were found, "no" means significant differences were not found, and a dash means the procedure was not used.

[a] Inferential analysis. Significant results were obtained for each of these two measures on the factor containing loadings for both i/d and i/d 8–9. The arithmetic measures were not so analyzed.

[b] Correlational analysis. None of the measures was significantly related to the factor containing i/d and i/d 8–9.

these experimental variables appear in the classroom observational systems which have been developed. This neglect is probably not due to any preference of the researchers; rather, they may be unable to translate experimentally developed variables into a classroom grammar. Thus Ausubel (1963) has investigated the importance of the stability and clarity of cognitive organizers as facilitators of classroom learning; but although he demonstrated the usefulness of his concept of cognitive structure, an investigator of classroom instruction cannot determine whether a teacher is adding organizers before the lesson— or during, or after the lesson—because the coding instructions needed to identify these behaviors have not been developed. In sum, until researchers can label the behaviors they observe, they cannot study either specific cognitive behaviors or the relationships between the behaviors and subsequent achievement.

Affective variables are also easier to code because they are more independent of a person's previous cognitive experience. Statements like "Shut up and sit down" and "Excellent" are relatively clear, and we do not have to assess the nature of the audience before we code them. But the question "How much is two and two?" is more difficult to classify. In a sixth-grade classroom, we should feel confident in classifying it as factual recall. But what if the question were asked of a five-year-old? This question might require convergent thinking or factual recall, depending upon the pupil's previous experience.

This problem of context has made it difficult to develop an observational system into which questions can be categorized reliably and meaningfully. Dichotomous classifications such as "narrow" and "broad" (Amidon & Flanders, 1967), "questions about content" and "questions that stimulate thinking" (Perkins, 1964), or "convergent" and "divergent" (Medley *et al.*, n.d.) appear to be oversimplifications of an area as complex as questioning, and they lead to different interpretations by different investigators. For example, Medley said that a divergent question admits of more than one answer, and that "Name one of the four freedoms" is, therefore, a divergent question; but some other investigators would probably modify these instructions. Classification systems which divide questions into more than two types seem necessary.

Investigators whose systems for coding questions have been more elaborate have been forced to use transcripts or tape recordings of the class proceedings as the source for coding, to allow coders the extra time necessary to categorize the behaviors (e.g. Bellack *et al.*, 1966; Solomon *et al.*, 1963, 1964a, 1964b). But even in these situations it has been difficult to develop categories whose boundary lines are clear, and as a result there are probably more differences between category systems in the methods for classifying questions than in any other variable.

Finally, problems on units of measure are even more difficult to handle in investigations of the cognitive aspects of instruction, because frequency alone does not seem a sufficient measure. In studies of cognitive aspects of instruction, the pattern would seem to be at least as important as frequency.

The Variables

One basic difficulty in exploring the research on the cognitive aspects of instruction is the enormous variety in the systems that have been developed to quantify cognitive interchanges. Some systems categorize questions, some classify statements, and others quantify combinations of statements and questions. Consequently, comparison and synthesis of the results are particularly difficult.

In order to present and compare the results of studies on cognitive variables, primary emphasis here will be given to questions. The variables in these studies are classified in three ways: the frequency of asking questions; types of questions asked; and results on other cognitive variables.

Frequency of Questions

The results of studies in which specific attention was given to the frequency of asking questions are summarized in Table 3.12. In five studies of instruction in the primary grades, the results are quite clear: in four of the studies the frequency of asking questions was significantly associated with pupil achievement (Conners & Eisenberg, 1966; Wallen, 1966; Harris *et al.*, 1968). In the only study in this group which did not use correlational statistics (Conners & Eisenberg), the results suggest a significant linear correlation.

Although these results suggest that frequent questioning is a component of effective instruction in the primary grades, we need more information about the nature of the questions. Such information is particularly difficult to come by. In three of the five investigations, the type of question was also observed (Conners & Eisenberg, 1966; Harris & Serwer, 1966; Harris *et al.*, 1968), and in none was any type of question a significate correlate of achievement (Table 3.13).

Types of Questions

The classification of questions and, as corollary, the classification of cognitive aspects of classroom interaction has been a most difficult task. Investigators have differed widely in their criteria and modes for

TABLE 3.12
SUMMARY OF RESULTS ON FREQUENCY OF ASKING QUESTIONS

| Investigator and Variables Studied | Subject Areas of Achievement Measures | | | |
	IQ	Arith.	Lang. Arts	Reading
Conners & Eisenberg (preschool) + frequency of intellectual interchanges	1/1			
Wallen (grade 1) + frequency of questions		0/1		2/2
Harris & Serwer (grade 1) + number of interchanges			2/2	1/3
Harris *et al.* (grade 2) 0 number of interchanges			0/1	0/3
Wallen (grade 3) 0 frequency of questions + percentage of questions		0/1 1/1		0/2 0/2

NOTE. The numerators in the column entries indicate the number of achievement measures with which the variable on the left was significantly, *positively* correlated. The denominators indicate the number of achievement measures used.

the classification of questions and in their statistical treatment of the data. The results of the investigations in which questions were classified are summarized in Table 3.13.

In general, three procedures were used in studying the effects of questions: linear analyses in which all questions were classified as to type; non-linear analyses; and analyses using only selected questions and cognitive interchanges.

Six of the investigators classified all questions by type, and subjected the results to a linear analysis. Conners and Eisenberg (1966) inspected teacher-pupil interchanges classified as devoted to intellectual growth, and further subdivided these interchanges into those which emphasized language, convergent reasoning, or divergent thinking. Harris and his associates (1966, 1968) divided questions into two types: those in which the pupils were asked to interpret the meaning of a word, symbol, or sentence (meaningful questions); and those in which the pupils had to recognize a symbol or word (form questions). One of the four "molar behaviors" in the observational system used by Spaulding (1965) was labeled "instruction," and technique of instruction was subdivided into a variety of behaviors including stating facts and explaining a process. Two types of questions appeared as instructional techniques: eliciting an answer the teacher had in mind; and eliciting a response in an open-ended way. Perkins (1965) classified questions as those in which the teacher wanted to find out "whether the student knows and understands material" (questions about content), or those which "encourage the student to seek explanations, to solve problems" (questions that stimulate thinking). In the study by Solomon, Bezdek, and Rosenberg (1963) on college teaching of American history, each teacher question was classified into one of seven categories: organizing, hypothetical, opinion, factual, interpretation, clarification, and non-specific. Transcripts of each lesson were coded. A teacher's frequency of use of these types of questions was expressed as a proportion of his total speech.

TABLE 3.13
SUMMARY OF RESULTS OF STUDIES IN WHICH
QUESTIONS WERE CLASSIFIED AS TO TYPE

Investigator and Variables Studied	Subject Areas of Achievement Measures				
	IQ	Arith.	Lang. Arts	Reading	Soc. Studies
Conners & Eisenberg (preschool) intellectual interchanges which emphasized					
0 language	0/1				
0 convergent reasoning	0/1				
0 divergent reasoning	0/1				
Harris & Serwer (grade 1)					
0 meaningful questions (pupil interpretation of word, sentence, or symbol)		0/2	0/3		
0 form questions (pupil recognition of symbol or word)		0/2	0/3		
Harris *et al.* (grade 2)					
0 meaningful questions		0/1	0/3		
0 form questions		0/1	0/3		
Soar (grades 3, 4, 5, 6)					
+ Factor 9		1/2		0/2	
+ teacher encourages elaboration					
+ Factor 3		1/2		2/2	
+ inquiry/drill ratio					
− drill [a]					
Thompson & Bowers (grade 4)					
+ convergent–divergent continuum [b]		1/1			0/1
Fortune (grades 4, 5, 6)					
+ probing		0/1	1/1		0/1

TABLE 3.13 (continued)

Investigator and Variables Studied	Subject Areas of Achievement Measures				
	IQ	Arith.	Lang. Arts	Reading	Soc. Studies
Spaulding (grades 4, 6)					
+ Component 6		0/1	1/1		
— eliciting response in open-ended way [a]					
0 Component 5 eliciting answer teacher has in mind		0/1		0/1	
Perkins (grade 5)					
0 questions about content		0/1	0/2	0/2	0/1
0 questions that stimulate thinking		0/1	0/2	0/2	0/1
Furst–Bellack (grades 10, 12)					
+ ratio of analytic and evaluative to empirical processes					1/1
Solomon *et al.* (adults)					
+ Factor 1 [b] hypothetical opinion non-specific organizing interpretation					1/2
+ Factor 2 interpretation factual					1/2

NOTE. The numerators in the column entries indicate the number of achievement measures with which the variable on the left was significantly, *positively* correlated. The denominators indicate the number of achievement measures used.

[a] Negative loading on this factor.

[b] Teachers who were moderate on this behavior obtained the highest class adjusted achievement scores.

Inspection of Table 3.13 indicates that except for the Solomon study, research on types of questions has not been extensive, and the number of categories in these studies is much smaller than the number of categories created for affective variables. It is difficult to compare these studies because of the problems in coding questions; but of the six investigators who studied linear relationships between pupil achievement and the use of a given type of question, only two found significant results. Spaulding (1965) found that eliciting responses in an open-ended way appeared negatively related to achievement, and Solomon and his colleagues (1963) found that two of the seven categories of questions loaded on a significant factor: questions of fact, and interpretative questions.

These non-significant results are puzzling. One would expect that the frequency of questions that encourage pupils "to seek explanations, to reason, to solve problems" (Perkins, 1965) or the frequency of questions related to interpretation (Harris & Serwer, 1966; Harris *et al.*, 1968) would be consistently related to achievement. Yet these non-significant results have been experimentally replicated. Hutchinson (1963) conducted an experiment in which four teachers taught the same material to two matched groups of seventh-grade pupils. The instructional period was three weeks, or 15 fifty-minute lessons. After the first series of lessons, the teachers were given special training to increase their use of convergent, evaluative, and divergent questions (Gallagher & Aschner, 1963). They then taught the same material a second time to new groups of pupils. All class sessions were tape-recorded, and the frequency of use of different types of questions was tallied. These tallies indicated that the teachers used more higher-level questions (i.e., convergent, divergent, and evaluative) when they taught the lessons a second time. Although the pupils who were taught the second series of lessons showed significantly more growth on some of the creativity tests, the two groups' mean scores on the achievement tests were almost identical.

Similar results were obtained by Miller (1966), although questions were not specifically categorized as such. Instead, all teacher statements were classified as "directive" or "responsive" according to an elaborate coding system. Under the responsive mode, the teacher asks more high-level questions and elaborates pupil responses. In this experiment, each of four teachers taught ten thirty-minute lessons to two groups of pupils—one set of lessons using the responsive mode, the second using the directive mode. Systematic observation of the teachers' behavior indicated significant differences between their behavior in the two settings, although the teachers were less consistent in following the responsive model. There were no significant treatment effects as measured by two criterion tests, one on mastery of facts and the other on "higher understanding."

The results suggest two conclusions: (1) no clear linear relationships have been found between the frequency with which the teacher uses certain types of questions and the achievement of pupils; and (2) the experimentally increased use of specified procedures or types of questions has not resulted in significantly increased achievement. As Conners and Eisenberg (1966) suggest from their study of the effect of teaching behavior upon IQ growth of preschool children, "It may be the total pattern of intellectual stimulation, rather than any specific adherence to . . . different patterns of questions, that is required to induce growth" (p. 10).

The optimal relationship between types of questions and pupil achievement may not be linear. Four investigators have studied this possibility: Soar (1966); Thompson and Bowers (1968); Furst (1967); and Solomon *et al.* (1963).

Soar did not have a variable based on the frequency of questions as such; he used frequencies in columns 3, 4, 8, and 9 to develop ingenious measures of "inquiry" and "drill." "Inquiry" was defined as the sum of the 3–3, 4–4, 8–8, and 9–9 cells (i.e., extended teacher behavior elaborating pupils' answers, extended questioning, extended pupil responses to teacher questions, and extended pupil-initiated responses). The pattern of questioning, elaborating, and answering was taken to represent inquiry. "Drill" was identified by the tallies in the 4–8 and 8–4 cells (i.e., pupil answers to narrow teacher questions plus teacher questions following pupil responses).

Soar developed three measures from these combinations—the amount of inquiry, the amount of drill, and an inquiry/drill ratio computed by dividing the frequency of inquiry behaviors by the frequency of drill behaviors. Two of these measures loaded on Soar's Factor 3, Discussion *vs.* Rapid Interchange, a factor which had a positive correlation with all achievement measures and significant correlations with vocabulary, reading, and arithmetic concepts. Inquiry did not load on this factor, but the inquiry/drill ratio had a positive loading and drill had a negative loading. Soar interpreted this finding as suggesting that a classroom which is high on this factor is not especially high on inquiry but is quite low on drill activities.

Thompson and Bowers (1968) classified questions into those for which more than one answer was possible (divergent) and those for which only one answer was possible (convergent). They also classified teachers as high, moderate, or low on a "convergent–divergent continuum" and found, using analysis of variance, that teachers classified as moderate had pupils whose achievement was highest in a test on word meaning.

One of the items in the cognitive composite developed by Furst (1967) was the ratio of analytic and evaluative to cognitive processes. She developed this ratio by using the descriptive data provided in the report by Bellack *et al.* (1966); the report gave the number of lines in the transcripts of the classroom interactions which Bellack and his associates coded as involving analytic, evaluative, or cognitive processes. "Analytic" refers to defining or interpreting the meaning of an item or statement; "empirical" includes fact-stating or explaining the relationship between events; and "evaluative" deals with personal judgments and/or the reasons for the judgments.

Furst hypothesized that the superior teachers would show greater variety in their use of these processes; she computed the ratio of the two least frequently used to the most frequently used cognitive processes (i.e., the ratio of the lines devoted to analytic plus evaluative processes to the lines devoted to empirical processes). Inspection of the original data (Furst, 1967, p. 203) indicated that the three most effective teachers were significantly superior to the remaining teachers with respect to variety of cognitive processes used.

Solomon *et al.* (1963) found that six of the seven types of questions loaded on Factor 1, labeled "permissiveness *vs.* control." (*Rated* items were also included in developing the factors, which accounts for the discrepancy in the label.) Although there was no significant linear relationship between teacher loadings on this factor and either of the achievement measures, teachers who were moderate on this factor had classes with significantly higher difference scores on the comprehension test.

The studies by Solomon *et al.* (1963) and Soar (1966) suggest that moderation in the use of questions is important. Soar found that the most effective teachers had a higher ratio of inquiry to drill activities, although inquiry itself was not a significant correlate and drill was negatively related to achievement. This suggests that the most effective teachers were moderate in their use of inquiry and low in their use of drill.

Thompson and Bowers (1968) found that teachers who used an equal mixture of convergent and divergent questions were the most successful; Furst (1967) found that the most effective teachers had a higher ratio of the most infrequently used types of interchanges (analytic and evaluative) to the most frequently used type (empirical). The results of these two studies suggest that the most effective teachers exhibited greater variety in their use of questions.

It is difficult to compare these last four studies discussed, because they involve widely disparate observational systems. Yet all four, using classrooms above the primary level, suggest that moderation and/or variation in the use of questions is important. These results also suggest that the patterns of behaviors are more important than single behaviors, and that the relationships of these patterns to achievement is not linear.

Three studies suggest that there may be merit in investigating the teacher's cognitive response to pupils' answers (Soar, 1966; Fortune, 1967; Spaulding, 1965). In the modified version of OScAR 2V used by Soar (1966), teacher questions and statements were coded into three categories: (*a*) teacher encourages further answers to fact questions, (*b*) teacher encourages further explanations, and (*c*) teacher encourages interrelationships, generalizations, and problem solutions. Only one of these three variables loaded on a significant factor.

Teacher encouragement of interrelationships and generalizations loaded on the unnamed Factor 9, which had a significant positive correlation with achievement in arithmetic concepts, and positive, although not significant, correlations with the remaining product measures.

In the study by Fortune (1967) of the effectiveness of student teachers in presenting short lessons to their fourth-, fifth-, or sixth-grade classes, the observational system contained eight items related to lesson development and discussion skills. Lesson development included stress on principal points, the development of discriminations unique to the concept being taught, the labeling of salient features, review and repetition, and the making of associations with prior experience. Discussion skills included "probing," a procedure of asking pupils to expand their answers or give reasons for their answers.

Only a few of these types of questions and cognitive procedures discriminated between the high-scoring and low-scoring teachers in the three subject areas: English, social studies, and mathematics. None discriminated significantly between the high-scoring and low-scoring teachers across all three areas. In English, the high-scoring teachers were rated as using probing behaviors more frequently. In social studies, the high-scoring teachers used review and repetition more frequently. In mathematics the high-scoring teachers emphasized principal points and reviewed more frequently.

We have already noted the positive finding by Spaulding (1965) for "teacher elicits clarification in a non-threatening way" (Table 3.4). All three investigators may be talking about a similar behavior, one which might be given the general label of "probing." That is, the teachers respond to student answers by asking further questions or by making statements which attempt to lead the pupils toward a more comprehensive response than the initial answer.

The teacher's cognitive response to pupil answers is a particularly puzzling area to investigate. Again, it is difficult to compare these three significant findings because the investigators used different observational systems. Furthermore, we have noted that in the investigation by Soar (1966) the variable "teacher encourages pupil elaboration and interpretation" was not related to the behavior "extended use of pupil ideas" (Table 3.9). In addition, Soar found that teacher use of inquiry, or the inquiry/drill ratio, was not related to the frequency of either type of cognitive response (Table 3.3). These perplexing results suggest that there is merit in continuing to study the teacher's cognitive responses to pupil statements, but that simple or even clear answers will be hard to come by.

Additional Cognitive Findings

Table 3.14 is a summary of results on the cognitive variables which were used in various observational systems and which cannot be easily grouped together because too few investigators studied them.

The results obtained by Conners and Eisenberg (1966) mainly substantiate their major finding that the frequency of teacher–pupil interactions concerned with intellectual growth significantly discriminated between high-achieving and low-achieving teachers. Interactions which focus upon property and materials apparently serve to reduce the time available for cognitive interactions. In addition, total com-

TABLE 3.14
SUMMARY OF ADDITIONAL COGNITIVE FINDINGS

| Investigator and Variables Studied | Subject Areas of Achievement Measures | | | | |
	IQ	Arith.	Lang. Arts	Reading	Soc. Studies
Conners & Eisenberg (preschool)					
— emphasis on property and materials	1/1				
+ total communication episodes	1/1				
Fortune (preschool)					
+ physical manipulation of materials					1/1
+ verbal manipulation of concepts					1/1
+ pupil practice					1/1
0 use of instructional set					0/1
0 use of introduction centering on rapport					0/1
0 concept development through emphasis on principal points					0/1
0 concept development through emphasis on discriminations and correct labels					0/1
0 patience to wait for pupil's response					0/1
Soar (grades 3, 4, 5, 6)					
+ Factor 3 steady-state lecture (cell 5–5) ratio of teacher activity to pupil activity		1/2		2/2	

TABLE 3.14 (continued)

Investigator and Variables Studied	IQ	Arith.	Lang. Arts	Reading	Soc. Studies
Fortune (grades 4, 5, 6)					
+ use of instructional set		0/1	0/1		1/1
0 use of introductions centering on rapport		0/1	0/1		0/1
+ emphasis on principal points		1/1	0/1		0/1
0 emphasis on discriminations or on correct labels		0/1	0/1		0/1
+ review and repetition		1/1	0/1		1/1
+ patience to wait for pupil's response		1/1	1/1		0/1
Bellack–Furst (grades 10, 12)					
+ Cognitive component moderate amount of structuring activities moderate number of cycles per minute					1/1

NOTE. The numerators in the column entries indicate the number of achievement measures with which the variable on the left was significantly, *positively* correlated. The denominators indicate the number of achievement measures used.

munication episodes had a significant correlation with only one group of activities, those related to intellectual growth.

Some of the variables developed by Fortune (1966, 1967) are fascinating teaching behaviors concerning concept attainment which might be considered in future investigations. These include: highlighting the difference between concepts; pointing out salient features; providing the correct label; and relating the material to some aspect of the child's life. The finding by Furst that the high-achieving teachers were moderate on the number of "teaching cycles" they went through is a partial replication of the finding by Soar that drill was negatively related to achievement. A drill situation would probably contain a high frequency of cycles per minute.

Four studies present some information on *structuring*. In two, Fortune (1966, 1967) attempted to quantify the teacher's use of an "instructional set," or introductory cognitive preparation. In only one of three subject areas—that of social studies in grades 4, 5, and 6—did use of this behavior discriminate between high-achieving and low-achieving teachers.

However, in the coding system developed by Bellack *et al.* (1966), "structuring" referred to the initial statements of the teacher which serve to initiate or focus a teaching cycle. These initial statements frequently precede a question. The finding by Furst that the high-achieving teachers were moderate in their use of structuring statements suggests that providing a moderate amount of structure was the most effective teaching procedure for these high school classes.

Soar (1966) believed that the positive relationship between steady-state lecturing (cell 5–5) and achievement reflects cognitive structuring activities on the part of the high-achieving teachers. Such a hypothesis cannot be investigated by inspection of an IA matrix, because both extended and relatively short lecturing would fit into the 5–5 cell. But Soar studied the original observer tally sheets and determined that four of the five teachers ranking highest on his Factor 3 followed a pattern in which they lectured at most for fifteen or twenty seconds, and then asked a question for pupils to respond to. Such a pattern—the posing of a situation or the providing of a limited unit of information, followed by the asking of a question, followed by response to the question—appeared to Soar to parallel the rationale of programmed instruction. It is possible that both Soar and Furst have identified such a pattern in some successful teaching. Gage and Unruh (1967) have also suggested a parallel between the structuring, soliciting, responding and reacting pattern described by Bellack *et al.* (1966) and the sequence of frame-presentation, question, response, and reinforcement which appears in programmed instruction.

There is a suggestion that for the primary grades *practice* is a component of effective instruction. This suggestion is supported by the finding of Fortune (1966) that the most successful teachers of pre-school children spent significantly more time asking the pupils to manipulate, physically or verbally, the concept being taught. The importance of practice in the primary grades is also supported by the findings by Harris *et al.* (1968) of a significant negative correlation between the amount of time the teacher spent reading and telling a story to the pupils and the mean class adjusted score on all four achievement tests. Additional support for the importance of practice can be inferred from the results shown in Table 3.12, suggesting the importance of the frequency of questions in the primary grades.

Summary and Discussion

Fifteen years ago Ackerman (1954) and Morsh and Wilder (1954) called for research on teaching which would employ systematic observation of specific teaching behaviors and would correlate these behaviors with measures of pupil achievement. Such research, they suggested, would be more productive than the previous studies which had utilized general rating scales and measures of teacher personality and characteristics as independent variables. The nineteen studies reviewed here which do relate systematically observed behaviors to measures of pupil achievement do not provide overwhelming support for the more systematic approach. Nevertheless these more recent studies do represent an improvement in two respects: they suggest several specific behaviors which appear to be somewhat consistently related to pupil achievement; and they do offer suggestions for future research that focuses on specific behaviors and details ways to study the effects of these behaviors.

Findings—Affective Variables

The results on the studies in which measures of teacher approval and disapproval were used as observational variables indicate a tendency for approval to be associated with higher pupil achievement and for criticism to be associated with lower pupil achievement. Of the two sets of variables, disapproval and criticism appeared to be more consistent in their effects than approval and praise. However, not all instances of approval facilitated learning, nor did all instances of disapproval hinder learning.

One of the most consistent findings was that extremes of criticism, such as continued disapproval (e.g., cell 7–7), appeared negatively related to achievement. However, milder forms of criticism (such as giving directions related to learning, telling a pupil his answer was incorrect, commanding conformance, or eliciting clarification of an incorrect answer) were usually not related, and were sometimes positively related, to achievement.

The results on instances and types of approval generally supported these behaviors, but not as clearly as those on criticism. Frequency of praise *per se* was not a significant correlate, and there were suggestions that minimal praise, such as "Uh huh," is at least as effective as stronger praise and encouragement. There are also suggestions that praise is more effective when coupled with a reason for its being given, or when it follows actions which indicate pupil independence, such as interpretation of ideas or pupil planning. This strongest type of approval was labeled "use of pupil ideas," and this behavior included repetition, summary, and modification of pupil ideas, and integration of a pupil's idea into the lesson. Such behavior appears to contain both affective and cognitive components. There is also a suggestion that some types of approval may be negatively related to achievement. These include use of the teacher-centered "I," use of a warm voice, and selection of topics related to pupils' interests.

Finally, the combination of approval and disapproval behaviors into an i/d ratio yields a score which is a relatively consistent discriminator between the most effective and least effective teachers.

Findings—Cognitive Variables

The two clearest results in this area of research are (1) the significant positive relationships of frequent questioning and of practice with achievement in the primary grades, and (2) the absence of a linear relationship between achievement and the frequency of use of specific types of questions.

Three other conclusions—which must be considered more tentative because it is difficult to compare studies on these teaching behaviors and because too few investigators have studied them—are these: (1) Moderation and/or variation in the use of questions facilitates achievement. (2) Pupil achievement is positively related to teacher responses that require pupils to probe or elaborate upon their answers to questions. (3) Achievement is positively correlated with a moderate amount of structuring, or short statements which serve to introduce or provide a focus for a series of teacher–pupil interchanges.

However, there are suggestions in this research that the most effective teachers do not merely emit a specified number of approving statements or types of questions; rather, they may be selecting certain behaviors and avoiding others in order to achieve particular cognitive ends. The most effective teachers studied by Conners and Eisenberg (1966) provided more interchanges involving intellectual content and fewer involving property and materials; the most successful teachers studied by Spaulding (1965) approved pupil responses which gave interpretation and judgment, but they asked few questions related to pupils' interests and few open-ended questions; the successful teachers studied by Soar (1966) and Furst (1967) gave short structuring lectures before they asked questions; the successful teachers studied by Solomon *et al.* (1963) emphasized *both* factual and interpretive questions; and in three investigations the most successful teachers responded to pupil answers by "probing," or asking the pupil or the class to elaborate and clarify what was said (Spaulding, 1965; Soar, 1966; Fortune, 1967).

In each of these cases, the teacher may have chosen the effective behavior because he thought the behavior would advance the attainment of specified cognitive ends. In other words, the teachers' behavior could perhaps be explained in terms of the following propositions: a moderate amount of structuring before a question was used because such structuring appeared to improve the quality of student answers; it was not pupil participation alone that the teacher sought, but a certain quality of response; only selected pupil responses were approved because these were the ones the teacher wished to encourage; pupils were asked to elaborate and extend their answers because such pupil behavior moved the class discussion toward certain ends that the teacher had in mind; at the same time, the teacher avoided behaviors (such as emphasis upon property and materials, questions related to pupils' personal interests, or excessive criticism) which did not contribute toward cognitive ends.

If ends-in-view are a critical component of effective teaching, then we should expect that simply increasing teachers' use of specific behaviors, as such, would have minimal effects. There has been insufficient study of this question; but the limited research indicates that teaching teachers to vary the types of questions asked (Hutchinson, 1963), or to vary both the types of questions and the types of teacher responses (Miller, 1966), has not produced significant differences in pupil achievement. The experimental studies may be showing that merely using certain behaviors is not sufficient. These behaviors may become effective only when the teacher sees them as *means* to cognitive achievement, not as ends.

One additional general suggestion emerges from the research on cognitive interchanges. After the primary grades, single cognitive behaviors are not significant correlates. Rather, the over-all pattern of behaviors is more important. Such a pattern includes the use of a variety of questions, moderate amounts of structure, lesser amounts of drill, and frequent requests for the pupil to elaborate his answer.

It is reassuring that the major conclusions of the research on the affective correlates of teacher effectiveness parallel the results in the experimental research developing under the general title of behavior modification (Ulrich *et al.*, 1966). Investigators in both areas of research have noted that approval is usually associated with higher achievement. It is possible that behaviors such as praise, rewards, and the attention of the teacher serve to develop the pupil's attention to task and persistence. Although attention and persistence may greatly facilitate cognitive achievement, in both areas of research the cognitive aspects of instruction have been relatively neglected. Approval behaviors of the teacher might have a greater effect upon achievement if they were joined with cognitive variables designed to focus, direct, and structure the practice of the pupils.

Each type of research contributes to the other. The correlational studies of objectively observed classroom behaviors produce new variables and new clusters of variables which might be used in experiments in behavior modification. The methods of behavior modification should be extremely useful in the training of teachers, because these methods focus upon precise, systematic use of significant variables in the classroom.

Future Research

Current research employing systematic observations of classroom behavior might be characterized as a shift from high-inference to medium-inference, a shift from subjective to relatively objective observation. The next shift should be toward greater precision in recording, reporting, and analyzing results.

Refinement of Variables

The reports of these studies need to contain much more specific descriptions of the behaviors included in any category. Without clear statements of the ground rules, comparisons between studies are hazardous. Excellent examples of this type of specification are contained in the final reports by Spaulding (1965), Snider (1966), and Bellack *et al.* (1966).

The reports should also contain the means and standard deviations of the behaviors investigated. Because of the possible curvilinear relationships between frequencies of a behavior and pupil achievement, we need to know more about the samples. It might be useful to avoid the practice of splitting a sample of teachers into "direct" and "indirect" teachers. Instead, more useful results might be obtained if teachers were stratified according to their use of certain behaviors. One stratification which would be particularly useful in studies in which an i/d ratio is used might be "i/d above 2," "i/d above 1," and so on. This stratification would facilitate more precise interpretations of the relationships between levels of a variable and achievement and would allow those involved in teacher education to describe "indirect" and "direct" teaching in more specific terms.

We are also interested in alternative procedures to achieve the same affective and cognitive results as the teacher's "acceptance and use of pupils' ideas" achieves. One procedure would be for the teacher to ask other pupils to summarize, compare, or elaborate what one pupil has said. Such repetitions might involve the same affective components of giving publicity and indicating that someone has listened to the pupil; they may have cognitive merit because they provide for the repetition and clarification of key points. In addition, requiring such pupil behaviors and approving their occurrence may facilitate the pupils' implicit rehearsal and practice of the major cognitive processes involved.

Additional alternatives for expansion and use of pupils' ideas have been discussed above in the section on cognitive results as related to teacher response to pupil answers (pages 86–87). There is some indication that a number of behaviors which appear to resemble "use of pupil ideas" are uncorrelated. Thus, two significant positive behaviors identified by Spaulding (1965) loaded on different factors: teacher approval of pupils' interpretation; and teacher disapproval by eliciting clarification in a non-threatening way. In the study by Soar, there were positive results for the teacher's encouragement of pupils' elaboration and generalization, although such behaviors were uncorrelated with teacher use of behaviors in Category 3. These similar but uncorrelated behaviors are further indication of the complexity of this particular area and the difficulty of separating the cognitive and affective components.

There is a need for future investigations which subscript the behaviors within Category 3 and which include behaviors that superficially appear to resemble "use of pupil ideas." Were such investigations completed we should have more specific knowledge about the number of factors which reside in Category 3 and in alternative forms of this behavior, and which of these factors are consistent correlates of certain pupil product measures.

Another variable that could be subscripted is criticism, which could be divided in to two types: extended criticism; and criticism for which a reason is given. There is also a need to separate "criticism and directions concerning academic activities" from "criticism and directions concerning personal control."

The theme of these suggestions for future research has been to emphasize the value of breaking categories into smaller units and learning the relationships of frequencies and patterns of these smaller behaviors with achievement. As knowledge accumulates, we shall be able to test whether certain combinations of these variables have greater predictability than the smaller parts. At present, we need to understand the parts better.

Combination of Variables

One of the major difficulties in interpreting the studies which have used IA or OScAR is the confusion which results from combining variables too soon. Not only are we unsure of the intercorrelations of the various i/d ratios, but using an i/d ratio which consists of 10 to 50 cells may be a premature step because such a combination obscures other relationships. Furst (1967) created the same problem when she formed *a priori* composites of three variables without first giving the results on each individual variable.

It may be true that an i/d ratio is a better predictor of achievement than any of its specific parts, but this empirical assertion has not been adequately tested. The assumption behind an i/d ratio is that indirect and direct behaviors have a substantial negative correlation so that the ratio of the two is more predictive than either set of behaviors taken separately. Inspection of the available matrices indicates that this assumption is tenable in only some of the studies. Further research utilizing the existing matrices of completed studies may help clarify a number of these questions; and this gold, or fool's gold, has yet to be mined.

It was relatively easy to describe current research and suggest new groupings of affective variables for future research. The problems are more difficult in the area of cognitive variables. For the reasons described before, these variables are considerably harder to categorize; therefore, there has been much less research in this area and the results are not easily compared.

Perhaps the best suggestion would be to conduct more research using cognitive systems. Several of these observational systems have been developed and have yielded high reliability coefficients across observers during the same lesson. But only a few investigators have attempted to correlate these cognitive variables with measures of adjusted pupil achievement. Until more data are available, specific recommendations for future research can be based only on speculation.

Yet, the cognitive areas have been most neglected in process-criteria research. Variables such as the relevance of the materials to the ability of the class, or the amount of time spent preparing pupils for future classwork, have not appeared in the systematic observational systems because these variables are extremely difficult to quantify. Indeed, most of the experimental research on instruction with human subjects and meaningful materials which is reported in educational psychology texts (even elementary ones) is not acknowledged in these category systems.

Conclusion

Nineteen studies are too few to reach comprehensive conclusions on the validity of a whole research form. Perhaps when sixty or eighty studies have been completed we might be able to consider their usefulness more closely. But future results may not be any clearer than those we have so far. First, we may continue to have trouble identifying the behaviors of good teachers because they are idiosyncratic. A wide range of superior teaching behaviors may be distributed among the superior teachers so that no single behavior or group of behaviors emerges as a correlate of good teaching or as a discriminating variable.

Second, too many potentially influential variables are not being considered in studies employing systematic observation. These variables include the textbooks and supplementary materials, organization of the lesson and sequencing of the materials, the cognitive learning styles of individual pupils, and the influence of the entire school environment upon academic achievement. It may be unrealistic to expect that the results of future studies employing systematic observation will be any stronger than the present ones.

Postscript

In the two studies reported by Flanders (1965) the results were analyzed using a critical ratio test comparing the achievement of the high i/d teachers with that of the low i/d teachers. In the study of sixth-grade teachers and pupils reported by Morrison (1966), only extremes, with respect both to teachers and to pupils, were used in the analysis. In a more recent (1970) book by Flanders, a reanalysis of these three studies is presented in which linear correlations are computed between teacher behavior variables and the adjusted achievement scores for all pupils in each class. In addition, the new report by Flanders contains correlations between teacher behaviors and adjusted pupil achievement for two additional samples: grade 2 and grade 4.

The linear correlations between a number of variables from the IA matrices and the measures of pupil achievement for the five studies are presented in Table 3.15.

This additional knowledge—the more complete analysis of three studies and the two additional studies—results in the modification of

TABLE 3.15
LINEAR CORRELATIONS BETWEEN IA VARIABLES
AND PUPIL ACHIEVEMENT

	Class Group				
Variable	Gr. 2 ($N = 15$)	Gr. 4 ($N = 16$)	Gr. 6 ($N = 30$)	Gr. 7 ($N = 15$)	Gr. 8 ($N = 16$)
i/d ratio	−.03	.33	.18	.47	.41
I/D ratio	−.07	−.08	.18	.25	.32
Teacher indirectness (Cols. 1+ 2 + 3)	−.04	.12	.37 *	.41	.30
Sustained acceptance (Cell 3-3)	−.45	.19	.30	.40	.19
Praise (Col. 2)	.25	−.13	.36 *	−.23	.30
Teacher directness (Cols. 6 + 7)	−.10	−.24	−.04	−.61 **	−.34
Small vicious circle (Cells 6-7 + 7-6)	.05	−.23	−.15	−.62 **	−.25

* $p < .05$ ** $p < .01$

some of the conclusions reported earlier in this paper. The variable "teacher use of criticism of pupils" had a significant negative relationship with some measure of achievement in 7 out of 13 studies, as compared with 7 out of 9 for the studies previously reviewed. Concerning the variable "teacher use of student ideas," it was previously reported that in 4 out of 5 studies significant results were obtained in some subject areas. Such a highly favorable conclusion must now be modified to 3 out of 8 studies; the trend remains quite favorable, but the results are not as strong. Finally, the lack of significant linear correlations between the i/d ratio and achievement is now clearer. Earlier it was stated that there were significant results in only one of 5 studies; now there are significant results in only one of 10 studies.

The moral of this postscript is that none of the summary statements is final, and that we can expect further revisions in any summary statements as new research results are reported and as existing data are reanalyzed.

Strategies and Approaches

FOUR

A Sociological Approach to Classroom Research

RAYMOND S. ADAMS

The suggestion has been made elsewhere that classroom research, in the face of the "specter" of automated education, is the ultimate gesture in futility. After all, what virtue can inhere in researching a phenomenon that tomorrow will be as dead as the proverbial dodo?

However, if education's future is machine bound, then rather than foresake research in today's classrooms, we should redouble our efforts —not indeed in order to solve pedagogical problems, but so that a quaint form of twentieth-century ritual can be preserved for posterity's interest, edification, and amusement. Such a prospect implies a stance rather different from the stances conventionally adopted. It suggests that rather than treating classroom research instrumentally, as a means for achieving a desired end, the intrinsic virtue of recording the "facts of educational life" should be recognized.

Education has, in the past, been rather schizophrenic about its own "facts of life." The facts of educational life, it seems, are not legitimate in their own right. It is not sufficient that they are, like Everest, there; they must be useful as well. Consequently, the educational researcher is torn between the scientific drive to investigate and his evangelistic drive to do good. He is increasingly pressured to show, and preferably in advance, the practical applications of his particular investigation. Funding agencies demand practical outcomes, teachers and administrators ask how can "it" improve education, and, more insiduously, educational researchers themselves feel that perhaps they *ought* to be doing this kind of good anyway. It hardly need be pointed out that in other fields of scientific endeavor, the criterion of demonstrable usefulness is not a necessary condition of legitimacy.

On the assumption that classroom behavior represents a phenomenon that is worthy of study in its own right (after all, it is probably quite as extensive às cigarette smoking), Bruce Biddle and I, in 1963, initiated a classroom research project making use of video-taped records. This research is different in a number of ways from most of the classroom studies that have been reported to date. This paper tells of the study, the kind of problems that prompted us to follow the path we did, and, with a small touch of whimsy, conjectures briefly about some of the educational implications.

The classroom research project was originally intended to be a "good" work in the best reformative sense. However, when it came to the point of making explicit the theoretical foundations of the study, the weaknesses of such an orientation became apparent. The value judgments implicit in the definition of "good" smacked too much of prejudice for our own comfort. After reevaluating the position, we came to accept description of classroom behavior as the initial "objective" of the study. We saw ourselves in the guise of conceptual cartographers.

A Structure and Some Terms

Description is a selective process which inevitably bears the stigma of the theoretical orientation adopted by the describer. Or, to put it another way, the observation of any phenomenon is always circumscribed by the perceptual blinkers of the observer.

For the analysis of classroom behavior, the orientation most comfortable for us was a sociological one. We were concerned primarily with the classroom as a group. The collective character of the institution rather than the individual characteristics of the members intrigued us most. We were seeking an objective interpretation of whatever it is that gives classrooms behavioral identity as classrooms.

The model upon which the study rested shares a certain amount of common ground with other research in this area. Like important studies by Flanders (1965), Smith *et al.* (1963b), and Bellack (1966), to name a few, its first assumption was that communication is a basic element. Unlike Ryans' recent work (1963), however, it does not rest on information theory.

For the study, communication is defined as *the transmission of symbolic meaning*. The transmission of symbolic meaning in turn implies (1) agents or actors who execute the transmission, (2) other agents who receive it, and (3) a process by which the transmission is made. It follows that the communication system of the classroom may be conceptualized in conventional sociological terms as having both function and structure. *Function* refers to the content of the communication and the mode or manner of the transmission. *Structure* refers to the patterning of elements involved in the transmission.

To recapitulate, the fundamental assumption on which the study rested was that the classroom as a system of communication is composed of members who engage in the transmission of meanings. The relationships among the members, and the relationships between the members and the process of communication, constitute the structural aspects of the situation. The functional aspects of the situation have to do with the nature of the communication—what it is about and how it is conveyed.

This basic model needs greater elaboration. *Function* was conceptualized as comprising two dimensions. The first, *content*, consisted of four rather gross categories: (1) *Scheduled subject matter* is concerned with task elements that are conventionally associated with the kind of lesson prescribed at that time. For example, defining a lesson as an arithmetic lesson also defines the nature of the scheduled subject matter. (2) *Nonscheduled subject matter* is communication content that can be identified with conventional school subjects other than the one scheduled at the moment. (3) *Sociation* communications are those whose content focuses on feelings or interpersonal relationships. Conventional greetings such as "Good morning" and "How are you?" fall under this rubric. So do exhortations to "Be good," "Stop fighting," or "Be polite." The occasions when friendly and supportive gestures are made or when hostile or threatening ones occur are also classified as sociation. (4) Finally, *organization management* communications refer to matters that involve classroom administration. They include directing and controlling the personnel and manipulating the various artifacts in the setting.

Some insight into the meanings of these content categories may be gained by comparing them with Bales' (1950) interaction analysis. Bales' coding system differentiated two general areas of content: instrumental–objective task area; and expressive–integrative social–emotional area. These correspond to subject matter and sociation in the current study. There are two features included in our model that are omitted from the Bales study, non-task communications and organization management communications. Whether Bales ever considered including such categories is a moot point, but there are several plausible reasons why he would not have done so. In the first place, Bales' groups were contrived, *ad hoc* adult groups that had no *raison d'être* outside the experimental situation. Neither did they have any permanency. Their organizational needs were minimal and their tasks, unlike those in most real-life situations, were well defined and single-faceted. He was not, therefore, forced to accommodate to some of the conditions existing in classroom groups.

The other functional dimension of analysis in the present study was called *mode*. There are three components: (1) *Information dissemination* communications are concerned with providing, clarifying, questioning, and elaborating facts. (Whether the facts are correct or not is incidental.) (2) Communications classifiable as *intellectualization* are those in which the message is devoted to the *process* of reasoning or conjecturing, or, if you prefer, to processes of induction and deduction. Whereas the emphasis in information dissemination is on symbol transmission, in intellectualization the focus is on the processes by which symbols can be related. (3) The third mode category, *operation*, is different from the others in some important respects. It will be recalled that the study is concerned primarily with the classroom as a collectivity. Conventionally, classroom members, from time to time, engage in some conjoint actions in which transmission of communications is private to the individual rather than public. For example, children engaged in seat work may be receiving symbolic meanings from the books they are reading or from the work they are doing. On other occasions they engage in activity in which symbols are being publicly displayed rather than transmitted. For instance, when the whole class is engaged in verbal drills, recitations, singing, honoring the flag, and so on, symbols are being transmitted by all actors simultaneously and in a way that suggests that the content is of little communicatory import. Such communication is clearly different from the other modes identified.

The three modes as they have been conceptualized here should *not* be interpreted as referring to the cognitive processes of individuals. Intellectualization is not equivalent to thinking. Operation is not equivalent to doing. Information dissemination is not equivalent to knowing. What is under consideration in this study is the character of communication in the classroom setting. To this extent, then, the individual members are incidental to the system of analysis devised.

It would be tempting to engage in a rationalization of these functional categories, showing their educational relevance and presenting a quite intuitively based defense of their incipient virtue. However, their ultimate justification is an empirical issue. If they can provide predictive power, then they too can be taken into account with the host of other concepts that will have to be considered before a technical language of education is developed and before theoretical sophistication can emerge. It should be noted in passing, however, that the present system makes no pretense of providing other than a set of very gross categories which can be operationally distinguished and which have the capacity for considerable refinement.

There are no doubt many ways in which the *structural* character of classrooms might be considered. One might, for instance, be concerned with different seating arrangements, the extent to which individuals in the setting interact, the utilization of various "props" in the situation, and so on. In the current study several structural components were conceptualized and identified.

The first and most molar of the structural components was concerned with the general pattern of communication prevailing over the whole classroom. This was called *communication system* structure.

One of the fundamental observable characteristics of classroom activity is that the members do not always constitute a single interacting group. Often classrooms may be observed in which some of the members are gazing elsewhere, are engaging in surreptitious conversations, are undertaking small group projects, and so on. The number and size of such *communicating groups* can be identified. In this investigation, the minimal basis for identification was that the members of a group are presumed to be communicating or are collectively engaged with a common stimulus. The three elements basic to this aspect of structural analysis were: (1) the *central group* (arbitrarily defined as engaging more than 50 per cent of the personnel present); (2) *peripheral groups* (fewer than 50 per cent); and (3) *noninvolved actors*.[1] In a given lesson, classrooms may exhibit each of these in varying combinations and for varying lengths of time.

At a more molecular level it is possible to attribute *communicatory roles* to actors in the classroom. Consistent with the analytic approach basic to the study, roles were identified in non-concrete terms. Three were selected: (1) *emitter*, (2) *target*, and (3) *audience*. An emitter is the source from which a communication emanates. Sources may be identified as consisting of single actors or multiple actors or even as being nonhuman (for example, a television set). A target is the subject or subjects (or the object or objects) toward whom (which) the communication is directed. An audience consists of those actors in the situation whose attention is engaged by the communication.

This system of analysis can be applied to each of the communicating groups identified earlier to yield what was termed *role allocation*. Thus, a central group might comprise a single emitter, no target, and a quorum (or majority) audience. A peripheral group, which perhaps was in existence at the same time, might comprise only a single emitter and a single target. During any class hour, various patterns of role structures may emerge, expand, diminish, and die.

In order to generate more information, provision was also made for mapping the teacher's participation in the three roles. This was called *teacher role assignment*.

The final structural characteristic provided for was concerned with the *physical location* of actors. An analysis grid, applicable in all classrooms of any shape, was devised to provide a consistent basis for classifying locations. The grid divided the floor space into twenty-five uniform segments which discriminated among locations on the basis of proximity to the front and sides of the room.

Several observations should be made about the types of concepts employed in the study. First, the concepts are analytic rather than concrete. Analytic concepts were preferred principally because concrete systems tend to provide few new insights, and because education's conventional terminology is most often semantically imprecise and not susceptible to operationalization. Secondly, the concepts taken are objective in that no assumptions about the intentions of the actors or the goals of the system are built in. This has the twin advantages of making data analysis less dependent on the observer's prior understanding of the system, and of facilitating subsequent incorporation of the findings with other more microscopic analyses of classroom behavioral phenomena that are planned for the future. Thirdly, the use of such concepts permits the utilization of analytic rather than arbitrary units of time in the actual coding.

Looking at Classrooms

Since this last point carries some important implications, it is now appropriate to move from the conceptual framework to an account of the methods of analysis employed. However, some description of the primary data and the way they were collected is a necessary prerequisite.

The primary data comprised video-taped recordings of lessons in live classrooms. These were obtained by means of two remotely controlled video cameras which were concealed in glass-fronted boxes. The boxes were placed at strategic positions in the classroom so that one, with a wide-angle lens, could record the faces of the children and the other, with a zoom lens, could focus on and track the teacher. The teacher wore a cordless microphone, and four other microphones were located judiciously throughout the room. All the recording was done in a control truck where the images from both cameras were monitored and blended for simultaneous reproduction onto tape. Two audio channels were used in the recording, one for the teacher's microphone and one for the four "public" ones.

Certain precautions were taken to try to ensure that the recorded lesson was as "natural" as possible. The camera boxes were placed in the classroom on the preceding day. The children were told that some of their lessons would be televised and were invited to ask questions (which were answered honestly). Finally, the participants were not informed of the actual time when recording would be undertaken. Whether these precautions were successful cannot be determined; the comparison of observed behavior with unobserved behavior is a more impossible task than getting toothpaste back in the tube. However, the teachers gave assurances that the lessons were relatively normal and that they themselves were usually unaware of the recording apparatus.

In all, 48 different classrooms were involved in the study. Each was recorded for two hours. Four independent variables were used to determine the composition of the sample: grade level (Grades 1, 6, and 11 were used); subject matter (social studies and arithmetic–mathematics); age of teacher (over forty and under thirty); and sex of teacher. We had a number of hypotheses or, more precisely, serendipities, about the relationships of these independent variables and classroom behavior. It is worth noting in passing that the independent variable that produced the greatest amount of significant difference was the one least often recognized in behavioral studies of teaching: the sex of the teacher.

The participating schools were selected with less regard for scientific utility. The criterion was willingness to become involved in the project. As well, the teachers chosen volunteered their cooperation. By chance the sample was a bland one. Most of the schools were located in areas that were not too socio-economically dissimilar from each other, and the teachers themselves were undoubtedly regarded as "competent." It is certainly true that the teachers had sufficient confidence not to be unduly threatened by the prospect of a "big brother" observation.

The obvious advantage of having primary data in the form of television tape recordings is that the behavior can be viewed and reviewed at length and at leisure. Control over the complexity of coincidental happenings can be exercised to a degree not possible with individual observers or, indeed, with large numbers of observers. The tape recorder used made rewinding and backing up extremely quick and simple. Repeated inspection of the same incident then posed no technical problems. On an average, each hour of classroom tape was subjected to twenty hours of analysis.

The analysis procedure itself was tedious and time-consuming, but relatively straightforward once the coding conventions had been determined and the coders trained. The task in its simplest form required that the times of origin and extinction of the behavior chosen for coding had to be identified and transcribed. A timing device attached to the tape recorder itself permitted times to be registered in quarter-second intervals.

For the broader coding task, each of the concepts discussed earlier was converted into a variable class consisting of varying numbers of component variables. The duration of each instance when any variable existed was recorded on master sheets and then converted to a form acceptable for IBM punching. The strategy used allocated column space for every variable class (and therefore every variable) on each card. The first card for any classroom, then, would contain a complete record of the state of every variable class, whether operative or in-operative, at that moment. It also would register the "time" and, of course, its own ID number. The second card would be created as soon as *any change* occurred *among any of the variables.* The new card would therefore contain a description of the state of all variable classes at this new point in time. This procedure, followed for the whole lesson, would yield a set of cards which, if read in sequence, could give a complete picture of the ebb and flow of functional and structural activity in the classroom. As well, individual variable classes could also be examined to determine the extent to which each variable occurred and how long it persisted.

A number of different kinds of basic units could have been employed in the analysis process, for instance, an arbitrary time unit (say three seconds) or a concrete unit that broke the lesson up into meaningful segments corresponding to "phases" of the lesson. However, the conventions adopted were different from these. The first basic unit was taken as a period of time during which no change, structural or functional, occurred. This homeostatic unit was called an "episode." Each card, of course, constitutes an episode. The second basic but less molecular unit is the "incident." The incidents take their character from the various variable classes, and they are defined as periods of time during which no change occurs in the particular variable class concerned. Thus a functional incident of, say, information dissemination would be uniform with respect to that function while many structural changes might be occurring throughout its duration. These basic units could be tallied either in terms of the number of times they occurred (instances), or as durational counts.

Some Findings

Understandably, the detail and complexity of secondary data resulting from this kind of analysis are immense, and this is not a proper place to demonstrate the nature of the complexity. However, some of the more intriguing findings from the pilot study are worth presenting. It should be noted that these findings were derived from 32 lessons given by 16 teachers. The sample, however, was balanced for each of the independent variables mentioned earlier (grade level, subject matter, age and sex of teacher).

The episode, as the smallest measurable unit employed, showed some variability over the whole sample. The number of episodes recorded for each lesson ranged between 176 and 654. The mean number of episodes was 371. When the average length of episode was calculated for each class, the resultant scores were found to range between 4.8 seconds and 17.6 seconds per episode.

Again taking a molar view of the data, it is possible to arrive at a general picture of the distribution of activity over the different variable classes. When each lesson was adjusted to equalize the duration of the lessons, the relative concentration of incident frequencies for the 24 variable classes in each lesson was obtained.

These are specific findings that can be reported for all of the classrooms studied:

√ For more than 85 per cent of the total time, the classrooms were organized so that a central communication system was in existence.

√ For 25 per cent of the time, some members were identified as being noninvolved.

√ The average teacher was: (a) an emitter in the central system 54.5 per cent of the time (and in peripheral systems 4 per cent of the time); (b) a target in the central system 24 per cent of the time (and in a peripheral system 2 per cent of the time); and (c) audience member for 7 per cent of the time. For another 8 per cent of the time he was noninvolved or out of the room.

√ Three types of role allocation dominated the data; namely: (a) teacher emitter with a quorum audience (42 per cent of duration); (b) single student emitter, teacher target, and quorum audience (26 per cent); and (c) teacher emitter, single student target, and quorum audience (16 per cent of duration).

√ The data on both emitter and target locations are uniform and striking. For 68 per cent of the time when emitters were in existence, they were located in one of three locations (the center front of the room, immediately behind center front, or immediately behind that). For 72 per cent of the time when there were targets, the targets were located in precisely the same locations.

√ The teacher occupied locations at the front of the room for 68 per cent of the total time. He spent 15 per cent of his time perambulating around the room. Of the remainder, he spent most time visiting three select locations.

√ Less than one-half of a per cent of time in the sample classroom was devoted to sociation functions.

√ Information dissemination covers 75 per cent of function time. Of this, information about subject matter accounted for 51 per cent and information dissemination about organization covered 15 per cent.

√ Intellectualization about subject matter accounted for 21 per cent of the total time.

√ Operation accounted for little time and was virtually confined to Grade 1.

The general impression these data convey is that the classroom is a remarkably busy place. Given the limited interpretation of structure and function accepted here, there is nonetheless evidence of frequent and rapid change. Even in the least active lesson, a change of one sort or another occurred, on an average, once every 18 seconds. It is also evident that the teachers do not readily accept the role of interested onlooker. They either take an active and central part or else they tend to withdraw from the situation, either physically or psychologically. Consistent with the teachers' tendency to participate persistently is the teachers' tendency to occupy front-of-the-room locations, thus assuring continued prominence. In fact, there appears to be a location principle operating which can be stated thus: *the further a location is from the center front of the room, the less likely it is to be visited by the teacher.* A second location principle that is almost identical can also be stated: *the further a location is from the center front of the room, the less likely it is that the occupant will be directly involved in the public communicatory action.*

In order to represent differences among the independent variables, the data were subjected to some 6,500 *t* tests. They provided details of the significance of differences for both number of incidents and duration. Again, it would not be proper to report results in detail here. It should also be noted that because of the smallness of the samples involved, the findings are presented merely as indicators of possible future lines of investigation. Each of the variable classes will be dealt with in turn.

Grade

In Grade 1, classroom life requires more overt educational activity than in the other grades. Compared with students in secondary classrooms, Grade 1 members spend more time more frequently on matters of organizational relevance. In Grade 1, too, the teacher will be talking to the whole class both more often and for longer periods than the teacher in Grade 6, but, interestingly enough, less than in Grade 11. Furthermore, whether the teacher is talking or not, the class in Grade 1 will be operating *as a class* more often and longer than in Grade 6, but again less than in Grade 11. Grade 1 students, in comparison with those of Grade 6, again are less frequently identifiable as "noninvolved" although the opposite holds good when comparison is made with Grade 11. Even so, Grade 1 students would also have more contact with the teacher in small groups, would have more opportunity to express themselves to other students, and would spend more time individually with the teacher.

To this extent the Grade 1 student would anticipate playing a more direct, overt part in classroom activities with opportunity for a continuing relationship with the teacher. However, the extent and nature of this relationship with the teacher would be influenced by the locations inhabited. Fringe-dwellers (not up and down the center line) would "but see her passing by." Even so, pass by she would, more frequently than would teachers in the other grades.

The Grade 6 student in the present sample experiences life a little differently from his junior and senior counterparts. In his classroom there will be significantly more exchanges concerned with the rationalization of organizational procedures. Presumably, where Grade 1 students had to "do," Grade 6 students have to both do and appreciate "why." (At Grade 11, it seems, the matter is no longer an issue.) As far as "understanding" subject matter (as distinct from knowing about it) is concerned, Grade 6 class members spend more time more often confronting this issue than do class members in Grade 1, but less than those in Grade 11. A final functional difference concerns sociation. Interestingly enough, there is greater likelihood that Grade 6 students will experience exchanges in which information is disseminated about sociation than will either Grade 1 or Grade 11 students.

In Grade 6 the opportunity for being "noninvolved" in the class is considerably greater than in the other two grades. There is, as well, a better prospect for being a member of a peripheral group than there is in the senior class. However, it may be said with assurance that if the existence of the central group is the dominant characteristic of Grade 11, the existence of noninvolved actors is that of Grade 6. Nonetheless, it is also more likely that the virtuoso performance will be more often required of Grade 6 pupils. The data showed that Grade 6 classes had single student emitters more frequently than the other grades. There was also an indication that the teacher communicated more often with a segment of the class or a single student in a segment. In Grade 1, the teacher more characteristically sought out students; it seems as if Grade 6 students seek out and communicate with the teacher more freely than do students in either of the other grades. As a corollary to this, however, more time is spent by the average Grade 6 member witnessing exchanges between the teacher and other students. In compensation, however (on the evidence of this study), the Grade 6 teacher will be "noninvolved or out of the room" for a longer time than the teachers of the other grades. Again, as in Grade 1, a student's location will have a great deal to do with the extent to which he becomes involved in classroom communication.

There are two functions at which Grade 11 scores more highly than the other two grades. These are information dissemination about scheduled subject matter and intellectualization about scheduled subject matter. To the secondary pupil, then, education is principally an intellectual affair. And, as an intellectual affair, it is very much a public one, with the existence of the central group being its most pervasive characteristic. Not surprisingly, the teacher is the dominant actor and his audience is (properly) the whole class. Single student communications (again properly, no doubt) are directed at the teacher. When these two are compared, the two-role situation with teacher emitter and quorum audience is most clearly shown to be the dominant one. The secondary teacher, furthermore, is less mobile, cherishes the front of the room more, and but rarely (comparatively speaking) either directs his communication at, or encourages contributions from, a particular student.

Age of Teacher

Three functional differences were exhibited in the data when the age of teacher crossbreak was employed. Classes with older teachers devote more time more often to disseminating information about scheduled subject matter. Classes with younger teachers spend more time on nonscheduled subject matter. Classes with younger teachers also devote more time more often to disseminating information about sociation. Communication structure data reveal an intriguing result. Younger teachers' classrooms are characteristically more attached to the use of central systems, while older teachers' classrooms produce a greater number of noninvolved actors.

The teacher's own role varies appreciably according to his/her age. The younger teacher more often plays a role in peripheral groups and is more frequently noninvolved or out of the room. The older teacher scores higher as a member of a central group audience and as emitter and target in the central subsystem. Age of teacher provides little basis for discriminating among the locations teachers use. Older teachers do move about a little more but settle in fewer locations.

Subject Matter

Analysis of significant functional differences, when the basis for distinguishing subsets was the subject matter of the lesson, reveals the following results. Social studies lessons produce (1) more and longer exchanges where information is disseminated on nonscheduled subject matter; (2) a greater amount of time spent on disseminating information about scheduled subject matter; and (3) more incidents involving intellectualizing about organization. Mathematics lessons produce (1) more and longer exchanges where information is disseminated about sociation; and (2) a greater amount of time intellectualizing about scheduled subject matter.

Quite a number of significant differences are revealed in the communication system structure data. However, these can conveniently be interpreted as two broad generalizations. Social studies lessons are more associated with the existence of central groups. Mathematics lessons are more associated with the existence of peripheral groups. But, within these structures, mathematics lessons seem to invite more teacher domination, in so far as this is represented by teachers as emitters and single student emitters with the teacher as the target. On the other hand, social studies lessons provide greater scope for role variety, for both teachers and students.

The role of the teacher seems clearly related to subject matter. Social studies teachers were more often and for a longer time targets, emitters, and audience members in the central subsystem. Mathematics teachers were more often emitters, targets, and audience members in peripheral subsystems. They were, as well, more often noninvolved or out of the room. However, mathematics teachers' participation in peripheral groups occurs from a safe distance. Mathematics teachers occupy front-of-the-room locations more frequently than do social studies teachers. Target location data suggest that members of social studies classes are more likely to have communications directed toward them if they inhabit locations that are not in the center of the room. The reverse holds good for those in mathematics classes.

Sex of the Teacher

The relationship between sex of teacher and teacher function proved more productive in terms of number of significant differences than any other of the crossbreaks used. (It should be noted that some of these findings reflect grade-level artifacts.) Results showed that

classrooms with female teachers had more (1) scheduled subject matter operation, (2) information dissemination about organization, (3)
intellectualization about organization, (4) intellectualization about sociation. Classrooms with male teachers had more information dissemination about sociation.

A rather distinct pattern emerges from role allocation data. Classes
with male teachers are clearly characterized by allocations that imply
greater teacher dominance. Male teachers scored higher than female
teachers in 7 of the 9 categories where the teacher was the target.
Correspondingly, female teacher classrooms were more acceptant of
non-teacher emitters, targets, and audiences. Data on the teacher's
own role show that male teachers are more frequently emitters in the
central system and are either noninvolved or out of the room more.
Female teachers are more often emitters and targets in peripheral
systems. They are also mobile more frequently than male teachers, but
for no significantly greater length of time. Male teachers, however,
occupy front-of-the-room locations more; female teachers voyage further afield than their male counterparts. The patterns discernible
among target locations reveal no marked differences for the two subsets. Female-teacher classrooms, however, score higher on diffuse target
locations.

Implications

At another level of analysis an attempt was made to ascertain the
extent to which some variable classes were found to coexist with others.
The findings from this investigation are detailed and, at the time of
writing, incomplete. However, some broad indication is possible. As
these results are presented, opportunity will be taken to conjecture to
a small degree about some of the educational implications of the study.

Surprisingly, analysis of coincidental data (variables existing at
the same time) showed that the link between structural and functional
characteristics of the classroom was rather tenuous. Changes in one—
either structure or function—seemed to generate no change in the
other. There are two basic implications.

First, given the teaching–learning interaction as a purposive one,
the teacher is trying to have the pupils learn. Presumably then, his
task is to so structure and manage the environment that learning will
in fact occur. It seems reasonable to assume that different kinds of
learning occur for different kinds of people under different kinds of
circumstances. What the current findings reveal is that whatever kind
of learning is envisaged, it is always supposed to occur under virtually
the same conditions. No matter what is taught, it is apparently always

taught under approximately the same conditions and in approximately the same way. This suggests an empirical question: Under what different kinds of structural–functional variations may the education output be varied?

Second, if there is uniformity in the way all structural variables associate with all functional variables, and vice versa, it seems reasonable to ask why. On the assumption that the behavior involved is subject to some control by members in the setting, does it follow that deliberately taken decisions have determined the pattern? Alternatively, have norms of behavior been set up (perhaps over the years) that in their way coerce and constrain individuals to conformity? These two general questions represent another way of asking the basic educational questions: What behaviors are associated with what outcomes? and What explains the existing form of behavior?

Less general and consequently less fundamental are some of the conclusions that can be drawn from specific findings in the study, particularly from the structural–structural associations.

The findings reinforce the impression that the teacher is constantly central, in both senses of the word, to the functioning of the classroom. If the teacher is absent, noninvolved, or a member of a peripheral group, there is likely to be no identifiable function in the central group. Again, if the teacher is emitter in the central group (as he usually is) when the central group is functioning, the teacher is likely to be in the center front of the room. When he is moving about the room (which he does much less frequently), then no central group function is likely. It also seems as if the members of the class attach ritualistic, formal, educational importance to the teacher's occupancy of front-of-the-room locations. When he strays from the front, interacaction is more likely to be concerned with nonrelevant subject matter. Perhaps a clue to the general formalization that characterizes the classroom may be gained from one small finding: when there is a central group in existence, then noninvolved actors are *not* likely to be in evidence. It is well known that "loss of control" is generally regarded as undesirable. The indicator of possible loss of control is the emergence of noninvolved actors who in their turn generate peripheral splinter groups. What better way to avoid loss of control, then, than to make use of structures that minimize the likelihood of noninvolvement? Consistent with this interpretation is the finding that when there is no central group, the teacher is likely to be diffusely located. Under such circumstances, it seems as if patrol and control are not disparate.

The structural data provided further details on the character of interaction. First of all, they show that the prevailing mode of behavior is a public one. Small enclaves emerge in the classrooms but they are typically transitory. Whenever they attract the teacher's participation, action for the majority of the class members is immediately suspended.

In the classroom it seems as if there is, in a real sense, a place "where the action is." It is to be found in the center band which stretches from the center front of the room to the back. Typically the amount of action diminishes further away from the front of the room. This finding suggests the frightening possibility that individual achievement may be a function of location in the classroom. There is a kind of fascinating horror associated with the thought that perhaps the children in the "action zone" might achieve less than those who are out of it.

There are several clearly marked distinctions between the role of the teacher and the role of the pupils. Not only is the teacher much more directly involved in the action; he is also involved differently. He is emitter nearly as often as are all pupils put together. He is target far more often than any other individual in the classroom. Furthermore, when he is actively involved in either role, there is a very strong likelihood that he will have an audience and an even stronger possibility that the audience will be a big one. When he is emitter, no matter where he is in the room, he will have an audience. Only rarely does the teacher join the audience, and then only for members of the "action zone"; there is a higher probability that the teacher will be noninvolved or out of the room than that he will be an audience member. Despite the fact that the teacher demands that his students be a constant audience, he rarely joins them in this role. Here is a situation where the aphorism "Do as I say and not as I do" is singularly appropriate.

Given these as facts of classroom life, it seems reasonable to conclude that both pupils and the teachers themselves cast the teacher into the roles of "ringmaster," "programmer," "prima donna." Such a vision does no violence to the common, stereotypical view of the teacher. It also justifies to some extent the conventional forms of teacher evaluation. If the teacher is "ringmaster," then he should be evaluated for control. If he is "programmer," then he should be evaluated for the systematic nature of his teaching. If he is "prima donna," then he (or rather she) should be evaluated in terms of the reaction of the audience. However, it is not unreasonable to ask what role learning occurs in situations like this. The data of this study do not tell, but they do suggest that the available model—that of the teacher—has some distinctive characteristics. The model, first of all, is a dominating and controlling one. It is also egocentric in that it demands both the biggest part to play and everyone's attention to it. It is also a model that characteristically rejects private, intimate interaction in favor of public interaction. Furthermore, the context in which the role is played seems to coerce pupils into conforming to this expectation of public behavior. In this sense the classroom is unique. There is no other situation (with the possible exception of evangelical witness ceremonies) where the persistent reference for individual behavior is an ever-present audience.

Again the definition of the situation requires a considerable amount of passive involvement for the pupils. The spectator pupils are, supposedly, empathizing with, identifying with, and thinking along with the select cluster of individuals who provide cue reactions to the teacher's continued promptings. They (the fringe-dwellers) learn and experience vicariously. Their involvement is apparently of little consequence to the teacher, to other class members, or to themselves.

Along with membership in the classroom goes a great deal of waiting, and it is subservient waiting. The pleasure of the teacher dictates when involvement, active or passive, may be resumed.

The educational consequences of classroom conditions like these are unknown. They are, nonetheless, testable. But adequate testing depends on setting up counter situations which are thought to be structurally and functionally different. It has already been implied that specific functions might proceed differentially under varying structural conditions. Some things might be undertaken more efficiently in small groups, others by individuals working alone, and others again by large collectivities. If the teacher is to manipulate situations that are other than central-group, teacher-emitter-cum-target situations, then obviously he will need management skills that were not exhibited in the classrooms of this sample. If passivity limits learning, then providing for simultaneous activity on the part of a number of actors is necessary. If the domain of non-public interpersonal interaction is being neglected, then norms different from those currently being sustained in classrooms will have to be established.

As a final footnote to this discussion, there is a point that needs to be made. The educationally minded reader may find some difficulty in accepting the assurance that by any "generally acceptable" criteria (of the intuitive type) these classrooms were "good" classrooms. Nonetheless, they were; and what is more, they exhibited the moments of humor, sensitivity, alertness, rapport, and inspiration that characterize the "good" classroom. The empathetic observer would note these and be enthralled by them. But these are *highlights*. And what is often missed is the recurring persistent background which is more pervasive and may eventually be shown to be more powerful. The data of this study tend to remind us of this sobering fact.

FIVE

Toward a Model
of Instructional Processes

T. A. BIRKIN

Introduction

Previous research into instructional processes seems to have produced a wealth of information that is not only diverse but also fragmentary. In consequence there is still no clear conception of the nature, the origins, and the effects of teaching behavior. There is a need for some framework that can provide a basis for both a theoretical structure and a set of explanatory principles for any future study of the teaching process. The exploratory work reported here seeks to examine the functional relations between classroom behavioral processes and the characteristics of the persons in classrooms, and in so doing suggest *one* framework for the analysis of teaching. Teaching processes are so complex, and so little explored in an objective and systematic way, that a search for a comprehensive theory of teaching cannot, at this point, be attempted.

Large numbers of teacher and pupil characteristics have been investigated, and more recently investigations of behavioral processes in classrooms have begun to proliferate. Unfortunately, there has been little organization or clear articulation of variables explored in these studies. The model outlined here suggests three sets of variables as an economical yet comprehensive way of organizing data to reflect the

The research on which this study was based was conducted at the New Zealand Council for Educational Research; the initial writing was completed at the School of Education, University of Birmingham, England; and the final writing was carried out at the Faculty of Education, James Cook University of North Queensland, Australia.

complexity of the problems in research into teaching. It seeks to organize and interrelate initially descriptive variables in a way that will enable research workers to generate further concepts.

If it can be accepted that it is a useful strategy to develop a model based on variables that are descriptive rather than interpretive, it follows that we need to provide for the expression of these variables in terms of actual behaviors. The technical possibility of distinguishing behaviors and validly conceiving basic dimensions in the process of teaching sets the stage for a range of experimental studies on the origins and effects of these same dimensions. A model so based offers a means for the achievement of a precision of concepts not immediately evident in much of the current research into teaching, where the variables used seem often to be only tenuous ideas clothed in sufficient factual demonstration to make them worth further investigation. Such verbal concepts are marked by intuitive rather than empirical bases; they derive solely from verbal notions rather than empirically established dimensions. Such intuitive notions are in fact budding hypotheses which may or may not be demonstrable.

In less complex and more unambiguous areas of research the postulation of such verbal hypotheses prior to investigation may be a feasible method of proceeding. However, in the more complex and less explored field of classroom behavior such simplicity is probably unproductive and possibly misleading. Investigation should begin closer to reality and derive its concepts from experimentally isolated phenomena; such concepts should have a clear behavioral basis. It should be possible to maintain a close and fruitful connection between verbal concepts and their experimental and statistical counterparts.

The first phase in theory-building, then, should be taxonomic, an attempt to define what variables can and do operate in teaching. The subsequent, operational phase must be the development of a tentative working model to describe events in significant form and sequence. The over-all task is to convert speculation into future dependable theory.

This conversion can best be done with a model based on measurement. Variables must be measured before they can be usefully related to one another, and, for statements of relationship to have any meaning, each measure must be validly related to the phenomenal world. Isolating what might be such variables is one of our major initial problems, but once this has been achieved, and given a metric, model-building becomes possible and has the potential of developing structures within which predictive relations between variables can be sought and explored. Such a model, with its implied predictive utility, contrasts with earlier "theories" which permitted enough error to allow a whole range of rival notions or interpretations to live together with little or no possibility of deciding between or amongst them.

Clearly, the kind of variable required for such theory-building must not be arbitrary in scope, must have stability from sample to sample, and must possess descriptive value. We have already suggested that the choice of such variables is difficult, particularly where phenomenal manifestations are complex and even apparently chaotic. Similarly, methods are needed which will reveal complex structural relations simultaneously, methods which can effectively handle interrelated patterns of concepts rather than single variables.

These requirements suggest a particular way of proceeding in research into teaching:

1. The exploration of the phenomena of classroom behavior and the consequent isolation of the major variables which constitute the phenomena.
2. The derivation of basic, operationally defined concepts relating to observations of classroom behavior. In this stage of investigation precise relationships and patterns existing between these concepts would be established.
3. The setting up of a descriptive model of classroom behavior and the examination of the type and nature of sequential or time-based patterns among the concepts.
4. The development of a predictive model of classroom behavior.

The eventual discovery of laws on which dependable theory can be built depends partly on fortunate choice of variables, yet this choice of variables must be largely arbitrary if no extensive previous observations exist. While there is considerable metric observation of individuals, the observation of characteristics of the behavior of these individuals *in situ* is to date relatively unsystematic, and generally not metric. Certain models have been used to characterize limited aspects of classroom behavior: these range from simple rote verbal learning to more complex activities such as problem solving. Such work, however, has limited application to the wider spectrum of classroom behavior. Other workers have ventured further. Lorge and Solomon (1960) have been concerned with problem-solving behavior as a function of the transactional relationship between groups of pupils; their model takes account of the sequence and stages of problem-solving and the distribution of problem-solving ability within the groups. However, the unreliable prediction deriving from their model indicates that the process is far more complex than this structure admits.

To date, little explicit or extensive use has been made of statistical models to account for the complex patterns of variables as they exist in classroom situations. There are, however, models and associated statistical procedures which immediately recommend themselves as allowing two conditions to be met: first, a requirement that a wide variety of classroom conditions and variables be taken into account in a clearly separable way; and, second, that variables be differentiated in terms of such relations as independent/dependent, and the like, and articulated one on another in systematically replicable ways. Procedures of the multivariate type meet these conditions, and as Cattell (1966a, p. 66) has pointed out, such procedures have tactical advantages: they have great potential for generating concepts and for structuring a domain which not only is little explored but is also likely to present some complexity in the form of patterns and relationships. Multivariate methods represent, in fact, an excellent device for probing into the complexity of classroom events—a device which isolates significant variables and indicates their interrelationships as these exist in reality rather than in intuition. Such analysis can then facilitate the use of the actual classroom situation as a source of variables, and eventually enable workable predictions to be made.

At the same time, however, the variables entertained in such theory-building must be linked to an appropriate theoretical context. Such a linking is possible only if taxonomies of classroom-relevant variables are developed in conjunction with reliable estimates of the main modalities of general psychological traits. An approach to such a context is presented in Figure 5.1. The diagram represents a hypothesis-derivation model, the hypotheses being derived to account for the relationships among variables, processes, and structures. These elements of the model are themselves located on a dimension of stability, ranging from highly stable (or structural) to highly fluid (or process). Some fifteen hypothesis points are located in Figure 5.1, and in Table 5.1 an indication of the form of these hypotheses is given. It should be noted that at this point, such hypothesis-derivation is logical, systematic, and non-definitive as to the nature of variables or the empirical form of relationships.

Hypotheses are derived from the model in a series of chains or cycles in the following manner. Fluid process variables may crystallize into various semi-stable internal structural characteristics; such structures will directly reflect, in part, particular combinations of population characteristics, and will constitute a description of the sociopsychological setting. These settings also reflect, indirectly, stable external structural characteristics such as administrative and physical requirements of the school and classroom setting. These intrinsic character-

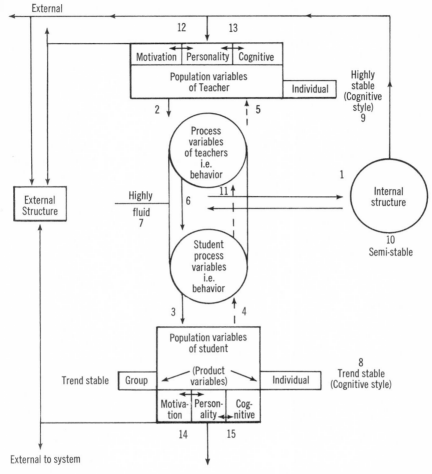

Figure 5.1 Model of the Instructional System

istics of the instructional system and the extrinsic characteristics of the external environment thus interact in complex but as yet largely unknown ways; the precise form of any functional relations we postulate between them cannot yet be specified. Indeed many functions may fit the data and we find it difficult to decide between them.

The most we can say is that the system is a closed one: i.e., trends in the population variables (which reflect the directive properties of past social experience outside the instructional system) will re-enter the system, so completing the cycle. In much the same manner, administrative arrangements such as size of school and class populations,

TABLE 5.1

RELATIONSHIPS THAT MIGHT BE HYPOTHESIZED
AMONG ELEMENTS OF THE MODEL

1. Process variables to internal structure.
2. Teacher population variables to teacher process variables.
3. Teacher and student process variables to student population variables.
4. (Converse of 3.) Student population variables to teacher and student process. Further subdivided into:
    a. Student population to student process.
    b. Student process to teacher process.
5. (In same derivation chain.) Teacher and student process to teacher population.
6. Teacher process to student process.
7. Nature of process stability.
8. Nature of stability of structure of student population variables.
9. Similarly for teacher population structure.
10. Similarly for internal group structure.
11. Student process to teacher process.
12. Teacher motivation to teacher personality.
13. Teacher motivation and personality to teacher cognitive variables.
14. Student motivation to student personality.
15. Student motivation and personality to student cognitive variables.

phasing of teacher and class contact, and the like, will in part be reflected in the internal structures set up in the system. Similarly, such physical components as space, lighting, and other spatial arrangements will have their directive effects in the instructional system.

The population variables used in this study were chosen on the grounds of their proven utility outside the instructional system. They include variables that have been useful in other parts of psychological theory and in predicting a range of criteria important in vocational selection, clinical diagnosis, and job performance. The population variables act, therefore, as an important link between the internal and external systems. The demonstrated external utility of these variables increases the likelihood of their internal utility. And, given this latter, it is more likely that the inferences we eventually make about the internal system will have some relationship to the wider body of inferences made about the external system.

With population variables of this kind in the model, it is possible to focus attention on the least developed part of the model, and proceed with examination of process variables. Such theoretical development is facilitated by a model which has its elements defined in relation to a time dimension so that variables are presumed to range from fluid through transitory to stable. Thus product parameters of the system are changes (complex or simple) over time in variables to be found in the population at large, and structural parameters are process variables in stable form. All such parameters can be seen as constructs derived from, and used to explain, behavior; constructs are used to explain the mediation of individual and group behavior.

Even at this point the model has potential as a device for ordering data and for generating possible relationships between variables that might be explored. For example, it is common in research into teaching to find that correlations are hypothesized between certain teacher behaviors and particular student attainment measures (or, in our terms, between teacher processes and student population variables), but there is little or no concern with the converse of this, the influence of student behavior on teacher behavior. There is no interest in the extension of this last hypothetical relationship into the influence of student-dependent teacher behavior on the teacher's general characteristics. While the usual, limited view is understandable, it is hardly adequate from the theoretical point of view. Not that the theoretical concern conflicts with the practical; quite the reverse. In fact, the important products of instruction may be either structural changes in the behavioral processes themselves or complex changes in the relationships obtaining amongst population characteristics.

To the extent that it opens up the possibility of these relations, the model enhances research possibilities. It also imposes certain conditions on the design and statistical characteristics of research. It both suggests and requires the application to classroom research of multivariate procedures with the opportunity they offer for the manipulation of concepts represented operationally by patterns rather than single variables. Such a possibility is particularly relevant to instructional processes research, where it seems "futile to seek laws joining single, specific, dependent or independent measured variables when the lawful relations really hold between dependent and independent concepts" (Cattell, 1966b, p. 7).

This is especially pertinent in classroom research where the important lawful relations must link concepts of process and structure while recognizing the time sequences involved and the insufficiency of experimental manipulation. Manipulation is not, however, the indispensable basis for causal inference: such inference may be sought by exploring patterns and relationships between events statistically. Such patterns may be explored in assemblies of large, comprehensive sets of variables representative of major segments of the domain and located in a time sequence. The range of multivariate methods meets these requirements.

This paper suggests some tentative steps toward a formulation based on principles of this kind. It is not a test of the theoretical principles or of the method used. Still less is it a thorough examination of the utility of the over-all model being proposed. Much work of a logical, technical, and empirical nature will be needed before even such a tentative working model as the one presented here can be regarded as theoretically useful. Nonetheless, because such a model seems tactically useful, it does seem worthwhile to venture an exploration of its likely problems and possibilities with as extensive a set of data as is available. This is the aim of this study. Although results of analysis are quoted to give substance to the framework of the argument, these results should not be seen as definitive; rather the intent is to be suggestive within the nature of the data and sample, and within the limits these impose on the methods of analysis.

The Experimental Study

Our initial requirement was that a full description of any classroom requires measures of three sets of variables: the stable population parameters of individuals, the processes involved in group interactional behavior, and the stable changes in the population parameters involved. Lists of these variables, designated *Population*, *Process*, and *Product* are set out in Table 5.2 and include measures of pupil and teacher personality, attitudes of teachers, success in teacher training, changes in reading comprehension of pupils over a five-month period, and *directness* versus *indirectness* of teacher classroom behavior.

This tripartite division allows for a basic model of the simplest kind commensurate with the known complexity of the phenomena we seek to investigate. We are at this stage postulating an input, a process, and an output, and have selected samples of variables to fill the three phases of the model. This ordering allows us to theorize about the underlying conceptual structure, and to be less than arbitrary in the choice of variables. Moreover, the variables have been chosen, wherever possible, from those extensively used in previous research. The population variables are drawn from Cattell's Primary Personality Factors, Guilford's divergent thinking factors, and the *Minnesota Teacher Attitude Inventory;* the product division is represented by measures of pupil reading comprehension and a further range of Cattell's Primary Personality Factors. The process variables used are those arising from Flanders' system of Interaction Analysis, a procedure that is widely used but has yet to be extensively explored and validated.

The data were collected from a sample of some 34 elementary school teachers of one grade level (corresponding to pupil age of ten years). Mean class size was 37, giving a pupil sample of approximately 1200. This figure was reduced to 822 (415 boys, 407 girls) for whom complete data were available. The product variables represent means for all children in a class for whom complete data were collected. The teachers sampled were all volunteers and represent approximately 50 per cent of all teachers of the relevant grade level in one New Zealand city.

TABLE 5.2
VARIABLES IN THE EXPERIMENTAL STUDY
(See Note for identification of variables.)

		Teacher Population Variables			
1.	(A—)	Aloof	vs.	Warm, outgoing	(A+)
2.	(B—)	Less intelligent	vs.	More intelligent	(B+)
3.	(C—)	Emotional	vs.	Mature	(C+)
4.	(D—)	Phlegmatic	vs.	Excitable	(D+)
5.	(E—)	Submissive	vs.	Dominant	(E+)
6.	(F—)	Serious	vs.	Happy-go-lucky	(F+)
7.	(G—)	Frivolous	vs.	Persevering	(G+)
8.	(H—)	Timid	vs.	Adventurous	(H+)
9.	(I—)	Tough	vs.	Sensitive	(I+)
10.	(L—)	Trustful	vs.	Suspecting	(L+)
11.	(M—)	Conventional	vs.	Eccentric	(M+)
12.	(N—)	Simple	vs.	Sophisticated	(N+)
13.	(O—)	Confident	vs.	Insecure	(O+)
14.	(Q1—)	Conservative	vs.	Experimenting	(Q1+)
15.	(Q2—)	Dependent	vs.	Self-sufficient	(Q2+)
16.	(Q3—)	Uncontrolled	vs.	Self-controlled	(Q3+)
17.	(Q4—)	Stable	vs.	Tense	(Q4+)
18.		Minnesota Teacher Attitude Inventory (MTAI)			
19.		Adaptive flexibility			
20.		Expressional fluency			
21.		Spontaneous flexibility			
22.		Power motivation			
23.		Word fluency			
24.		Associational fluency			
25.		Divergent production of semantic implications			
26.		Divergent production of figural implications			
27.		Divergent production of figural systems			
28.		Originality			
29		Age			
30.		Divergent production of semantic units			
31.		Ideational fluency			
32.		Anxiety vs. Adjustment			
33.		Introversion vs. Extraversion			
34.		Fitness for elected leadership			
35.		Success in teacher training			

	Process Variables
36.	Percentage teacher talk
37.	Percentage steady-state cells
38.	I/D ratio (Indirect to Direct ratio)
39.	Percentage content
40.	i/d ratio
41.	i/d 8 ratio
42.	i/d 9 ratio
43.	i/d 8–9 ratio

(Continued overleaf)

TABLE 5.2 (continued)

Product Variables
(Student Population Variables)

44.		Reading Comprehension			
45.	(A—)	Aloof	*vs.*	Warm, outgoing	(A+)
46.	(B—)	Less intelligent	*vs.*	More intelligent	(B+)
47.	(C—)	Emotional	*vs.*	Mature	(C+)
48.	(D—)	Phlegmatic	*vs.*	Excitable	(D+)
49.	(E—)	Submissive	*vs.*	Dominant	(E+)
50.	(F—)	Serious	*vs.*	Happy-go-lucky	(F+)
51.	(G—)	Frivolous	*vs.*	Persevering	(G+)
52.	(H—)	Timid	*vs.*	Adventurous	(H+)
53.	(I—)	Tough	*vs.*	Sensitive	(I+)
54.	(J—)	Vigorous	*vs.*	Internally restrained	(J+)
55.	(N—)	Simple	*vs.*	Sophisticated	(N+)
56.	(O—)	Confident	*vs.*	Insecure	(O+)
57.	(Q3—)	Uncontrolled	*vs.*	Self-controlled	(Q3+)
58.	(Q4—)	Stable	*vs.*	Tense	(Q4+)

NOTE: *Variables 1–17 and 45–58* are Cattell's Primary Personality Factors (Cattell, 1957, pp. 84ff.). *Variable 18:* see the Manual for MTAI. *Variables 19–21, 23–28, and 30–31* are Guilford's divergent thinking factors (Guilford, 1967, pp. 138–70). *Variable 22:* see Torrance (1963). *Variables 32 and 33* are Cattell's second order factors (Cattell, 1957, pp. 317–18). *Variable 34:* see Cattell & Stice (1954). *Variable 35:* see Handbook for Sixteen Personality Factors Questionnaire, Supplement No. 9 (1963). *Variables 36–43:* see Flanders (1965). *Variable 44:* see Fieldhouse (1954).

The teacher data were gathered immediately prior to the experimental period; the pupil data were gathered at the beginning and end of this period. Classroom observations were made over the thirteen-week experimental period so as to secure a sample of about 5 per cent of the total relevant teaching time for each teacher observed. This was done by breaking each teaching day into four equal periods of approximately one hour each, two in the morning and two in the afternoon, and then observing systematically so as to fill all of the resulting twenty cells over the thirteen-week period. A group of observers trained in Interaction Analysis was broken into subgroups so that each observer saw each teacher in rotation.

Three overlapping multiple regressions were performed on the sets of data in order to begin stipulating the functional relations between the sets of variables. These attempted to predict process criteria from population variables, product criteria from population variables, and product criteria from process variables. At this point the goal of the study was an organization of the mass of data into more homogeneous subsets which could, in their turn, become the starting points for further investigations. Such subsets, and their placing within the model, may reveal that we lack important variables, have included non-focal variables, or have incomplete or unrefined data; or, by pooling data from previously diverse sources, they may suggest new interpretations of the phenomena.

Given these goals and samples that were, in the main, unsuitable for the precise computation of multiple R's, it seemed satisfactory to investigate only the relative weight of variables from the different sets in predicting the criteria, rather than attempt an investigation of the amount of variance each of the predictors accounted for. For this albeit limited purpose, the ranking of predictors according to beta weight was both sufficient and possible. Only such rankings are reported for the three hypothetical predictions investigated.

Results

Prediction of Process Criteria from Population Variables

The results of the attempt to predict process criteria from teacher population variables are set out in Table 5.3. The best predictors, and those occurring most frequently, were the MTAI, Stable *vs.* Tense (variable 17), Anxiety *vs.* Adjustment (variable 32), and Fitness for Elected Leadership (variable 34).

Only two of the four subsets of predictors—personality variables, divergent thinking variables, an attitude variable, and an age variable—entered substantially into the prediction of the process criteria. Personality and attitude variables entered into the predictions about equally, with personality playing the greater part, possibly because there were more variables in this subset of the total set of predictors. However, in all but one criterion (number 41) the attitude variable accounts for a substantial amount of variance. In summary, then, the most efficient and economical prediction of classroom processes would seem to be derived from the use of personality variables and the attitude variable.

Prediction of Product Criteria from Population Variables

The prediction of the fifteen product criteria was also highly significant, with a substantial amount of the criterion variance again being predicted in each case. The results of this analysis are set out in Table 5.4. As before, the major predictors are listed under each criterion. Computation of multiple R's was restricted due to zero degrees of freedom.

As in the prediction of process criteria, two of the four subsets of predictors were in evidence. There was a tendency for the personality subset to figure prominently in the prediction of the product criteria. Again the attitude variable was in evidence in the prediction of about half the criteria. Thus, the most frequent best individual predictors were again Stable *vs.* Tense (variable 17), Anxiety *vs.* Adjustment (variable 32), and MTAI (variable 18). On this occasion, however, Fitness for Elected Leadership (variable 34) was not prominent although Cattell's Submissive *vs.* Dominent (variable 5) and Success in Teacher Training (variable 35) were. The age variable was only in evidence in the prediction of one criterion (number 50).

The most obvious difference suggested by these results between prediction of process and product criteria from the same set of variables is increasing complexity; more predictor variables are required to account for the variance on each criterion. An explanation of this result can only be speculative at this point; but one possibility, and one which is particularly interesting for the construction of a model of instruction, centers around the interaction of particular personality factors in the teacher as these might affect student product variables.

Prediction of Product Criteria
from Process Variables

The prediction of gains in product criteria from classroom process indices was much less successful than prediction of the same products from characteristics of the teachers. In no case, for example, was an F ratio significant at the .05 level, and uncorrected multiple R's range from .36 to .63, accounting for only about 13 to 40 per cent of the criterion variance.

The results of the analysis are set out in Table 5.5.

There are, no doubt, a number of technical reasons for these less than helpful results. The smaller number of predictors used, and a restriction in criterion variance due to the comparatively short time (four months) over which product gains were measured, may account for some of the reduced significance of the multiple R's. It might be that the high intercorrelations of the process variables explain the small proportion of the criterion variance they seem able to account for (see Table 5.6). However, these intercorrelations of process variables are at best confusing; without considerable refinement of our understanding of what these variables might be it is difficult to clarify this possibility. These problems are, in fact, serious enough to raise suspicion about the predictive utility of the process variables in their present form.

There is some warrant for suspicion about the usefulness of all indicators derived from the Flanders instrument. There are problems, for example, with the reliability of the measure that are not easily explained as statistical artifacts (Westbury, 1967). Given the apparent phenomenal ambiguity of these measures, research workers with stringent theoretical needs and requirements might be forgiven if they pursued a different or modified approach to the process realm.

TABLE 5.3
PREDICTION OF PROCESS CRITERIA FROM POPULATION VARIABLES

Predictor Variable Number	Variable Description [a]	Beta Weight
Criterion 36.	Percentage of Teacher Talk	
35	Success in teacher training	−2.86
18	M T A I	−2.60
32	Anxiety *vs.* Adjustment	2.01
Criterion 37.	Percentage Steady-State Cells	
32	Anxiety *vs.* Adjustment	−2.39
12	Simple *vs.* Sophisticated	1.75
18	M T A I	1.61
Criterion 38.	I/D Ratio	
17	Stable *vs.* Tense	2.85
34	Fitness for elected leadership	2.26
18	M T A I	1.79
Criterion 39.	Percentage Content	
18	M T A I	1.67
32	Anxiety *vs.* Adjustment	1.66
17	Stable *vs.* Tense	1.34
Criterion 40.	i/d Ratio	
17	Stable *vs.* Tense	3.37
34	Fitness for elected leadership	2.16
5	Submissive *vs.* Dominant	1.93
18	M T A I	1.65
Criterion 41.	i/d 8 Ratio	
17	Stable *vs.* Tense	3.64
34	Fitness for elected leadership	2.09
32	Anxiety *vs.* Adjustment	−1.63
Criterion 42.	i/d 9 Ratio	
35	Success in teacher training	−2.75
21	Spontaneous flexibility	1.33
18	M T A I	−1.32
Criterion 43.	i/d 8–9 Ratio	
17	Stable *vs.* Tense	3.90
18	M T A I	2.58
34	Fitness for elected leadership	2.28

[a] Generally popular labels rather than technical titles have been used. For the technical details see appropriate manuals.

TABLE 5.4

PREDICTION OF PRODUCT CRITERIA FROM POPULATION VARIABLES

Predictor Variable Number	Variable Description	Beta Weight
Criterion 44.	Reading Comprehension Gain	
35	Success in teacher training	3.42
5	Submissive *vs.* Dominant	2.95
18	M T A I	2.86
Criterion 45.	Reserved *vs.* Easygoing	
32	Anxiety *vs.* Adjustment	−1.17
17	Stable *vs.* Tense	1.08
8	Timid *vs.* Adventurous	−0.93
Criterion 46.	Less Intelligent *vs.* More Intelligent	
17	Stable *vs.* Tense	7.38
34	Fitness for elected leadership	4.31
5	Submissive *vs.* Dominant	3.73
32	Anxiety *vs.* Adjustment	−3.15
Criterion 47.	Emotionally Unstable *vs.* Emotionally Mature	
35	Success in teacher training	−3.00
13	Confident *vs.* Insecure	2.40
5	Submissive *vs.* Dominant	−2.27
18	M T A I	−2.10
Criterion 48.	Phlegmatic *vs.* Excitable	
17	Stable *vs.* Tense	4.61
32	Anxiety *vs.* Adjustment	−4.44
35	Success in teacher training	3.80
5	Submissive *vs.* Dominant	3.32
Criterion 49.	Submissive *vs.* Dominant	
17	Stable *vs.* Tense	2.10
21	Spontaneous flexibility	−1.67
32	Anxiety *vs.* Adjustment	−1.61
18	M T A I	1.45
Criterion 50.	Serious *vs.* Happy-go-Lucky	
35	Success in teacher training	2.84
21	Spontaneous flexibility	2.56
6	Serious *vs.* Happy-go-lucky	2.43
17	Stable *vs.* Tense	2.35
29	Age	2.31
Criterion 51.	Frivolous *vs.* Persevering	
17	Stable *vs.* Tense	−1.96
32	Anxiety *vs.* Adjustment	1.49
11	Conventional *vs.* Eccentric	1.32
9	Tough *vs.* Sensitive	−1.23
12	Simple *vs.* Sophisticated	−1.08
Criterion 52.	Shy *vs.* Venturesome	
17	Stable *vs.* Tense	−2.37
32	Anxiety *vs.* Adjustment	2.13
16	Uncontrolled *vs.* Self-controlled	1.63
Criterion 53.	Tough *vs.* Sensitive	
17	Stable *vs.* Tense	−6.29
5	Submissive *vs.* Dominant	−3.95
18	M T A I	−3.88
32	Anxiety *vs.* Adjustment	3.83
21	Spontaneous flexibility	3.18

TABLE 5.4 (continued)

Predictor Variable Number	Variable Description	Beta Weight
Criterion 54.	Vigorous *vs.* Internally Restrained	
35	Success in teacher training	1.77
33	Extraversion *vs.* Introversion	1.73
18	M T A I	1.02
Criterion 55.	Simple *vs.* Sophisticated	
17	Stable *vs.* Tense	−2.88
32	Anxiety *vs.* Adjustment	2.37
34	Fitness for elected leadership	−2.10
Criterion 56.	Confident *vs.* Insecure	
12	Simple *vs.* Sophisticated	1.41
34	Fitness for elected leadership	−1.35
28	Originality	1.30
32	Anxiety *vs.* Adjustment	−1.26
35	Success in teacher training	−1.26
Criterion 57.	Uncontrolled *vs.* Self-controlled	
35	Success in teacher training	−2.04
5	Submissive *vs.* Dominant	−1.64
22	Power Motivation	−1.34
18	M T A I	−1.05
Criterion 58.	Stable *vs.* Tense	
17	Stable *vs.* Tense	2.75
32	Anxiety *vs.* Adjustment	−2.69
16	Uncontrolled *vs.* Self-controlled	−1.73
33	Introversion *vs.* Extraversion	−1.68
18	M T A I	−1.37

TABLE 5.5

PREDICTION OF PRODUCT CRITERIA FROM PROCESS VARIABLES

Predictor Variable Number	Variable Description	Beta Weight
Criterion 44.	Reading Comprehension	
40	i/d ratio	0.61
41	i/d 8 ratio	−0.49
36	Percentage of teacher talk	0.43
$R = 0.47$ $R^2 = 0.22$		
Criterion 45.	Aloof *vs.* Warm, outgoing	
43	i/d 8–9 ratio	−0.59
42	i/d 9 ratio	0.50
38	I/D ratio	0.49
$R = 0.60$ $R^2 = 0.36$		
Criterion 46.	Less Intelligent *vs.* More Intelligent	
38	I/D ratio	0.58
36	Percentage of teacher talk	0.38
$R = 0.44$ $R^2 = 0.18$		

(*Continued overleaf*)

TABLE 5.5 (continued)

Predictor Variable Number	Variable Description	Beta Weight
Criterion 47.	Emotional *vs.* Mature	
38	I/D ratio	0.86
41	i/d 8 ratio	0.67
43	i/d 8–9 ratio	−0.48
$R = 0.51$	$R^2 = 0.26$	
Criterion 48.	Phlegmatic *vs.* Excitable	
41	i/d 8 ratio	−0.69
43	i/d 8–9 ratio	0.68
40	i/d ratio	0.64
38	I/D ratio	0.52
$R = 0.43$	$R^2 = 0.18$	
Criterion 49.	Submissive *vs.* Dominant	
37	Percentage steady-state cells	0.51
38	I/D ratio	0.38
$R = 0.46$	$R^2 = 0.21$	
Criterion 50.	Serious *vs.* Happy-go-Lucky	
40	i/d ratio	−0.98
$R = 0.59$	$R^2 = 0.35$	
Criterion 51.	Frivolous *vs.* Persevering	
41	i/d 8 ratio	0.39
$R = 0.36$	$R^2 = 0.13$	
Criterion 52.	Timid *vs.* Adventurous	
39	Percentage content	−0.79
43	i/d 8–9 ratio	−0.65
38	I/D ratio	0.64
36	Percentage of teacher talk	0.61
$R = 0.58$	$R^2 = 0.33$	
Criterion 53.	Tough *vs.* Sensitive	
36	Percentage of teacher talk	−0.64
39	Percentage content	0.54
$R = 0.46$	$R^2 = 0.22$	
Criterion 54.	Vigorous *vs.* Internally Restrained	
41	i/d 8 ratio	−0.28
$R = 0.41$	$R^2 = 0.17$	
Criterion 55.	Simple *vs.* Sophisticated	
38	I/D ratio	−0.85
40	i/d ratio	0.60
$R = 0.62$	$R^2 = 0.38$	
Criterion 56.	Confident *vs.* Insecure	
37	Percentage steady-state cells	0.37
$R = 0.47$	$R^2 = 0.22$	
Criterion 57.	Uncontrolled *vs.* Self-Controlled	
40	i/d ratio	−0.75
41	i/d 8 ratio	0.53
39	Percentage content	−0.41
$R = 0.63$	$R^2 = 0.40$	
Criterion 58.	Stable *vs.* Tense	
40	i/d ratio	0.59
41	i/d 8 ratio	−0.50
$R = 0.38$	$R^2 = 0.15$	

TABLE 5.6
SOME INTERCORRELATIONS OF PROCESS VARIABLES

Variables		36	37	38	39	40	41	42	43
36	Percentage Teacher Talk		−.35	—	.90	—	—	—	—
37	Percentage Steady-State Cells			.54	—	−.50	−.51	—	−.39
38	I/D Ratio				—	.85	.80	.37	.85
39	Percentage Content					—	—	—	—
40	i/d Ratio						.85	.47	.82
41	i/d 8 Ratio							.56	.90
42	i/d 9 Ratio								.47
43	i/d 8–9 Ratio								

Conclusions

This all too brief exercise had two broadly related aims: to search for some of the difficulties and deficiencies in teacher and student behavior research; and to explore some strategies which might systematically generate, or eliminate, promising conjectures. The objective of the exercise was to help provide a communicable basis for experimental, and ultimately practical, control of variables characterizing the domain of classroom behavior. These goals stem from an assumption that research into classroom processes is at present neither as firmly based empirically nor as extensive as experimental or practical control require.

These weaknesses in classroom research derive from a lack of adequate theory. Construction of theory necessarily involves an inductive logic as the basis for generalizations; the model presented in this paper is intended to function as such a theory constructor. The model (Figure 5.1) generated a set of predictive statements about consistent relations between the two main roles in the classroom, teacher and student, as part of an attempt to specify consistent effects between behaviors associated with each position.

These relations in the model were directed, since, in a formal instructional system, we are primarily interested in that change brought about by the teacher on the student. While the model was in this sense unidirectional (hence the term "product variables"), there is the possibility of two-way, or mutual, influence in the process section of the model. Theoretically, of course, one might consider changes in the teacher population variables as important outcomes of the system, and indeed consistent changes in the internal process structure might be a significant product. Nonetheless, the practical importance of the model was expressed in terminology designed to reflect contemporary classroom arrangements; if these typical arrangements change, so may the direction of interest in the model. Thus, the model is flexible in that all major directions of influence may assert themselves without presuming any necessary influence.

Three sources or modalities of teacher influence—motivational, temperamental, and cognitive—were postulated. These were assumed to be the origins of the behavioral acts which function as consistent influences, and the structure of these acts should reflect their sources. In any event, the unidirectional aspect of the present model was revealed by the assumption that teacher acts generate pupil acts, and it is the consistent cycles of these acts that is the process of the instructional system. Stable aspects of this process (called "internal structure") were assumed to result in consistent changes in the tri-modal sources of pupil acts. These changes may be of two kinds: simple quantitative changes in one or more of the source variables, or more complex structural changes in the pattern of interrelations among the source variable. The empirical results reported here constituted a very limited examination of some aspects of the proposed model. Nonetheless they represented the most complete range of variables available.

To this extent the model can facilitate the development of theoretical frameworks within the context of which particular sets of hypotheses might be posited or alternatively be seen to be fruitless. Thus, our predictions of product criteria from process variables were not sustained. The observational categories used to provide indices of process do not appear to express the postulates of the model adequately; the range of possible behavioral acts must be regarded as too limited (particularly in the case of student acts) to express the richness of the source traits presumed to give rise to them. Such limitations in the complexity of variables must seriously inhibit the generation of concepts expressing classroom processes. If this is an accurate assessment of what this study has revealed, it points out clearly the need to attend again to the description of classroom processes and questions the usefulness of proceeding further with sets of arbitrarily derived variables as representations of complex interactions.

This suggests an alternative way of proceeding. A wide selection of behaviors covering various possible manifestations of the three modalities of source traits is available. It should be possible to apply to the behavior of classroom groups the multivariate methods used to establish the dimensionality of individual behavior. If this can be accomplished systematically, research on classroom groups with differing external structural characteristics should then establish the most important dimensions within which experimental manipulation for particular requirements can be pursued. Bereiter (1966) has described how such a search might be undertaken.

Since models are used, and advocated, for a variety of purposes, we should remind ourselves that the objective of the work being reported here is an empirically based theory of instruction. This general aim can be given diverse interpretations, and it is necessary to conclude this paper by examining the implications of the approach outlined here for future theory in research into classroom behavior.

This discussion has implied that implicit formalization of existing verbal propositions which relate sets of interdependent variables, yet specify only one direction of relationship between variables, is less than fruitful. Such an approach seems useful only when existing concepts are both extensive and more than superficial. Without such a rich body of existing concepts, formalization may well produce frameworks which are psychologically, and practically, trivial and which cannot be used to give the kinds of quantitative predictions about classroom behavior necessary for unambiguous deduction. The present body of research into classroom processes is not able to offer any generalizations which can claim quantitative precision, yet it is only through testing of hypotheses derived from such generalizations than an adequate explanatory scheme for instructional processes might be derived.

Quasi-formal model-building of the kind suggested in this paper offers one approach to production of generalizations necessary for explanatory theories of the instructional process. Postulates can be developed within this structure which are not so much based on earlier experiment, but rather are logically drawn. These reasonable postulates can then be used to construct a framework for a model which, in its turn, can be used deductively to construct hypotheses which can be tested by observation. It is hoped that this tentative first investigation has indicated not only the direction of such research, but also some of the procedures that might be appropriate.

SIX

A Model for
Strategies of Instruction

JOHN R. GINTHER

This model for strategies of instruction was first presented formally at the University of Rochester in June, 1964. It was the topic for a symposium at the 1965 annual meeting of the American Psychological Association in Chicago. Such consideration of the model has resulted in several studies, and that portion of the Rochester presentation dealing with the materials of instruction has since been published (Ginther, 1965, pp. 43–54). Some clarification of the model has occurred during the years since 1964, and findings of interest to practitioners as well as important in testing the validity of the model have been generated. This paper reviews the work that has been done to date with the model for strategies of instruction.

First there will be a review of the model as it was presented in the *materials modality* at the Rochester Conference. Next will come information helpful in seeing how this model is applied in the *teacher modality,* that is, when a live teacher is guiding the class. Finally, there will be a discussion of some of the research which has sprung from consideration of this model.

The Model

As shown in Figure 6.1, the model has three dimensions. The first is the dimension called *Degrees of Freedom.* This runs from an "errorless" pole to a "dialectical" pole. Materials at the errorless pole on this dimension could be characterized by saying that the student is locked in when he confronts these materials, i.e., he has no opportunity to alter the sequence or content of presentations which are about to be

139

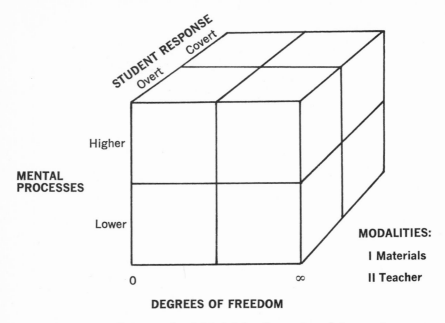

Figure 6.1 Framework of Model for Strategies of Instruction

made. Nor does he have leeway in altering the form or content of responses which will be considered correct in the instructional material. Such materials have often been referred to as "linear" programs, but this designation fails to point to the critical characteristic of the materials, the fact that the student is offered no alternatives, no opportunities to alter his pathway through the program. As one moves along this first dimension toward the dialectical pole, one could place Norman Crowder's (1959) work near the center of the scale. His branched, programmed materials were constructed specifically for the purpose of eliciting many incorrect responses from students. These responses are dealt with differentially as the student is shunted to different points in the material. In book form these programs came to be known as "scrambled books." In the Rochester presentation examples were given of other materials which moved us further toward the dialectical end of the dimension. Suffice it to say that as one moves toward the dialectical end of this dimension the materials of instruction require more complex consideration when they are being developed. Such materials have built into them more and more options which the student may choose to follow. Thus the student is given greater and greater opportunity (i.e., more and more degrees of freedom) to make decisions which will set the course of instruction from that point forward. At the time of the Rochester presentation, consideration was limited to books, loose leaf material, and programs for inexpensive teaching machines. Since then, high-speed computers have become a potentially important factor in instruction and so could be included here as instruments capable of providing even greater degrees of freedom for the student, if instructors so developed the material and so programmed the computer. In other words, the amount of freedom which can be provided for the student seems theoretically boundless because of the almost frightening speed of response, the potential memory storage, and the simulation capability of these machines. However, their instructional potential can be encompassed by the construct under consideration.

The second dimension of the model is called *Mental Process*. This dimension is divided into the subcategories "lower" and "higher"; these are definable in terms of *The Taxonomy of Educational Objectives* (The Committee of College and University Examiners, 1956), or in terms of the eduction of relations and correlates (Spearman, 1923), and, perhaps, in many other ways. The third dimension, *Student Response*, is dichotomized by the categories "overt" and "covert." In his criticism of the model during the APA symposium in 1965, Ross Green of Emory University said he thought that student response was not a dimension, or at least not an important dimension. However, an extensive survey of research on learning and instruction (Rippey, 1965a) revealed that the largest group of studies, 53 out of 103, focused on the categories of this third dimension. Green may have correctly evaluated this dimension; if so, psychologists and educational psychologists should take note.

The model has been used in the analysis of a large number of research studies. A summary report on that activity is presented later in this paper. However, further understanding of the model in the materials modality may be gained by seeing it specifically applied. To this end, one of our research analyses is presented in outline, as recorded by the analyst, in Figure 6.2.

The Teacher Modality

Assuming the reader has either some knowledge of my 1965 exposition of the model in the materials modality or an intuitive sense of it, we shall now examine the teacher modality. If one substitutes the term *listening point* for reading point (Ginther, 1965, p. 48) it is possible to sort accurately much of what transpires in classrooms in the teacher modality. In the main, students listen to information broadcast orally by teachers. Typically, they are later required to recall or recog-

Title, Investigator and Reference				Reviewed by
Krumboltz, John. "The Nature and Importance of the Required Response in Programmed Instruction." Paper presented to American Educational Research Association, Chicago, Feb., 1963 (mimeo).				Sayegh

Modality	Degrees of Freedom	Mental Process	Response	Subject Area
Materials ✔ Teacher __	Near zero	Higher __ Lower ✔	Covert __ Overt ✔ (Reading)	Educational measurement

Grade Level	Social Class	IQ	No. of Subj.	School Prescription	Date of Study
University students	Most prob. middle and upper	Above average	120	University	1963

Variables: Mode of Response:
> (1)Key-word response vs. (2)trivial-word response vs. (3)reading the material in paragraph form.

Instruments: Linear program (89 frames).
> Immediate and delayed posttests.

Findings: On immediate and delayed posttests the key-word and paragraph-format scored about the same, and both were significantly higher than the trivial-word response group.

Evaluation of Procedures:
1. Short program used, and consequently short experimental period.
2. A fairly large sample of students.
3. No information in abstract on retention period, kind and length of text, and technique of analysis of data.

Figure 6.2 Sample Review of Experiment on Instruction

nize this information. However, more interesting classroom operations lead us to discuss first the dialectical pole of the dimension *Degrees of Freedom.*

At one time or another most of us have been exposed to classroom procedures which require verbal participation from the student. But verbal participation permitting great freedom to the student differs immensely from verbal participation in an errorless classroom. The following list of student behaviors, developed by a group at The University of Chicago concerned with teaching through discussion, suggests the kind of verbal participation which might flow from the dialectical classroom. A teacher could structure or program a lesson so that the following behaviors might be elicited:

1. The student listens to the instructor expound a point.
2. The student asks questions in order to clarify in his own mind what the instructor has said.
3. The student challenges the instructor's statement.
4. The student propounds his own solution to a problem and has it approved or corrected by the instructor; if corrected, he listens to the instructor's reasons for modifying or rejecting.
5. The student propounds his own solution to a problem and is led by the instructor to elaborate and to defend it against attack, to relate it to other ideas, to modify it, if necessary, in the light of the attacks, etc.
6. The student *participates* in a *group effort* in which #5 is done by other students as well as by himself. (Axelrod, 1949, p. 24)

Discussion, of the kind suggested by the list, was advocated by Axelrod's Chicago group. The behavioral outcomes which they feel stem from discussion were summarized in F. Champion Ward's Foreword to Axelrod's publication:

One of the salient characteristics of the recent history of the College of the University of Chicago has been the shift from "lecture" to "discussion" as the dominant mode of instruction. The chief reason for this shift has been a steadily increasing emphasis upon the student and eventual adult as acquiring by actual exercise those basic competencies which all educated men and women should command. It is obvious that the lecture system is not well adapted to this end (p. 5).

These investigators in the College at The University of Chicago provided a framework of generic competencies which encompass some of the more specific behavioral outcomes of what I would label "higher" mental processes. They believe that the generic competencies cannot be developed through lectures but can be developed through discussion, a mode of instruction which itself leads to intellectual freedom for the student.

One could easily document the assertion that there are many studies which involve large numbers of degrees of freedom for students. One investigator has gone so far as to adapt Rogerian client-centered therapy to the classroom; he cast the teacher in the role of a reflector of comments from students. Surprisingly, on the other hand, the variety of classroom methods in the *teacher modality* that are based on zero degrees of freedom is, judging from the literature I have read, quite limited. The lecture is probably the most widely used method at this zero pole of degrees of freedom for the student.[1] The challenge was to create a different classroom situation of this type, for the construct validity of the model was at stake. We feel we were successful, and we called the product an *errorless classroom,* borrowing from Professor Skinner's lexicon.

Our conception required overt behavior from students, as opposed to the covert behavior in the lecture room.[2] In an attempt to establish whether or not a teacher could operate a classroom of this character, a teacher at the University of Chicago Laboratory School undertook the preparation of a script which he used while teaching a fifty-minute class period in errorless fashion. The script was very similar in format to the errorless *materials* mentioned earlier. However, the range of cues to correct responses was broad, including overhead projections, laboratory equipment, oral suggestions, and blackboard presentations. The topic under consideration was "The Atmosphere—A Sea of Air." The teacher's purpose in the instruction was to show students that "air is real, takes up space, and has weight."

During the errorless class session, the teacher asked 50 non-procedural questions, and the students responded with correct answers 92 per cent of the time. During the more conventional control class, the teacher asked 70 non-procedural questions and the students responded with correct answers 76 per cent of the time. In the control class, the teacher called on only those students who expressed a desire to answer a question. This, no doubt, resulted in a higher proportion of correct answers than would have resulted had the students been called on in a more random order, as they were in the errorless class. (A transcription of a portion of the errorless class is in the Appendix to this paper.)

Guided by cues, the errorless class moved towards the answers that the teacher desired. The conventional class, however, showed many tangential thrusts even by students who were volunteering. Thus Axelrod's behavior number 4 ("The student propounds his own solution . . .") was demonstrated, at least roughly, in the conventional class, but avoided by the same teacher in the errorless class. We were satisfied that we had created, in the teacher modality, an errorless class of a kind seldom seen.

Studies Based on the Model: 1964–66

Several studies based on my model will be reviewed here (Sheehan, 1965; Berlin, 1965; Bhushan, 1965; Rippey, 1965b; Rippey, 1966). In addition to providing a reality test for the model, these studies were undertaken to correct shortcomings we had found in an extensive sample of research into programmed instruction.[3]

Perhaps the most significant of those weaknesses was the undefined and therefore non-reproducible nature of instructional procedures in conventional "control groups." It has always been my belief that the model could lead to the development of reproducible instructional environments, an exciting possibility if one is attempting to accomplish experimental research on instruction. Most of the authors of the model-based studies were unwilling to accept my belief without evidence, and they used the Flanders–Amidon method of analyzing classroom inter-action to check on the validity of the assertion that reproducible classrooms were being established. Various cells in the model result in characteristic patterns of interaction, and an intuitive sense of the proper operation stemming from a cell, combined with objective in-formation about classroom interaction, enabled the researchers to keep a tight check on the instructional cell being used or viewed.

Another shortcoming that we carefully guarded against in the model-based studies was the instruction period of short duration, de-fined as "less than 50 frames of programmed materials, or less than an hour of instruction by a teacher" (Rippey, 1965a, p. 2).

The third weakness, dealt with in several of the studies to be reviewed here, was the failure to contrast instruction by teachers with instruction by materials in otherwise comparable situations. This inade-quacy is reflected in item 4 of the following categorization of the earlier studies:

1. Studies investigating the contrast between overt and covert student responses: 53
2. Studies contrasting errorless and dialectical procedures: 27
3. Studies contrasting higher and lower mental process instruction: 17
4. Studies contrasting teacher–materials instruction: 6

Commenting on this categorization, Rippey (1965a) says, in part:

> It seemed almost as if a kind of dogmatism was controlling experi-mentation—few investigators seemed anxious to risk ventures into the uncharted wilds of higher process and even fewer wanted to mess around with teachers . . . maybe there were few teachers who wanted to be . . . in experimental situations.

As a group, our studies yield some interesting generalizations; first, however, the individual studies will be reported.

Sheehan (1965) investigated the possibility of developing higher mental processes through the exclusive use of instruction in the materials modality. He used the errorless–dialectical distinction of the model to define the degrees of freedom assigned to the student and the categories of the *Taxonomy of Educational Objectives* to define lower and higher mental processes. "By varying the student's degree of freedom along the errorless–dialectical dimension, its influence upon higher mental process learning will be studied" (Sheehan, 1965, p. 12). The study extended over a period of five weeks. The content was mathematics, and the contrast in the experimental variable was provided by two widely different types of programmed materials. A pair of classes taught by regular teachers provided information on the relative amounts of achievement demonstrated in the experiment. Sheehan concluded that "significantly different methods in the materials modality have not produced significantly different results in achievement" (p. 76).

Thus, instruction by materials alone failed to generate markedly different patterns of achievement when contrasting lower and higher process achievement or when considering higher process achievement resulting from instruction by errorless and dialectical materials. But Sheehan did report a fact which was to bear fruit in Berlin's study (1965) when he said: "In this case, the results of the analyses of the experimental effects were not statistically significant at the required level, although they were in the predicted direction. Future studies might now focus upon the comparisons and contrasts between the materials and teacher modality" (Sheehan, 1965, p. 79).

In a study involving a unit in mathematics and one in English grammar, composition, and usage, Rippey (1965b) developed four classroom environments from the model. He characterized them as follows:

1. The errorless-teacher classroom exerted much control over the student and encouraged much interaction between student and teacher. This interaction was highly structured and stylized.
2. The dialectical-teacher classroom exerted a minimum of control and encouraged high interaction between student and teacher.
3. The errorless-materials classroom exhibited high control and low interaction.
4. The dialectical-materials classroom had low structure and low interaction.

The restriction of classroom procedures to the behaviors allowed by the model of instruction did indeed result in the explanation of a considerably higher percentage of the variance of final scores on the achievement test in the experimental classes than in the regular class. These percentages of explained variance were (1) regular class, 19 per cent; (2) errorless teacher, 40 per cent; (3) dialectical teacher, 42 per cent; (4) dialectical materials, 54 per cent; and (5) errorless materials, 50 per cent (Rippey, 1965b, p. 377).

Further, the important contrast in the mathematics class was between errorless and dialectical procedures, with the former favored by an F ratio significant at the 10 per cent level. However, the English class data indicated the importance of the teacher by yielding an F ratio significant beyond the .025 level on the teacher–materials effects. The entire study was aimed at the development of lower order processes.

Pursuing a question which arose during the above study, Rippey carried out a study contrasting the effects of a carefully defined role for a teacher and a similarly defined role for materials of instruction (Rippey, 1966, pp. 283–91). Using the model as the basis for structuring replicable instructional situations he created two highly structured classrooms characteristic of the point zero degrees of freedom, lower order mental process, overt student response. He used the following protocols suggested by the model:

1. The instructor limited himself to reading, or projecting by means of an overhead projector, the frames of the Plumb program.
2. Students were called upon from a randomized list of names, after the stimulus question was asked.
3. If the student was correct, his correct reply was acknowledged. If he was incorrect, he was told so. In either event, instruction proceeded to the next frame.
4. No students were allowed to volunteer answers or to ask questions. Volunteers were either ignored or reprimanded.
5. The pace of instruction was kept as rapid as possible. Each student recited at least ten times during the course of a two-hour period. Where the author became verbose, appropriate elisions were made in the text.
6. Students were expected to maintain a rate of correct responses of at least 90 per cent.

He evaluated broadly, using seven tests of varying orientation. Tests 1 and 6 were directly related to the instruction provided by the program. Tests, 2, 3, and 4 were higher-order-process transfer tests. Tests 5 and 7 were related to attitudes and depended on the verbal facility of the student in expressing his attitudes.

The teacher modality seemed to emerge clearly superior to the materials modality for instruction in lower order mental processes. The mean scores on all seven tests were higher for the teacher modality, although only tests 1 and 6 yielded acceptably significant differences. "For variable 1, F was 8.79, significant beyond the 0.01 level, and F for variable 6 was 3.712, significant beyond the 0.1 level. . . . The other test scores, consisting of higher-order-process transfer and attitudinal items, were not affected by differences in method" (Rippey, 1966, p. 288). This tended to confirm my suspicion that a very great number of studies contrasting linear programs (errorless materials) and teachers (procedures undefined) were really contrasting structured and (in the worst sense) unstructured instruction.

While a postdoctoral fellow with the Center for the Cooperative Study of Instruction, Vidya Bhushan completed a study of the effectiveness of errorless and dialectical materials when used exclusively to instruct graduate students (Bhushan, 1965). He commented on other studies based on the model as follows:

In these four studies the time to learn the two kinds of material was kept constant. But this writer feels that for learning tasks sufficient time should be given so that nearly all the subjects may be able to finish the task. The present study was conducted keeping this point in mind and using four cells of the Ginther model: errorless versus dialectical materials, and higher versus lower order mental process (p. 3).

Three groups of students were used in the experiment. These groups had almost identical pretest scores in algebra (9.46, 9.00 and 9.00 with σ's $= 4$) and essentially zero scores on a pretest in matrix algebra. The dialectical group spent an average of nearly three hours more than the errorless group in completing the programs over a period of six weeks (one two-hour session per week was scheduled for each group). The criterion test was divided into "part I consisting of 36 items for measuring lower mental process" (defined as "simple recall of information learned from the program") and "part II consisting of 26 items for measuring higher mental process" (defined as "generalization of information learned from the program"). Bhushan also refers to the items in part II as requiring application. The rounded mean percentage scores for the errorless materials group on parts I and II of the test were 76 and 54; for the dialectical group, 80 and 53. Thus "both groups did better on simple recall of the material than its application" (p. 8). His main conclusion was that "no significant differences were found between the two treatments." Bhushan dealt with small groups of homogeneous students, graduate students at a major university, deprived temporarily of human instruction. His findings fit an emerging pattern perfectly.

The most comprehensive experimental study based on the model was completed in 1965 (Berlin, 1965). The general question Berlin addressed was: "Is there a relationship between learning experiences and certain structured learning situations?" He was careful to differentiate between "the encountered situations [which] are what we call the learning situations, [and] . . . the reactions of the students to these situations [which] are the learning experiences of the students." Berlin used the Flanders–Amidon technique to check on the validity of placement of the classroom situation along the degrees-of-freedom dimension of the model. He used stimulated recall to elicit information from students. This information was categorized on the basis of definitions in *The Taxonomy of Educational Objectives,* and this categorization was treated in terms of the "lower" and "higher" categories of the mental-process dimension of my model. Finally, Berlin required overt responses in all the structured situations.

Following a pilot study in a suburban high school, Berlin conducted his study at two private high schools in the Chicago area. He established four different classrooms in one school and replicated them in the second school: (1) materials-controlled, with little freedom of response by the student (materials–errorless); (2) materials-controlled, with much greater freedom of response by the student (materials–dialectical); (3) teacher-controlled, with little freedom of response by the student (teacher–errorless); and (4) teacher-controlled, with great freedom of response by the student (teacher–dialectical). Each class type was operated for three regularly scheduled, consecutive class sessions. The same subject matter, an introduction to the study of plants, with focus on algae, was covered in the four differing situations.

The significant findings, i.e., statistically significant at or beyond the 5 per cent level, were reported as follows:

1. In the teacher modality (teacher–errorless or teacher–dialectical):
   A. The number of *unrelevant* (i.e., a combination of nonrelevant and irrelevant thought processes) experiences is greater than in the materials modality;
   B. There was a higher mean number of comprehension experiences than in the materials controlled classes;
   C. Errorless classes produced a higher number of unrelevant experiences than did the dialectical classes.
2. In the materials modality (materials–errorless or materials–dialectical):
   A. There was a higher mean number of knowledge experiences than in classes in the teacher modality;
   B. Errorless classes produced a higher number of irrelevant experiences than the dialectical classes (Berlin, 1965, pp. 83–84).

The findings are represented graphically in Figure 6.3. One feature of the figure requires a word of explanation. The scheme used for cate-

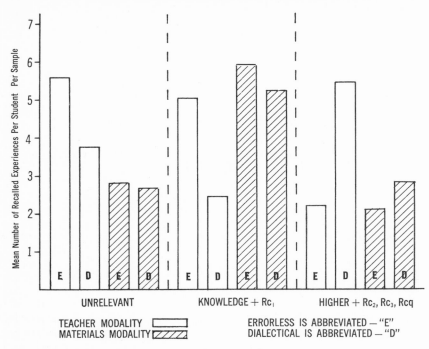

Figure 6.3 A Comparison of Reported Learning Experiences
in the Errorless and Dialectical Classes in the
Different Modalities (Berlin, 1965, p. 63)

gorizing reported thoughts included a category ("comprehension")
with several subcategories which Berlin labeled Rc_1, Rc_2, Rc_3 and Rc_q.
The data showed that Rc_1 reported thoughts looked like "lower-process
thoughts" and that the remainder of the Rc's looked like "higher-
process thoughts." He reclassified them accordingly when constructing
Figure 6.3.

An added feature of Berlin's work is the fact that he also categorized the students as *rationals* or *stereopaths* (after Stern *et al.*,
1956). The significant findings in terms of personality types were as
follows:

a. stereopaths reported a higher mean number of unrelevant experiences
than rationals in dialectical situations;
b. rationals reported a higher mean number of experiences in both the
Comprehension and Higher categories of experiences than stereopaths in
the dialectical situations;

c. rationals reported the greater number of relevant experiences in dialectical situations, while the stereopaths reported the greater number of relevant experiences in errorless situations;

d. rationals have a higher mean number of unrelevant experiences than stereopaths. The difference between the means is significant only in the teacher modality (Berlin, 1965, pp. 84–85).

One additional finding is of particular significance. Berlin states: "Students in the dialectical situations reported a greater number of Higher learning experiences than students in the errorless situations. This finding is significant only in the teacher modality, although the data from the materials modality follow the same trend." Over and over we fail to find significant higher-process outcomes stemming from the materials modality. Although the involvement of a teacher by no means insures the generation of higher-process thoughts in learning, it seems to be a necessary condition for such learning.

About the model, Berlin has this to say:

We have shown that this construct is useful in designing learning situations which have clearly defined characteristics. Possibly even more important, these learning situations are reproducible, as indicated by the important similarities in recalled experiences reported by students [in both schools] (p. 87).

It may be fair to say that evidence suggests some construct validity for the model. Consistently, investigators fail to get significant findings involving higher-process learning unless a teacher is involved in instruction; such involvement, although not sufficient, does seem necessary. This tentative conclusion has set the direction for an investigation I hope to pursue. Could one be more successful in generating or inducing higher thought processes in the materials modality by using the great potential of high-speed computers in instruction? Clearly a negative finding here would bolster the ego of teachers. Secondly, although not all psychological variables generate exciting results, some classifications of students by means of psychological variables yield consistent, reliable results in terms of the dimensions and modalities of the model. And thirdly, the classrooms structured on various cells do seem to be reproducible. This has been demonstrated in terms of (1) intuitive sensing, (2) objective evidence from Interaction Analysis, and (3) reproducibility of findings in supposedly very similarly structured classrooms.

Two other generalizations seem fair at this time. First, teachers following a regime suggested by the model compete more successfully with instructional materials than when they use "typical procedures."

Second, the regime seems to permit the investigator to reduce the amount of variance assigned to error.

All of the work up to this point has been stilted, perhaps artificial; and deliberately so. If one cannot generate reliable differences between situations based on the polarities of a dimension, there is little hope that closer points along the dimension would be useful. Having established some semblance of construct validity, it becomes reasonable to experiment with shifting patterns of reproducible instructional procedures. Some of the finest teaching I have seen, although I have no evidence that it was effective, was describable as shifts from one cell to another of my model, even from one modality to another, within the span of a single fifty-minute period. We have stayed with "pure cell" instruction not because we believed it to be superior, but only to establish a reasonable basis for believing such instruction might be useful for short periods for certain purposes and with particular kinds of students.

It is my belief that teachers may be trained to be versatile by using this model, or construct: first to determine the natural style of the teacher-in-training, and then to require him to practice using procedures from cells different from his "home-cell" and procedures involving instruction exclusively by materials created or selected by the trainee. Perhaps the information stemming from consideration of this model will stimulate a few to regard a roomful of students as requiring more than a single method of instruction. Perhaps the demonstration of a variety of useful tactics will lead to consideration of strategies for instruction.

Appendix:
Part of a Transcript from an "Errorless" Lesson

Teacher: [*Demonstrating a balance, calling one side "A" the other "B".*]
   If you have a balance and push down here (at A) and here (at B)
   with equal force [*demonstrates with his hands*], does A go down
   while B goes up, or does B go down while A goes up, or do they
   remain level, Carl?

C: They remain level.

T: Right. If we reduce the weight or pressure of B, what will happen?
   Will B go down, or will it go up, Mary?

M: Go up.

T: Yes. Good. It will go up [*demonstrates*]. Now we are going to
   consider a lift pump. [*Shows small lift pump, projects diagram of
   lift pump with air pressure labeled "A" outside the pump and "B"
   inside the pump.*] When the pump handle is down the pressure at
   A is equal to the pressure at B. [*Places pump into glass container
   of water.*] We have just put the pump in the water. We have not
   changed anything. Is the pressure at A equal to the pressure at B,
   John?

J: Yes.

T: All right. When the handle is lifted, what happens to the pressure
   at B? Is it greater or less than at A, Fred?

F: Less.

T: Good. Now remember what happened when the pressure at B on
   the balance was reduced by the removal of weights. What happened, Ernie?

E: B went up.

T: That's right. What do you suppose will happen to the water at B
   when the pressure at B is reduced, Edna?

E: It will rise.

SEVEN

What's Happening in the Elementary Classroom?

PAUL V. GUMP

Introduction

The title of our symposium commits us to a discussion of next steps in research into teaching processes. Clearly, next steps depend upon the conception held by researchers regarding "the teaching process." At present, educational investigators have only partial and inadequate conceptions of what happens in the classroom; next steps in research must include development of a more realistic and more comprehensive picture of this activity.

The teaching process, as understood here, is that which teachers do in classrooms; what they do from morning openers to reading time, to recess, to spelling drill, to getting ready for lunch—and so on throughout the day. When one has described what's happening in the classroom, and the teacher's relation to what's happening, one has the basic information upon which to build a theory of the teaching process.

Researchers now are attempting to arrive at a theory of teaching by study of selected parts of the process. There are laboratory studies in which a stripped-down model of a teaching–learning phenomenon is manipulated; there are studies in the classroom in which some kind

This discussion was stimulated by a symposium sponsored by the Department of Curriculum of The Ontario Institute for Studies in Education in May, 1967. The data referred to were derived from an investigation entitled *The Classroom Behavior Setting: Its Nature and Relation to Student Behavior* and supported by the U. S. Department of Health, Education and Welfare, Office of Education, Bureau of Research, Project No. 5–0892.

of incident (Kounin & Gump, 1958) or certain academic portions of the classroom day (Biddle & Adams, 1967) are examined.

Certainly, models or pieces of actual events are legitimate objects of study. Much can be gained by focus upon narrowed research targets. However, total investment in such partial approaches cannot, *in principle*, bring adequate understanding of the total phenomenon. The words *in principle* are emphasized in order to deny that improvements in the partial approaches can lead to adequate theory. There are deficiencies in the manner in which past investigations have been carried out: recording of events based upon inadequate methods, failure of investigators to clarify terms and develop concepts applicable across investigations, inadequate control of possible contaminating variables, insufficient rigor in making inferences from data, and so on. However, the position taken here is that *if all such deficiencies were eliminated, we would still remain unable to theorize adequately about the teaching process.* A theory of the teaching process must rest upon what happens in the classroom over its real span, not on what happens during particular lessons or incidents.

We must develop scientific descriptions of the total run of classroom activities; if we enter classrooms to study and describe particular lessons or incidents, we must miss other pieces of reality that are equally part of the teaching process. Study of teacher or pupil behavior in academic lessons, for example, leaves out large blocks of classroom time when teachers and pupils are engaged in other, presumably useful, or at least necessary, activities. Furthermore, there are some matters that cannot be understood if parts are studied in isolation. If the parts have some dynamic relationship to one another, then understanding demands that the parts be considered simultaneously. In the classroom, a kind of lesson *can* be the object of study, but in reality it is not an isolated package; the lesson was preceded by other events, it may be accompanied by non-lesson events, and it will be followed by different events. These enclosing phenomena are themselves parts of the classroom; the relationships they have to the lesson are matters of interest. For example, the junctures between the lesson and other parts form transitions; and Kounin, Friesen, and Norton (1966) have data to show that teacher behavior at transitions is highly related to pupil involvement in subsequent lessons. Yet the idea of transition hardly arises if one restricts his attention to individual behavior during a sample of classroom activity called a lesson. The idea of transition requires concepts for extra-individual parts and for the junctures between these parts.

Extra-individual Units in the Classroom

We propose that the ordinary self-contained elementary classroom is a *behavior setting*, as this eco-behavioral unit has been described by Barker (1968). A full exposition and justification of this idea of behavior setting unit is beyond the scope of this discussion. However, since the way of conceptualizing environment that is represented by the unit has fundamental relevance to educational research, five saliencies of the unit's quality are stated here:

1. The behavior setting unit accepts the reality-given integration of behavioral and milieu elements. An example from human engineering can illustrate the point. In this field, functioning units are often man-machine couplings; a psychologist *could* study the relation of man to his machine but, for particular problems, this would be neither necessary nor fruitful. The appropriate unit may be a milieu-behavioral, a machine-man combination. Taylor (1963) has described the content of human engineering in *Psychology: A Study of a Science*, where he discusses the unwillingness of academic psychology to accept a man-machine unit; he maintains that the thinking behind such a unit is "quite foreign to anthropocentric psychology for it places the mechanism on a par with the man who controls it and creates a new unit which is hierarchically superior to both" (p. 880). The thinking behind behavior settings places matters of milieu alongside those of behavior and recognizes a unit which is "hierarchically superior to both."

   The mixture of milieu and behavior puts a different light on person-environment interaction. Persons are seen as being *in* environments in the sense that people are *in* basketball games (as opposed to simply contained by a physical milieu such as a gymnasium). When we see persons reacting to their game environments, we see them reacting to something they also create and maintain. As Barker (1965) explains it, persons have two positions in their environments: (*a*) they are component parts of media used by the setting, and (*b*) they are individuals using the setting for individual purposes.

2. The behavior setting units are primary, relatively unabstracted sections of reality. They have substance, they can be seen directly, they can be entered and their parts touched. They are not units like power structures or sociometric patterns. These latter units are schemata representative of certain more primary realities—they are abstractions, not ecological realities. Abstractions are necessary but

they start from primary phenomena. What kinds of abstractions become possible obviously depends upon which sections of reality form their starting-point. Units which are persons or behaviors give rise to abstractions different from those arising from eco-behavioral or behavior setting units.

3. The units have internal dynamics; changes in behavior in one part of the setting have clear reverberations in other behaviors; the addition or subtraction of physical objects also affects certain behaviors. The units represent encompassing wholes which have coercive effects on their interior parts: the total setting constrains individuals and objects within it. This fact is significant because the establishment of viable settings means that teachers can depend upon the setting to guide behavioral elements within it. The teacher's task becomes one of setting creation and maintenance—not one of dealing with the infinity of pupil behaviors which could occur in the setting.

4. The milieu-behavioral units are ubiquitous: events of interest to psychologists and educators occur somewhere in space and time; they occur in one behavior setting or another. The operations of a school or of a classroom can be mapped in terms of their eco-behavioral units. A map is often useful; it can organize complex data arrays, but its potential far exceeds this outlining function. A map which shows parts and their relationships can suggest new understandings.

5. Milieu-behavioral units of the behavior setting type can serve as links in the causal chain between institutional and behavioral variables. For example, a major variable describing high schools is population size; one outcome for students is a difference in satisfaction patterns; investigation (Barker & Gump, 1964) shows that qualities of the inhabited behavior settings carry the effects from school size to pupil satisfaction.

Entire schools may be described in terms of behavior setting units; it is also possible to describe particular classrooms in terms of behavior setting *sub*units which we designate as *segments* (defined by Webster as "the constituent parts into which a body, entity or quantity naturally divides"). Segments appearing in classrooms include such activity structures as Morning Song and Salute, Red Bird Reading Circle, Social Studies Seatwork, Spelling Test, Getting Organized for Gym, and so forth. A complete description of a segment would include a *site* (e.g., main part of room or circle in back), *temporal boundaries* (e.g., 9:05 to 9:22), *behavior objects* (pencils, papers, text), *participants* (pupils, teacher), *behavior or activity format* (kinds and relationships of participant actions) and *concern* (the "business" of the segment). As one looks at segments it becomes obvious that events within them are highly interdependent, that boundaries surround segments; in short, segments have the qualities of true units. Of importance to the task of describing what is happening in classrooms is the ubiquity of segments: teachers, pupils, and behavior objects function in one segment or another throughout the classroom day. This means that the comprehensive picture of classroom phenomena suggested as necessary for a theory of the teaching process can be given in terms of the organization and the qualities of segments.

Classroom Description in Terms of Segment Organization

We endeavored to record the major events in six classrooms on two different days. These twelve records, or chronicles, described teacher behavior and certain other events such that all the segments could be identified and described. The chronicles also described each teacher act in sequence. Time-lapse photography provided visual samples of pupil behavior; from these samples it was possible to code pupil involvement in the on-going activity. A full explanation of the method and findings is available (Gump, 1967). Here we should like to refer to certain findings to illustrate the sort of research effort being recommended.

When an entire classroom day is segmented, the result may be mapped as has been done in Figure 7.1. The duration of segments is indicated down the left column in each of the four vertical sections corresponding to divisions of the day. This spatial representation of the segments in Mrs. Carr's third grade generates a number of interesting observations. First, since segments represent activity environments, a day with segments of short duration provides more breaks, more change of pace, than one in which segments are long. Duration, then, is one measure of temporal differentiation. Secondly, there are occasions when a larger segment has clear divisions within it. In Mrs. Carr's room, one of the reading groups in the first morning seatwork period contained two activity segments within the general reading work: Discussion of New Words and Worksheet Instruction. Thirdly, there is the issue of simultaneous operation of segments. In Mrs. Carr's day, the activity was similar for the total class until a little after 9:20; at this point the class was divided into two major spheres: one devoted to Morning Seatwork, the other to a series of small groups, first for reading, then for arithmetic. At 10:30 the class again shared one segment (Going to Recess).

Whether or not the teaching process should include simultaneous

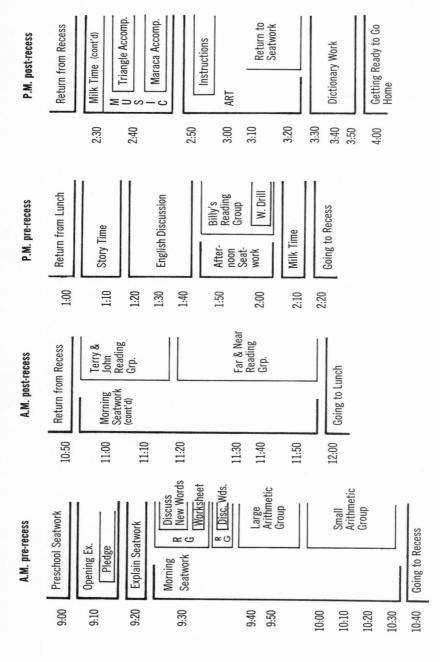

Figure 7.1 A Day in Mrs. Carr's Third-Grade Class: A Segmental Map

160

operation of segments is probably a significant issue. Building simultaneous segments is one way of fitting instruction more closely to interests and capacities of particular pupils. Further, with simultaneous segments, a teacher can form small units; available data indicate that pupils in smaller teacher-led groups are more highly involved than those in full-class teacher-led groups. On the other hand, simultaneous segments are not without their problems. The teacher has more arenas to keep in mind and she can act only in one at one time; this requires that means other than continuous teacher input must be developed for guiding pupil action. Teachers may have more to do for simultaneous segments. Activity in one segment may interfere with activity in another. For these reasons we would speculate that operation of simultaneous segments, as compared to *en masse* ones, requires more teacher preparation and more on-going vigilance and effort. Research is needed on this point. Our data do show that the teachers we observed were consistent in the amount of simultaneous segmentation they arrange for their classroom days.

A final aspect of segment structure made visible by Figure 7.1 is the occurrence of transitions. Each pair of adjacent horizontal lines marks an occasion for which an on-going segment—with its particular site, behavior objects, participants, activity format and concerns—must be dissolved and a new segment, with new elements and patterns, established.

Our data indicate that these transitions create sharp changes in the teaching process. Prior to transitions, a large proportion of the teacher's activities consist of pedagogical acts (asking questions, giving feedback, imparting information), and a much smaller proportion are structuring moves (directions regarding placement of attention or behavior—where to go, what to attend to, tools to procure or put away, and so forth). At transitions, the proportions are radically reversed; pedagogical moves are far fewer and structuring ones much more frequent. The result is not surprising; reflection tells us that transitions, by their nature, require structuring. But when we look at transitions, specifically, the "teaching process" appears quite different than when we look simply at an over-all on-going "lesson."

Less obvious changes in teaching behavior at transitions occur in the realm of control of divergent behavior. Before transitions, teacher moves to counter, to criticize, or to forbid behavior are relatively infrequent; at transitions these moves increase; they increased at transitions for each of the 12 different classroom days observed. Although more research is required, it is already clear that qualities of the structure of segments are highly relevant to the teaching process.

Classroom Description in Terms of Segment Qualities

Certain aspects of segments tend to persist throughout their existence. For example, a segment has a "business," a *concern* which is the reason for its establishment. When the on-going segment is no longer concerned with a given business, a new segment is usually formed. An array of segments can be categorized according to their concerns; these may be *academic* (e.g., reading, arithmetic), *artistic* (music, art), *recreational and social* (milk and story time, sharing), or *procedural* (preparation for gym, cleaning up at end of day). A day may be described in terms of the relative prominence of segments of various categories. Although prominence of segments of a particular category can be represented by their number and duration, another measure is *pupil occupancy time*. A group of 25 students may occupy a classroom for a total of 200 pupil hours a day. The proportion of this time spent in segments of given concerns is one representation of "what's happening in the elementary school classroom."

Table 7.1 presents our own data for two days in each of six third-grade clasrooms in terms of the means and ranges of pupil occupancy time in segments of various concerns.

TABLE 7.1
PERCENTAGE OF PUPIL OCCUPANCY
TIME SPENT IN SEGMENTS OF VARIOUS CONCERNS

Concern	Mean	Low	High
Academics	72	65	83
Music, Art	7	2	13
Social, Recreational	7	4	12
Procedure	12	7	16
Other (Ritual Group "Talks")	2	trace	8

NOTE. Each "Low" and "High" represents a classroom average for two days of observation.

Although the classrooms observed were in the same school system, the variability in exposure to different concerns was rather impressive. For example, pupils in one teacher's class spent one-third of their time on segments concerned with things other than academic study, and pupils in another teacher's class spent only one-sixth of their time out of the academic arena. When the effectiveness of particular teachers or of methods of instruction becomes a research target, pupil occupancy time in the pertinent subject matter would be a necessary statistic.

Table 7.1 also reveals differences in how much time pupils spent in particular categories of nonacademic concerns; one category of possible interest is the procedural one. These segments most probably represent "educational losses." They do not directly advance any curricular goal; they are preparations and closings-down; yet the average proportion of occupancy time here was rather high: 12 per cent. Pupils in the classrooms of the two most experienced teachers spent only 7 per cent of their time in such segments while pupils of one teacher had 16 per cent of their time tied up in procedural segments.

One implication about the "teaching process" which can be drawn from the data on pupil occupancy time and segment concern is that a respectable portion of teaching is *not* related to academic and artistic environments; the "teaching process" includes establishment and maintenance of social, recreational, and procedural environments. Further, the fact that experienced teachers can cut their losses to procedural segments implies that this might be one way of measuring effectiveness of the teaching process.

There are other aspects of segments which persist through their operation: extent of direct, continuous teacher leadership required by the segment's type, extent of required pupil-pupil interdependence in the segment's interaction pattern, kind of perceptual and motoric behavior demanded of participants, and so on. One further aspect of segments which can be employed in describing their coercivity is *pacing*. To explain: In some activities, the participants receive continued elicitation from the outside; they are required to track and to respond to an externally controlled input. Segments which offer oral quizzes, group singing, or recitations have such a pacing arrangement. Other activities may specify the task but leave the timing of particular acts up to the participant; for example, in seatwork, the task is usually defined but there are no persisting external calls for action. Such an activity is self-paced. Segments of the self-pacing type required over 40 per cent of pupil occupancy time. The fact is significant because the percentage of pupils rated as involved in the segment's activity is clearly lower in self-paced segments than in externally paced ones. In general, the teacher is faced with more difficult pupil motivation problems in self-paced segments.

The issue of motivation and the teacher's response to it is even more crucial when facts of segment pacing and segment structure are brought together. Percentage of pupil involvement tends to be low at the very beginning of the segment. (Beginnings, as referred to here, are the three-and-a-half-minute periods following the start of a segment or following the resumption of an interrupted segment.) At points where self-pacing and beginnings coincide, effects are additive. Our data showed that the percentages of pupils involved in the various combinations of self- or external-pacing and beginning or remainder of segments were as follows:

Beginnings of self-paced segments:	63%
Remainders of self-paced segments:	74%
Beginnings of externally paced segments:	75%
Remainders of externally paced segments:	81%

The same pupils were measured in all of the above comparisons; statistical tests of differences between beginnings and remainders and between self-paced and external-paced were highly significant. Clearly, the kind of segment and the point in segment structure are both relevant to pupil involvement.

We have offered data to illustrate how the classroom day might be described; further data have shown that meaningful relations obtain between those variables relating to the structure and content of units and variables of the teaching-learning process. Strictly, the data apply only to third-grade elementary classrooms of the type studied. However, the approach to educational research, it is contended, has a much wider relevance.

Ecological Structure and Educational Research

The general orientation proposed is one in which the educational environment is permitted to run a full course during which a comprehensive (not necessarily highly detailed) record is made of "what happens." Examination of the record will *not* show a homogeneous or a random array of milieu and behavior; it will show a pattern of extra-individual units to which particular kinds of teacher and pupil behaviors are sensibly correlated. The organization and content of these units provide a systematic and coherent way of stating what happens in the classroom.

The nature of the units employed in the description is highly crucial; if these are merely convenient partitioning devices, then units are simply helpful in outlining complex data arrays. However, if units are dynamic and cohesive, the implications are quite different. Then it may be expected that the units will coerce and guide particulars within their boundaries; they will shape their many interior elements.

On a less abstract level, segments, once under way, take care of many things for the teacher. The infinite number of events which could occur (and create chaos) will *not* occur. There is evidence that teachers understand this quality of segments because they devote a good deal of effort to segment creation and maintenance. Teacher acts which reflect this effort are structuring acts. In our own data, teachers engaged in an average of 1300 acts per day, and 40 per cent were of the structuring type.

A good look at complete cycles of the educational process indicates that educators are in the business of creating extra-individual behavior-milieu units. Research in the teaching process must come to terms with this fact; it must recognize "what's happening in the classroom."

EIGHT

A Perspective on a Theory of Urban Teaching

LOUIS M. SMITH

Introduction

Classroom procedures seldom are altered on the basis of educational theory and research (Miles, 1964). Waves of innovation and reform respond to other than research influences. In contrast, however, some critics believe that fundamental change in classroom practices is almost nonexistent. In their eyes, the urban public schools are very stable institutions in our society. Sociologists have commented upon other institutions:

> . . . the foregoing analysis has direct implications for *social engineering*. It helps explain why the periodic efforts at "political reform," "turning the rascals out" and "cleaning political house" are typically (though not necessarily) short lived and ineffectual. It exemplifies a basic theorem: any attempt to eliminate an existing social structure without providing adequate alternative structures for fulfilling the functions previously fulfilled by the abolished organization is doomed to failure (Merton, 1957, p. 81).

The fundamental thesis of our recent work has been precisely that. I believe that if significant and lasting changes in urban teaching are to be made, we need to see clearly the latent as well as manifest

This paper presents material adapted from *The Complexities of an Urban Classroom*, by Louis M. Smith and William Geoffrey (Copyright © 1968 by Holt, Rinehart and Winston, Inc.), with the permission of the publishers. The original research was based upon Project S–048, supported by the Bureau of Research, U.S. Office of Education, *Teacher Decision-Making in an Urban Classroom*.

functions of the urban classroom. In our research we have tried to describe carefully the day-to-day events in the life of a middle-class teacher working with a group of sixth- and seventh-grade pupils in a school located in a lower socio-economic urban neighborhood. As these events are conceptualized they can be entered into a functional analysis of the classroom and become part of a theory of teaching.

Methodology

In these times of emphasis on quantitative procedures, large-scale investigation, and computer programs, our procedures were embarrassingly simple. We followed the uncomplicated suggestions of George Homans (1950) and tried to observe carefully the concrete, the familiar, and the obvious events of social behavior and attempted to talk about these events as consistently as possible. We hoped to present a case study of a specific group, an urban public school classroom.

The most succinct statement summarizing the methodology of the investigation is contained in this sentence: "Recently I spent all day, every day, observing *one* seventh grade school teacher and his class of children." My university commitments were lightened; my days were reasonably free. I attended the public school opening day exercises, faculty meetings, daily informal staff coffee klatches, and daily lessons in reading, writing, and arithmetic. It was the most fascinating professional experience that I have ever undertaken.

Briefly, two points should be clarified concerning the methodology: one of these concerns what I call the logic of this approach, and the other concerns the "how to do it" aspect. While both of these issues have been elaborated into papers of considerable length, two paragraphs will suffice for our purposes.

One of my colleagues has called the approach *the micro-ethnography of the classroom*. That has a nice ring to it; it makes what one does sound academic and important. Beyond this, it puts the methodology into the anthropological tradition, with the benefits and liabilities that that suggests. More recently this research orientation has been described by sociologists as participant observation. Within psychology the parallels to the methodology are to be found in naturalistic observation and clinical method.

The how-to-do-it aspects of the method were that I made contact with an intraceptive teacher who had some interest in the idea. He checked first with his principal, then later I talked with the principal and other responsible parties in the school and secured their permission. In the class, I sat at a table on the side and toward the back of the room. I took copious freehand notes of the events of the class, focusing basically on the teacher; my conceptual bias originally centered on his behavior and on social system theory. More particularly, I had just finished writing an educational psychology text (Smith & Hudgins, 1964) in which we had spent considerable time with McClelland's personality theory, Homans' conception of the human group, and Skinner's descriptive behaviorism. Most certainly my perception was guided selectively by the ideas from these men.

To the pupils I was introduced as a university teacher who was interested in finding out how children learn, what they find hard, interesting, and so forth. In the day-to-day relationships, as I lived in the class, I never told on them for things they did which the teacher did not see or for what they did when he was out of the room. As I lived in the class, I did not pry into their affairs but was always willing to listen and to talk with them. To the other teachers, I was a naive but persistent observer of Mr. Geoffrey's class. As we became friends, they told me more and more about what life was like in their school. I tried to listen carefully and to understand the nuances of the latent as well as manifest things they were saying. I was around as the day-to-day trials, tribulations, joys, and excitements occurred, but in general I tried to stay out of the way of the flow of events.

In the classroom, I kept copious field notes of the events of the day. Using a portable Stenorette I dictated long, daily statements of observations and interpretations. These daily records grew to a horrifying quantity. The field notes were typed into multiple copies, and ultimately these were the raw data processed as we built our models.

The class I observed was located in a school in a metropolitan slum community where mostly the homes were tenements in need of repair. The school had the reputation of being "a good school in a difficult neighborhood," and the teacher, who had taught for five years in the building, had the reputation of being a good, and a strong, teacher. He lived in a suburban middle-class neighborhood and commuted by car to the school. The children were not atypical for this community. Of the original 34 children all but three had tested IQ's below 100. One child had a Kuhlman-Anderson IQ of 137. Approximately one-fourth had failed seventh grade last year and over half at some time had failed at least one grade. All but three of the children were white. Many of the children were migrants from the rural south, and conversations with some of them suggested that their families were originally from lower socio-economic levels of the communities they had left. Many of the children spent weekends and holidays "in the country" visiting relatives. After the first month of school a room was closed in the building due to less than anticipated enrollment and 20 of my original seventh-grade group were replaced with sixth-grade pupils. This meant that the teacher taught a split class—approximately 14 seventh-graders and 20 sixth-graders—for the remainder of the semester. This new group was a "difficult group" in the eyes of the sending teacher. They had been giving him trouble since the beginning of the year. "I can't get any work out of them" were his words. He was pleased to have a different group of children.

Results

Our more lengthy accounts of the research detail the substantive findings of the project (Smith & Geoffrey, 1965, 1968). Here I would like to accent the kind of theory for which we were striving, the kind of theory needed ultimately for guiding innovation and change. The psychology of teaching seems to have suffered from at least three problems: (1) evaluative exhortations—the "good" teacher does this or that; (2) dustbowl empiricism—"workbooks yield more learning than dittoed exercises"—with little attempt to conceptualize the latent variables involved; and (3) taxonomies of classroom events which "don't go anywhere" in terms of sequentially linked propositions. Our focus has been toward a fourth option.

While Homans (1950) provided a model for substantive concepts and, to a degree, for the formal characteristics of a theory, it was Zetterberg's (1965) conception of social science theory that more explicitly became our target. For us, he made clear distinctions among primitive and derived concepts, propositions, and theory. A theory is an interrelated set of propositions; a proposition is a relationship between two or more concepts; and a concept, or term, is the primary language unit. The initial set of concepts is undefined [1] or primitive; the broader set of concepts used in the propositions is derived from combinations of the undefined or primitive concepts. Further, Zetterberg states that propositions may be organized or related in various ways: inventories of determinants, inventories of results, chain patterns, and axiomatic formats.

Our procedures have been essentially these. As we have tried to abstract from our observations and our operational definitions, we have named phenomena. Then we have tried to define theoretically the new term we have coined or borrowed. As we wrote down our conceptual definitions, we found that they usually contained some terms already in our growing glossary and also some new terms. Ultimately we found our way back to our "undefined" primitive list. While this process has a circular quality to it, it seems to us to be the essence of a theory. Eventually the glossary becomes larger and larger as it becomes more all-embracing.

As an illustration of our theory-building, we present an example growing out of a concept we have called *personalized interaction*. The reduction proceeded this way:

1. By personalized interaction we mean the interaction between the teacher and a single pupil.[2]
2. Interaction—a minimum sequence in which the behavior of one or more persons follows another.
3. Behavior—a primitive term, the things people do.
4. Person—a primitive term, an individual.
5. Teacher—an incumbent in a role in the school in which an individual attempts to change the learning of another, the pupil.
6. Pupil—a role in which one is expected to learn.
7. Role—a pattern of activities, interactions, and sentiments bound together by a group belief.
   . . . (Et cetera)

As is evident, the list of concepts grows and grows. We have tried to account in our glossary for all the terms we have used, and in this manner we have "derived" more and more complex concepts which are relevant and related to our other concepts.

In general we have tried to develop concepts which Zetterberg calls "variates." The conceptions are susceptible to quantification in more and less amounts; they represent continua, and they also fit within a functional or propositional theory rather than in a descriptive schema or taxonomy.

As a further step we tried to find in our data the antecedents and consequences of the conception. This led us to the formation of hypotheses that used concepts already in our theory while, at the same time, forcing us to create new concepts. The new ones had to be defined conceptually as we have just indicated with our concept of personalized interaction. As we sketched out our propositions, we found we were drawing diagrams. For instance, we have hypothesized that an increasing amount of personalized interaction leads to increased pupil satisfaction, increased pupil esteem for the teacher, a more highly differentiated role structure in the classroom, and increased clarification of learning barriers. Our data were striking in their indications of a tremendous variety of roles that were played out in the classroom. Sam became the court jester, Pete became the troubled and troublesome one, Henry adopted the no-work stance, and so forth. In our case study, Mr. Geoffrey's high degree of personalized interaction seemed to precipitate this highly differentiated role structure. As the role structure became part of the social equilibrium, it became a potent factor in its own right.

In addition, we hypothesized that pupil satisfaction and pupil esteem for the teacher lead to classroom control and that clarification of specific barriers to pupil learning leads to enhanced pupil achievement. Similarly, we hypothesized several antecedents affecting the amount of personalized interaction; these included administrative organization (intact or split-level classes), teacher personality structure, "liking children," and staff norms regarding teaching styles. In short, we have what might be called a miniature theory of personalized teacher-pupil interaction. We diagrammed the hypothesized relationships in Figure 8.1. The concepts were all within the broader theory included in our glossary.

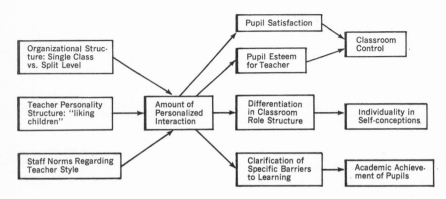

Figure 8.1 A Miniature Theory of Personalized Interaction

Stated in a more axiomatic form, we have ten hypotheses which constitute the basic postulates of our miniature theory of personalized interaction. They are listed below.

1. As organizational structure shifts from a single class to a split-level class the amount of personalized interaction decreases.
2. As teacher liking of pupils increases then the amount of personalized interaction increases.
3. As staff norms increase in intensity and crystallization and decrease in range of tolerable behavior regarding personal interaction then amount of personalized interaction increases.[4]
4. As amount of personalized interaction increases then pupil satisfaction increases.
5. As amount of personalized interaction increases then pupil esteem for the teacher increases.

6. As amount of personalized interaction increases differentiation in classroom role structure increases.
7. As amount of personalized interaction increases clarification of specific barriers to learning increases.
8. As pupil satisfaction and esteem for teacher increase then classroom control increases.
9. As differentiation in classroom role structure increases then individuality in self-conceptions increases.
10. As clarification of specific barriers to learning increases then academic achievement increases.

Our concept of personalized interaction has suggested ten propositions that can serve as postulates. The number of theorems open to test is considerably larger. For instance, personalized interaction should be related to each of the more distal consequences, and thus give three testable theorems. Each of the antecedents of personalized interaction should relate to each of the four immediate consequences and to each of the three more distal consequences, a total of twenty-one additional theorems which would be testable hypotheses. Less apparent theorems include the interrelationships among the consequences themselves, e.g., classroom control and individuality in self-conceptions. Later, as we present additional concepts, we hypothesize further interrelationships which in turn increase the complexity of the theory and hopefully present a more valid map of the reality of the classroom.

Zetterberg (1965) argues that several important values arise from this kind of theorizing. First, ". . . a theory can be used to provide the most parsimonious summary of actual or anticipated research findings" (p. 161). In our research the relationships are hypotheses; they reflect what we believe existed in this case. As we have said several times, they need verification through quantitative research in the laboratory and the field. Second, ". . . a theory can be used to coordinate research so that many separate findings support each other giving the highest plausibility to the theory" (p. 163). In effect, each piece of support accents the plausibility of related aspects of the theoretical structure. Third, ". . . a theory can be used to locate the most strategic or manageable proposition for testing" (p. 164). Without question, some concepts have more readily available and valid indicators than other concepts. As one has the more general theoretical picture, one's research tactics can be made more flexible and presumably more productive. Finally, Zetterberg proposes "a fourth virtue of theory for the researcher: a theory provides a limited area in which to locate false propositions when an hypothesis fails to meet an empirical test" (p. 166). As theorems do not stand the test of carefully drawn data, the specific postulates which are in error can be excised or reconceptualized. The total theory is not dissolved. In this way "negative results" can contribute to the cumulative enterprise.

While Zetterberg (1965, pp. 159–166) argues that each one-step relationship becomes a postulate and each two-step relationship becomes a theorem and that one need only test empirically the end points to verify indirectly the postulates, we have less confidence in this degree of formalization and verification. However, verification can proceed more systematically by obtaining valid indicators of each concept: for instance, measures of norms based on Jackson's return potential model, attitudes via an MTAI, and class organization through a questionnaire. The amount of personalized interaction can be obtained from frequency counts in direct observation. Pupil esteem for the teacher should be obtainable from questionnaires, and the degree of differentiation of role structure of the classroom from observation or modified sociometric instruments. Similarly, operations can be devised for other parts of the model; our intent here is to show how the theory can be moved from the formulation and development stage in which we have been engaged to the verificational stage of tested propositions.

Conclusion

At a time in history when educational change or innovation is salient for parts of our profession and when "rigorous, quantitative, experimental" research is salient for others, I am suggesting additional alternatives. My colleague, William Geoffrey, and I have found the urban classroom to be a tremendously complicated social *organism*. We think that other careful descriptions of naturalistic settings are imperative if long-term change is to be effected. Also, as we have tried to think more abstractly about our classroom, we have talked about many phenomena (such as personalized interaction and differentiated classroom role structure) representing important concepts that need to be put into the language system of teachers and researchers. The range and variety of the concepts needed seems much larger than those currently finding favor with educational researchers. Finally, we argue for a kind of theory, an axiomatic one, necessary for a psychology of teaching. As competing middle-range theories are developed and tested, the psychology of teaching will make important strides.

NINE

Explorations of the Teacher's Effectiveness in Lecturing

This chapter presents four studies by associates of the Stanford Center for Research and Development in Teaching, with an introductory essay by N. L. Gage and concluding comments by John B. Carroll and Robert Glaser. The individual studies, whose authors are identified at the appropriate section headings, were made independently on the same data.

The Microcriterion of Effectiveness in Explaining

N. L. GAGE

The four studies described in this report explored the role of the teacher as explainer. The studies were based on a modification of the "criterion of effectiveness" paradigm. This paradigm, used successfully

The researches reported herein were performed pursuant to a contract between the United States Department of Health, Education, and Welfare, Office of Education, under the provisions of the Cooperative Research Program, and the Stanford Center for Research and Development in Teaching. The study reports are adapted from presentations made at a symposium at the meetings of the American Educational Research Association in February, 1968. The Comments by John B. Carroll and Robert Glaser were also presented at that symposium.

The authors of Study I are indebted to Katherine Baker for editorial assistance.

More complete reports of Studies II and III are available in the doctoral dissertations of Unruh (1967) and Rosenshine (1968).

in other areas of research, has been dominant in the study of teaching. The paradigm is one in which the investigator undertakes to:

Identify or select a criterion (or set of criteria) of teacher effectiveness. This criterion then becomes the dependent variable. The research task is then (1) to measure this criterion, (2) to measure potential correlates of this criterion, and (3) to determine the actual correlations between the criterion and its potential correlates (Gage, 1963, p. 114).

In many studies, the criterion of teacher effectiveness has been a rating assigned by the school principal, and the potential correlates have been measures of the personality and characteristics of the teacher. Many attempts to identify good teachers have been made in this manner; hundreds of studies yielding thousands of correlation coefficients have been carried out. But reviewers of this research have not been impressed. "In the large, these studies have yielded disappointing results: correlations that are non-significant, inconsistent from one study to the next, and usually lacking in psychological and educational meaning" (Gage, 1963, p. 118). Similarly, Getzels and Jackson (1963), after reviewing research on teacher personality, concluded that:

Despite the critical importance of the problem and a half-century of prodigious research effort, very little is known for certain about the nature and measurement of teacher personality, or about the relation between teacher personality and teaching effectiveness. The regrettable fact is that many of the studies so far have not produced significant results (p. 574).

Under such circumstances, researchers have sought to refine the paradigm, shifting to different types of potential correlates and criteria. In place of personality traits, the potential correlates have become objectively denoted classroom behaviors of pupils and teachers; in place of a global rating of effectiveness, the criterion has become a measure of pupil achievement. Researchers who followed this approach (e.g., Medley & Mitzel, 1959; Spaulding, 1963; Soar, 1966) have usually conducted their research during a school year, sampling the teacher's behavior two to five times during the year, and otherwise imposing no restrictions on materials to be used or objectives to be achieved.

"Microcriteria" of Effectiveness

A further refinement in the criterion-of-effectiveness paradigm was suggested by Gage (1963). He advocated reducing the complexity of the problem through the use of "microcriteria" of effectiveness:

Rather than seek criteria for the overall effectiveness of teachers in the many varied facets of their roles, we may have better success with criteria of effectiveness in small, specifically defined aspects of the role. Many scientific problems have eventually been solved by being analyzed into smaller problems whose variables were less complex (p. 120).

The studies conducted by Flanders (1965) and Bellack (1966) may be regarded as exemplifying an approach toward microcriteria. Both investigators reduced their criteria to pupil achievement over a short period (two weeks and one week, respectively) and attempted to standardize the investigation by providing all teachers with identical and previously unused curricular materials.

But it may be argued that their criteria were still highly complex. Many aspects of the teacher's role were being considered; the designs permitted a wide range of behaviors. That is, in the investigations of Flanders and Bellack, the teacher was expected to (*a*) motivate the reading of prepared materials, (*b*) promote discussion, and (*c*) maintain discipline, as well as (*d*) engender a cognitive grasp of the material. The teachers were also allowed unrestricted freedom to choose their own methods, and the consequent differences in methods made comparisons difficult. Some teachers spent most of the class time lecturing, while others promoted decision-making by the students.

It is too early to draw conclusions as to the most effective design for determining the correlates of teaching effectiveness because too few studies have been completed. But the concept of microcriteria of effectiveness suggests that we study teaching by using criteria even simpler than those used by Flanders and Bellack. Simplifications might include the reduction of teaching time, focus upon only one type of teaching behavior and its outcomes, and further control of teaching procedures.

The Teacher's Effectiveness in Explaining

The present four studies are attempts to investigate teacher effectiveness with the microcriterion approach. The specific teacher behavior selected for investigation was "explaining." Explaining is the skill of engendering comprehension—usually orally, verbally, and extemporaneously—of some process, concept, or generalization. Explaining occurs in all grade levels and subject matters, whether it is a fifth-grade teacher explaining why the time in New York differs from that in San Francisco or a geologist explaining how the ice age may have been caused by volcanic eruptions. Everyday observation tells us that some people explain aptly, getting to the heart of the matter with just the right terminology, examples, and organization of ideas. Other explainers, on the contrary, get us and themselves all mixed up, use terms beyond our level of comprehension, draw inept analogies, and even employ concepts and principles that cannot be understood without an understanding of the very thing being explained. Explaining may come close to being the essence of instruction, so that when a teacher is attempting to explain proportionality to his geometry class or irony to his English class, he is behaving more purely as a teacher than when he is attempting, say, to motivate, promote discussion, or maintain discipline.

The teacher's "effectiveness in explaining" was defined operationally as the ability to present ideas in such a way that the pupils would be able to respond to questions testing the comprehension of those ideas. Explanation as defined by philosophers of science was not the focus of these studies. Rather, these investigations were concerned with the kind of pedagogical "explaining" discussed by Swift (1961), Thyne (1963, pp. 126–155), Meux and Smith (1964, pp. 146–148), Nuthall and Lawrence (1965, pp. 33–48), and Bellack and his associates (1966, pp. 24–25).

The same basic data were used in all four studies. After the initial data were gathered, the investigators independently studied specific problems:

Study I, by Belgard, Rosenshine, and Gage, focused on three questions: How reliable and general is the teacher's ability to explain? How reliable and general are pupil ratings? Which pupil ratings are related to the teacher's effectiveness in explaining?

Study II, by Unruh, dealt with the question: Which type of protocol, or record of the teacher's behavior, is the most effective source of cues that observers can use in rating teacher effectiveness? This study also included an exploration of the validity of free-response and structured ratings in an attempt to determine new variables, perceptible by pupils, which are related to the teacher's effects.

Study III, by Rosenshine, and Study IV, by Dell and Hiller, were investigations of specific behaviors whose frequency of occurrence might be related to teacher effectiveness in explaining. Both investigations were innovative in that they dealt with verbal behaviors not customarily measured in systematic studies of teaching behavior. In the study by Rosenshine, human coders counted the frequencies of the various syntactic, linguistic, and gestural events in teachers' behavior. In the study by Dell and Hiller, computers and specially developed dictionaries were used in the search for correlates of effectiveness; the capabilities of an IBM 7090 computer as a high-speed clerk were exploited. Different variables were measured in the two studies.

All of the studies were exploratory and correlational, and it would be hazardous to infer that the significant findings reflect causal relationships. Much experimental and correlational work will be necessary to confirm and expand the present findings. Nonetheless, the studies demonstrate a set of techniques that may yield knowledge on how to improve the effectiveness of classroom explanations.

Method

The basic records of teacher behavior and effects, which were used in all four studies, were collected by Rosenshine and Belgard. Fifty-eight experienced social studies teachers and their twelfth-grade classes in public schools in the San Francisco Bay Area participated in the study as volunteers. Only classes in which pupils were grouped heterogeneously according to general ability were used; class size ranged from 10 to 31, with a mean size of 21. Complete data were available initially for 43 teachers and 898 pupils, but due to the deterioration or loss of some video tape recordings, the number of video-taped lectures on each topic ranged in the four studies from 26 to 38. There was nothing to suggest that the elimination of the recordings was not random.

All teachers taught lessons based upon identical materials. The materials were "Atlantic Reports" in issues of the *Atlantic* magazine between November 1964 and August 1965; they were judged by curriculum experts to be suitable for twelfth-grade social studies classes. The teachers were asked to explain the material in the reports, which dealt with economic, political, and social conditions in Yugoslavia and Thailand. The term "explain" was operationally defined as the process whereby a teacher's fifteen-minute lecture on the prescribed curriculum material would enable his students to answer ten multiple-choice questions on the content. The pupils' mean adjusted score on the test was used as the index of the teacher's effectiveness in explaining. The adjustment procedures are explained below.

Standardization of lesson procedure. A week before his explanation of the material to his class, each teacher received a copy of (*a*) the Atlantic Reports on Yugoslavia and Thailand, (*b*) the five odd-numbered items of each multiple-choice test, (*c*) a modified version of the Stanford Teacher Competence Appraisal Guide, (*d*) the Attention Report, and (*e*) the following instructions:

Explain the important ideas and principles contained in the article. You may organize the lecture in any way you wish. The 10 test items will probe comprehension of main ideas and not test for knowledge of little pieces of information. For your guidance, you will be given five of the ten questions which will be used on each of the student tests.

Limit yourself to the content of the article. Do not do any additional reading or research on the topic covered by either article, or add material to your lecture. This rule is intended to save you unnecessary effort, and to insure that all teachers work with identical curricular material, no more and no less. The 10-item test will deal only with material in the article.

Limit yourself to lecture and use of the chalkboard for purposes of this study. In subsequent studies, we may investigate the effects of such other procedures as questioning, discussion, questions from students, study sheets, student note-taking, and use of various types of projectors. But in this study, if teachers use techniques other than lecture with the chalkboard, it will be impossible to perform an adequate analysis of the data. For some teachers this restriction may require a difficult departure from their customary teaching style. We hope that you will bear with us, since the purpose of this study is to investigate explaining behavior *per se* and not to evaluate any teacher or groups of teachers. We also hope, therefore, that you will discourage student questions during the lecture.

The 15-minute restriction is necessary to equate time conditions for all of the 50 teachers participating in this study. You may pace yourself, or you may have the equipment operator give you a signal when there are two or five minutes remaining. (The lecture must end after 15 minutes.)

During the 15-minute lecture period you will be in complete charge of the classroom. The Stanford research assistant will be available to aid you. You will signal the start of the lecture.

On the second day, the procedure will be exactly the same, except that you will lecture on the Thailand article.

On the third day, the procedure will vary slightly. To make possible the control of differences in student ability, all students will hear an identical 15-minute tape-recording of an article on Israel. The only responsibility of the teacher during the playing of this tape will be that of maintaining class order. The testing will be carried out as usual.

The Yugoslavia and Thailand lessons were taught by the teachers to their own pupils in their regular classrooms on each of the first two days of the period of the study. Video tape recordings were made of all the lessons. On the third day, an audio tape record of an Atlantic Report on Israel was played for all the classes. Immediately after each of the three lessons, a comprehension test, the Stanford Teacher Competence Appraisal Guide, and the Attention Report were administered by the investigators.

Measures. The comprehension tests consisted of ten-item multiple-choice tests constructed for a previous study (Fortune, Gage, & Shutes, 1966). The adjusted mean score of each class on each test was used as an index of the teacher's effectiveness in explaining the Atlantic Reports on Yugoslavia and Thailand.

Because there were no teacher effects in the audio-taped lesson presented to all classes, in Study I the mean test scores on Israel were used to adjust the mean class scores on Yugoslavia and Thailand for differences between classes in aptitude for achievement on lessons of this type, and the ratings given to the Israel tape-recorded lecture were used to adjust the ratings given to the other lectures for tendencies to rate teachers favorably or to report high or low attention.

In Studies II, III, and IV, the raw mean posttest class scores on Yugoslavia and Thailand were adjusted for two predictor variables: (1) the mean test scores on Israel, and (2) a score developed by using content analysis procedures to assess the relevance of the material in each lecture. This second adjustment was made to insure that the differences between classes were not due merely to differences in the pertinence of the presentations of the teachers. In making all adjustments, the between-groups regression slope was used.

After each lesson, the pupils rated the lesson on an adaptation of the Stanford Teacher Competence Appraisal Guide, which deals with the following dimensions: (1) clarity of aims, (2) organization of the lecture, (3) beginning the lecture, (4) clarity of presentation, (5) pacing the lecture, (6) pupil attention, (7) ending the lecture, (8) teacher-pupil rapport, and (9) amount of learning. For each dimension, the ratings were made on a seven-point scale ranging from "truly exceptional" to "weak," with an additional category for "unable to observe." The class mean of the pupils' ratings for each of the nine dimensions was computed for each lesson, and this mean was used as an index of how the class rated the lesson on each dimension.

After each lesson, pupils also filled out the Attention Report, which solicited self-report information on four items, of which the following is an example:

During this lecture, my mind wandered and I began
to think about other things:
    0. all of the time.
    1. most of the time.
    2. some of the time.
    3. a little bit of the time.
    4. none of the time.

The mean of the pupils' total scores on the four items was used as the attention score of the class for a particular lesson.

Study I. Effectiveness in Explaining:
Evidence on Its Generality
and Correlation with Pupil Ratings

MARIA BELGARD | BARAK ROSENSHINE | N. L. GAGE

The teacher's effectiveness in explaining was defined in this study as the teacher's ability to present ideas to his pupils in such a way that the pupils would be able to respond to questions that assessed the comprehension of ideas. Given this definition, one can ask: How consistent is the teacher's effectiveness? Effectiveness in explaining in any given instance may be only a function of the particulars of that instance and hence predict nothing about effectiveness in other situations. But if effectiveness is general in some significant degree, generalizable findings as to its determiners, correlates, and consequences are more likely.

Results

The report of the results of this study will deal first with the reliability and generality of effectiveness in explaining over lessons; second, with the reliability and generality of pupils' mean ratings and attention reports over lessons; and third, with the correlations of effectiveness in explaining with class ratings of teacher competence and with measures of pupil attention.

Correlations among mean comprehension test scores. The means, standard deviations, Horst coefficients, and intercorrelations (zero-order, partial, and part correlations) of the mean comprehension scores of the classes participating in this study are shown in Table 9.1. The Horst coefficients ($r = .77$, $.76$, and $.76$) show that the three sets of mean scores differ from class to class with substantial reliability.

The three correlations among unadjusted mean scores indicate that classes with high mean scores on one test tended to get high mean scores on the other two. For example, the correlation between unadjusted mean scores on Yugoslavia and unadjusted mean scores on Thailand was $.63$, which indicated that the proportion of variance among the means on one test predictable from the means on the other test is $.40$.

The predictable variance of the mean scores on Yugoslavia and Thailand can be seen as having two components, one which is specific to the Yugoslavia and Thailand scores and another which is shared by all three—the Yugoslavia, Thailand, and Israel scores. The variance

TABLE 9.1

INTERCORRELATIONS AMONG TOTAL MEAN COMPREHENSION SCORES, UNADJUSTED AND ADJUSTED, ON YUGOSLAVIA, THAILAND, AND ISRAEL TESTS (N = 43 classes containing 10–31 students)

	Mean of Means	S.D. of Means	Horst Coeff.	(2) Thailand	(3) Israel	(4) Yugoslavia	(5) Thailand
(1) Unadjusted Yugoslavia Total	6.91	.92	.77	.63 [b]	.58 [b]	.81 [d]	.37 [d]
(2) Unadjusted Thailand Total	6.24	.76	.76		.52 [b]	.40 [d]	.84 [d]
(3) Unadjusted Israel Total	5.17	.81	.76			−.01 [d]	−.03 [d]
(4) Adjusted Yugoslavia Total [a]							.47 [c]
(5) Adjusted Thailand Total [a]							

[a] Adjusted for class mean score on Israel test. [b] Zero-order correlation. [c] Partial correlation. [d] Part correlation.

TABLE 9.2

CORRELATIONS BETWEEN UNADJUSTED AND ADJUSTED MEAN SCORES OF ODD-NUMBERED AND EVEN-NUMBERED STUDENTS ON THE YUGOSLAVIA, THAILAND, AND ISRAEL TESTS (N = 43)

	Mean of Means	S.D. of Means	Unadjusted Mean Scores						Adjusted Mean Scores			
			Odd-numbered			Even-numbered			Odd-numbered		Even-numbered	
			Yugo. (1)	Thai. (2)	Isr. (3)	Yugo. (4)	Thai. (5)	Isr. (6)	Yugo. (7)	Thai. (8)	Yugo. (9)	Thai. (10)
(1)	6.87	.94		.56	.52	.59	.34	.33	.86	.32	.49	.21
(2)	6.25	.92			.35	.39	.36	.06	.45	.87	.43	.44
(3)	5.19	.81				.44	.43	.58	.01	−.15	.14	.14
(4)	6.95	1.05					.57	.55	.43	.18	.83	.35
(5)	6.23	1.06						.65	.15	.16	.24	.84
(6)	5.28	1.00							.04	−.25	−.01	.14
(7)										.47	.48	.16
(8)											.38	.33
(9)												.38
(10)												

183

which is common to all three scores is presumably due in large part to between-class differences in mean student ability, since no variance attributable to teachers entered into the tape-recorded lecture on Israel.

The correlation between the adjusted mean comprehension scores on Yugoslavia and Thailand ($r = .47$) represents the relationship between the mean scores on Yugoslavia and Thailand which remains when the effects of student ability and other irrelevant factors measured by the comprehension scores for Israel have been removed. Of the total proportion of variance common to both tests (namely, .40), the proportion which is common to all three lessons is .18. The proportion common only to the Yugoslavia and Thailand lessons, presumed to be due to teacher effects, at least in large part, is .22.

The part correlations shown in Table 9.1 indicate the relationship between the adjusted and unadjusted means. The part correlations involving the same variable are high ($r = .81$ and .84) because the effects common to the live lessons and the lesson on Israel are not high. The part correlations between mean scores on Israel and adjusted mean scores on Thailand and Yugoslavia are, as expected, about zero, since all the variance in Yugoslavia and Thailand scores which is predictable from Israel scores had been removed.

The other part correlations, which are less meaningful, are those of unadjusted mean scores on Yugoslavia with adjusted mean scores on Thailand ($r = .37$), and unadjusted mean scores on Thailand with adjusted mean scores on Yugoslavia ($r = .40$).

The foregoing method of estimating the generality of the teacher's effectiveness, as measured by the adjusted mean comprehension score, may not completely eliminate covariance due to the pupils' ability, since the same pupils are involved in both measures of mean comprehension. That is, the adjustment on the basis of the Israel mean may not completely eliminate covariance irrelevant to a measure of the *teacher's* effectiveness. To obtain an estimate of generality less influenced by such irrelevant covariance, we made the following additional analysis. Each teacher's students were divided at random into odd-numbered and even-numbered students. Separate means were computed for the odd-numbered and even-numbered subclasses on the Yugoslavia, Thailand, and Israel tests. The means on the Yugoslavia and Thailand tests were adjusted so as to eliminate the effects of variance between classes on the Israel test. Then correlations were computed between the adjusted mean of the odd-numbered students on Yugoslavia and that of the even-numbered students on Thailand ($r = .16$), and vice versa ($r = .38$). (The full array of obtained r's is shown in Table 9.2.)

These two coefficients each represent the "reliability" of the adjusted mean score for a class half as large as those actually tested. To estimate from these coefficients the reliability of the adjusted means based on the entire class, the Spearman-Brown formula was applied. The adjusted r's obtained in this way were .28 and .55. The mean of the latter two r's is .41, which represents an estimate of the generality of teacher effectiveness over two different topics and two subsets of students whose differences in ability have been adjusted for. This estimate ($r = .41$) is lower than that obtained when the same students were involved ($r = .47$) because irrelevant covariance due to students was more effectively eliminated. The degree of generality reflected in this coefficient may be considered to characterize the teacher's effectiveness in explaining when both subject matter and pupils are varied.

These results indicate that the teacher's effectiveness in explaining had some consistency across different topics and different groups of pupils. The correlations were not high enough to indicate that the effectiveness of individual teachers can be measured with adequate reliability with only two lessons, ten-item tests, and classes of about 21 students. For such reliability, higher than about .40, additional lessons, longer tests, and larger classes would be needed.

Correlations among pupils' mean ratings and attention scores. The second question concerned the reliability and consistency of pupil ratings. We were interested in knowing the degree to which the ratings were reliable, consistent from occasion to occasion, and influenced by general tendencies of pupils to give high or low ratings.

The means, standard deviations, and Horst coefficients of the mean ratings on the Appraisal Guide are shown in Table 9.3. The Horst coefficients, averaging about .7, indicate that the mean ratings of the classes on the various items have substantial reliability; only three of the 27 r's are below .50.

Table 9.4 shows the zero-order and first-order partial correlations between the mean ratings of the Yugoslavia, Thailand, and Israel lessons on each Appraisal Guide item. Also shown are the r's between the self-reported attention scores for each of the three lessons. The zero-order r's between ratings of Yugoslavia and Thailand range from .60 to .83, except that for Item 7, which is .21. But the correlations between the mean ratings of these lessons with that of the Israel lesson are much lower, ranging from .00 to .36. The correlations show that students tend to rate their teacher similarly on the two lessons, but there is little or no tendency on their part to give the same rating to the taped lesson. For example, the correlation between the mean ratings of the Yugoslavia and Thailand lessons on Item 5, "Pacing the Lesson," is .62, which indicates that classes which rate the teacher high on the Yugo-

TABLE 9.3

MEANS AND STANDARD DEVIATIONS OF STUDENTS' RATINGS ON ATTENTION REPORT
AND ON EACH APPRAISAL GUIDE ITEM OF THE YUGOSLAVIA, THAILAND, AND ISRAEL LESSONS

	Yugoslavia			Thailand			Israel		
	Means	S.D.	Horst Coeff.	Means	S.D.	Horst Coeff.	Means	S.D.	Horst Coeff.
Appraisal Guide Items									
1. Clarity of Aims	3.69	0.55	.68	3.78	0.46	.55	2.96	0.60	.71
2. Organization of Lesson	4.07	0.50	.65	3.95	0.42	.69	3.37	0.57	.68
3. Beginning the Lesson	4.00	0.59	.36	3.83	0.59	.68	2.52	0.56	.56
4. Clarity of Presentation	4.26	0.53	.68	4.13	0.45	.71	3.04	0.56	.73
5. Pacing of Lesson	4.01	0.38	.82	3.88	0.40	.73	3.02	0.48	.63
6. Pupil Participation and Attention	4.29	0.74	.77	3.69	0.64	.75	2.05	0.54	.69
7. Ending the Lesson	3.54	0.77	.74	3.70	0.68	.52	2.87	0.56	.73
8. Teacher-Pupil Rapport	3.80	0.73	.67	3.67	0.66	.56	1.65	0.58	.70
9. Amount of Learning	3.56	0.59	.49	3.49	0.47	.43	2.38	0.58	.67
Attention Report	16.46	0.95		16.37	1.05		12.77	1.45	

slavia lesson tend to rate the teacher high on the Thailand lesson for this item. The mean ratings of the Yugoslavia and Israel lessons on Item 5 correlated only .06, and the mean ratings on the Thailand and Israel lessons correlated only —.02. When the mean ratings on Yugoslavia and Thailand are adjusted for the mean ratings on Israel, the correlation remains the same, .62, indicating that a negligible amount of their variance was associated specifically with the ratings of the Israel lesson. This pattern of relationships prevails for all the Appraisal Guide items. Such results are reassuring in indicating that the correlations between the Yugoslavia and Thailand ratings do not arise merely from consistent class tendencies to rate more or less favorably.

The mean scores of the students on the Attention Report for the three lessons correlate substantially ($r = .68, .47, .48$). The correlation between the mean scores on the Attention Report for the Yugoslavia and Thailand lessons, after the scores were adjusted for the mean score for attention to the Israel lesson, is .59. The latter r indicates that the level of attention attributable to the teachers is fairly consistent, even when variance due merely to consistent class tendencies, as measured by mean self-reported attention to the Israel lesson, has been partialled out.

The foregoing method, used to estimate the consistency of ratings and attention scores over lessons, employed an adjustment on the basis of ratings and attention scores on the Israel lesson. This method could be improved by eliminating additional irrelevant covariance due to students. The adjusted mean ratings by *odd*-numbered students on *Yugoslavia* were correlated with the adjusted mean ratings by *even*-numbered students on *Thailand;* similarly, the adjusted mean ratings by *even*-numbered students on *Yugoslavia* were correlated with the adjusted mean ratings by *odd*-numbered students on *Thailand*. The means of these two r's—corrected to obtain an estimate of the r's between means based on *all* students—are shown in column 5 of Table 9.4. These correlations, though still substantial, are somewhat lower than the correlations in column 4, since more irrelevant covariance has been removed.

The correlations in Table 9.4 can be taken to indicate that student ratings of teachers and pupil attention over two different topics and two subsets of students are fairly consistent, even when the effects of consistent rating tendencies on the part of the students in various classes have been removed.

Correlations of comprehension with ratings and with attention. The final question dealt with the correlations of the students' mean ratings and attention scores on the lessons with their mean comprehen-

TABLE 9.4

GENERALITY OF RATINGS OVER LESSONS: CORRELATIONS BETWEEN STUDENTS' MEAN RATINGS OF THREE LECTURES, ON EACH APPRAISAL GUIDE ITEM AND ON THE ATTENTION REPORT, UNADJUSTED AND ADJUSTED FOR MEAN RESPONSE TO ISRAEL LESSON

(N = 43 classes containing 10–31 students)

	Unadjusted			Adjusted	
	Yugo. vs. Thai.	Yugo. vs. Israel	Thai. vs. Israel	Yugo. vs. Thai.	Yugo. Odd vs. Thai. Even & Yugo. Even vs. Thai. Odd — Mean of 2 r's between Mean Ratings, Correlated for Full "Length" [a]
	(1)	(2)	(3)	(4)	(5)
Appraisal Guide Items					
1. Clarity of Aims	.60	.34	.16	.59	.49
2. Organization of Lesson	.64	.28	.00	.66	.45
3. Beginning the Lesson	.70	.15	.21	.70	.52
4. Clarity of Presentation	.65	.17	.24	.64	.56
5. Pacing of Lesson	.62	.06	−.02	.62	.47
6. Pupil Participation and Attention	.69	.14	.20	.68	.55
7. Ending the Lesson	.21	.22	.06	.21	.14
8. Teacher-Pupil Rapport	.83	.15	.09	.83	.73
9. Amount of Learning	.71	.36	.15	.72	.56
Attention Report	.68	.47	.48	.59	.52

[a] This mean r was computed by (a) obtaining the two r's between mean ratings each based on half the number of students, (b) using the z-transformation to obtain the mean of the two r's, and (c) adjusting this mean r for increased "length," or the total number of students (Guilford, 1954, p. 407, Formula 14.39).

sion scores on Yugoslavia, Thailand, and Israel. These correlations are shown in Table 9.5. Almost all the *r*'s are substantial for all three lessons, indicating that teachers whose classes achieved higher scores on the comprehension test also tended to receive more favorable ratings on each Appraisal Guide item. These correlations remained substantial even when general tendencies to achieve highly and rate favorably, as measured by performance on and ratings of the Israel lecture, were adjusted for. Thus, the correlation between mean ratings on Item 9, "Amount of Learning," and the students' mean achievement test scores, or what they actually learned, on Yugoslavia is .61, on Thailand is .59, and on Israel is .66. The first two correlations drop only slightly, to .59 and .56, respectively, when both the mean ratings and the mean comprehension scores are adjusted for the mean ratings and mean comprehension scores on Israel. Hence the relationship between what the students thought they learned and what they actually learned is not attributable to general attitude and achievement.

The mean ratings on Item 1, "Clarity of Aims," and Item 4, "Clarity of Presentation," correlate second and third most highly with the mean comprehension scores, in terms of the average *r* for both Yugoslavia and Thailand. The mean ratings on Item 5, "Pacing the Lesson," and Item 8, "Teacher-Pupil Rapport," correlate least with the comprehension scores.

The correlations between self-reported attention scores and mean comprehension scores are much the same ($r = .59, .57,$ and $.52$) for all three lectures. Adjustment by use of the scores for the Israel lesson has little effect on the other two correlations. This result again indicates that the correlation is not attributable to general tendencies to report attention and achieve comprehension in the same degree on all lessons.

The relationships of comprehension scores to mean ratings of the teacher and self-reported attention were also estimated by calculating the mean of four *r*'s—namely, the *r*'s between the following pairs of adjusted mean comprehension scores and adjusted mean ratings: (1) Yugoslavia comprehension of odd-numbered pupils *vs.* ratings by even-numbered pupils; (2) Yugoslavia comprehension of even-numbered pupils *vs.* ratings by odd-numbered pupils; (3) Thailand comprehension of odd-numbered pupils *vs.* ratings by even-numbered pupils; and (4) Thailand comprehension of even-numbered pupils *vs.* ratings by odd-numbered pupils (see column 6, Table 9.5). These correlations—corrected to obtain an estimate of the *r*'s between means based on *all* students—show the relationship of achievement to ratings and attention when covariance due to involvement of the same students has been removed.

TABLE 9.5

CORRELATIONS OF COMPREHENSION WITH RATINGS AND ATTENTION: CORRELATIONS BETWEEN STUDENTS' MEAN RATINGS OF LECTURES, ON APPRAISAL GUIDE ITEMS AND ON ATTENTION REPORT, UNADJUSTED AND ADJUSTED, AND THEIR MEAN COMPREHENSION SCORES, UNADJUSTED AND ADJUSTED

(N = 43 classes containing 10–31 students)

	Correlation of Unadjusted Mean Rating with Unadjusted Mean Comprehension Score			Correlation of Adjusted Mean Rating with Adjusted Mean Comprehension Score		
	Yugoslavia (1)	Thailand (2)	Israel (3)	Yugoslavia (4)	Thailand (5)	Mean of 4 r's Correlated for Full Length [a] (6)
Appraisal Guide Items						
1. Clarity of Aims	.64	.56	.47	.50	.39	.36
2. Organization of Lesson	.48	.48	.23	.24	.34	.27
3. Beginning the Lesson	.53	.41	.33	.46	.19	.28
4. Clarity of Presentation	.60	.44	.43	.53	.31	.35
5. Pacing of Lesson	.32	.28	.10	.21	.11	.17
6. Pupil Participation and Attention	.44	.23	.41	.47	.15	.31
7. Ending the Lesson	.24	.39	.34	.10	.35	.23
8. Teacher-Pupil Rapport	.46	.25	.02	.32	.10	.24
9. Amount of Learning	.61	.59	.66	.59	.56	.52
Attention Report	.59	.57	.52	.57	.55	.51

[a] Mean of the following four r's: (1) adjusted mean comprehension scores of odd-numbered pupils on Yugo. vs. adjusted mean ratings by even-numbered pupils on Yugo.; (2) odd-numbered mean comprehension scores on Thai. vs. even-numbered mean ratings on Thai.; (3) even-numbered mean comprehension scores on Yugo. vs. odd-numbered mean ratings on Yugo.; (4) even-numbered mean comprehension scores on Thai. vs. odd-numbered mean ratings on Thai. Each r based on half the students was adjusted for full "length" (see Guilford, 1954, p. 407, Formula 14.39) and then the four adjusted r's were averaged, using the z-transformation.

190

The most striking results in columns 4, 5, and 6 of Table 9.5 are the consistently positive correlations between the adjusted achievement scores and student ratings. The ratings have about the degree of correlation with achievement that should be expected for assessments of components of teaching performance. These correlations indicate that the specific behaviors defined by the Appraisal Guide are relevant to teacher effectiveness in explaining as measured by adjusted student achievement. The correlations are not so high, however, as to eliminate room for improvement by defining even more relevant behaviors. Some hints as to what these might be can be seen in results of Study II.

Discussion

On the question of generality, the foregoing results warrant a positive conclusion. Generality was indicated by the correlation of .47 between the mean comprehension scores on one lesson and those on another, after adjustment for the mean ability of the students. When corrected split-half r's were obtained across topics (the adjusted means being based on random halves of the students), they averaged .41. Such generality indicates that the teacher's effectiveness in explaining does not depend entirely on the particular lesson being taught on a particular day to a particular group of students.

Beyond this finding, the present study demonstrated a method for estimating the degree to which various dimensions of the teacher's performance, as measured by mean student ratings, correlate with the teacher's effectiveness, as measured by mean student achievement. The method entails adjusting both the mean rating and the mean achievement for student characteristics, as measured by their ratings of, and achievement on, a lesson taught without teacher variance, i.e., a tape-recorded lesson. The method also entails splitting each class into random halves to reduce irrelevant covariance due to basing two means on the same students. Estimated in this way, the r's between students' mean ratings and attention, on the one hand, and their comprehension, on the other, were positive and substantial, ranging from about .2 to .5.

Study II. The Modality and Validity of Cues to Lecture Effectiveness

W. R. UNRUH

Teacher behavior can be recorded in various forms, or types, of protocol: typewritten transcripts of lessons, audio-taped lessons, video-taped lessons, or combinations of these. Which of these kinds of record provides the basis for the most valid ratings of teacher effectiveness? Does the accumulation of cues, by involving additional sensory and perceptual modalities, improve the validity of judgments made about teachers?

Further: What are the correlates of effective explaining behavior? If it is found that raters can accurately judge teachers over all on a criterion of effectiveness, what are the bases on which their judgments are made? For example, are such rated characteristics as the teacher's warmth, vocal qualities, and pre-planning related to the teacher's effectiveness?

This investigation had three major parts: (*a*) an initial "postdiction rating study" to determine the relative effectiveness of seven kinds of protocols; (*b*) the "AV study"—similar to the initial postdiction rating study except that it was based on the use of audio-video protocols only; and (*c*) a study of correlates of effective explaining behavior as rated on a free-response instrument and a check list of teacher characteristics.

Comparing the Protocols

In relation to the first question, seven types of protocols were compared in order to determine which type yielded the most accurate prediction of teacher effectiveness. The teachers' lectures were available in the form of typewritten transcripts, audio tapes, and video tapes, and the seven types of protocol were prepared from various combinations of these records.

The initial postdiction rating study. Four teacher-lessons were chosen randomly from each quarter of the distribution of adjusted mean comprehension scores on the Yugoslavia lesson, and four were similarly chosen from the Thailand group of lectures. Each of these lectures was then rated by eight twelfth-grade high school students randomly selected from a pool of 112 such students. Each group of eight raters was assigned to one of seven different protocols and to one of the two subject matters. Thus, different groups of eight judges each were assigned to the following seven kinds of protocol:

> *T*—Typewritten transcript only
> *A*—Audio record only
> *V*—Video record
> *TA*—Typewritten transcript plus audio record
> *TV*—Typewritten transcript plus video record
> *AV*—Audio record plus video record
> *TAV*—Typewritten transcript plus video record
>   plus audio record

Each student rater read the article on which the lesson was based, and took the ten-item test based on that article. Then the raters were exposed to the complete lessons of the four teachers in the type of protocol and in the subject-matter group to which they had been assigned. Following this they were exposed to a second six-minute portion of each of these lessons. Then they were asked to rate each teacher on a scale from one to ten by postdicting the mean score they thought each teacher's class had obtained on the ten-item criterion test. The accuracy of this rating, when correlated with the actual mean scores made by the students of the four teachers, was used to evaluate the validity of the protocol.

The data derived from the initial postdiction rating study were analyzed in three different ways. First, rank-order correlation coefficients between the actual teacher ranks and the rater-assigned ranks were determined for each rater. The results of this analysis are presented in Table 9.6. The median rank-order correlation coefficient for the AV protocol group was .6 for the Yugoslavia sample and .7 for the Thailand sample. The median correlation coefficients for all other protocols were either negative or near zero.

TABLE 9.6

RANK-ORDER CORRELATION COEFFICIENTS BETWEEN POSTDICTED AND
ACTUAL RANKS FOR FOUR YUGOSLAVIA AND FOUR THAILAND
TEACHER-LESSONS

($N = 4$ teacher-lesson protocols per rater)

Protocol	Raters								Median
	1	2	3	4	5	6	7	8	
				Yugoslavia					
T	.0	−.6	−.6	−.6	−.6	−.8	−.8	−1.0	−.6
A	.8	.4	.4	.2	.0	.0	−.2	− .4	.1
V	.8	.8	.4	.2	.2	.2	−.2	− .4	.2
TA	.6	−.2	−.4	−.8	−.8	−.8	−.8	−1.0	−.8
TV	1.0	.8	.4	.2	−.4	−.4	−.4	− .8	−.1
AV	.8	.8	.6	.6	.6	.2	.0	− .8	.6
TAV	1.0	.8	.4	.4	.2	−.4	−.4	− .6	.3
				Thailand					
T	.4	.2	.0	.0	−.4	−.4	−.4	− .4	−.2
A	1.0	.4	.4	.2	.0	.0	−.4	− .4	.1
V	1.0	.8	.4	.2	.2	.0	−.2	− .4	.2
TA	.4	.4	.2	.0	−.4	−.6	−.8	− .8	−.2
TV	.8	.4	.4	.2	.2	.2	−.4	− .8	.2
AV	.8	.8	.8	.8	.6	.4	.4	− .6	.7
TAV	.8	.4	.4	.2	.0	−.2	−.4	− .4	.1

Second, an analysis of variance was carried out to determine within each protocol (*a*) whether there was a significant difference among the ratings for each of the four teacher-lessons and (*b*) whether the mean ratings increased monotonically as the actual teacher scores increased. Variances significant at the .05 level were found among teacher-lessons for both content groups, and the mean ratings did increase monotonically as actual scores increased.

Third, accuracy-of-rating scores were computed as the sum of squared differences between the actual teacher ranks and the rater-assigned ranks, and these scores were subjected to analysis of variance. Differences in accuracy among protocols significant at the .01 level were found for Yugoslavia, and at the .08 level for Thailand. Tests of paired means, however, showed that *AV* was significantly different ($p < .01$) only from *T* and *TA* in the Yugoslavia group and only from *T* ($p < .10$) in the Thailand group. In view of the findings noted above, and because the accuracy of ratings based on the *AV* protocol was highest in both subject-matter groups, it appeared reasonable to conclude that the *AV* protocol was the best basis on which to collect further data.

The AV study. An additional 60 judges (30 assigned randomly to the four lessons on Yugoslavia, and 30 to the four Thailand lessons) then rated the *AV* protocols. The ratings by these 30 judges were pooled with those of the eight judges used in the two *AV* groups in the initial rating study, thus providing responses from a total of 38 raters in each *AV* group.

These ratings were analyzed in the same way as those in the initial postdiction rating study, except that no comparison between protocols was made. The median rank-order correlations between actual and postdicted ranks were .56 and .55 for the Yugoslavia and Thailand samples, respectively. *F*-ratios significant beyond the .001 level were obtained for differences in mean rating assigned each of the four teachers, and the postdicted means increased monotonically as the actual means increased, with the exception that Teachers 1 and 2 of the Yugoslavia sample and Teachers 2 and 3 of the Thailand sample were reversed. Apparently, the twelfth-grade students who served as judges could rate the teachers with reasonable validity.

Correlates of Explaining Effectiveness

The second purpose of the study was to determine correlates of effective explaining as perceived by the judges. In view of the findings noted above, only the data derived from the *AV* protocols were analyzed in this phase of the study.

The free response study. After the judges had supplied their over-all rating for each lesson, they were asked to write on a blank form at least six adjectives or phrases describing strengths or weaknesses of the teacher, the lesson, or the way in which the raters had made their judgments. Analysis of the resulting 1,768 responses made it possible to assign responses either to one of 17 positive categories or to one of 18 negative categories.

The discriminatory value of each category was determined according to whether it showed a significant difference among teacher-lessons in the frequency of responses, and whether there was a substantial correlation between these frequencies and the actual teacher scores. Whether the first requirement was met was tested by means of the chi-square one-sample test, as indicated in Tables 9.7 and 9.8. Whether the second requirement was met was determined in terms of

TABLE 9.7

CHI-SQUARE TESTS OF SIGNIFICANCE AND PEARSON PRODUCT-MOMENT CORRELATION COEFFICIENTS FOR POSITIVE FREE-RESPONSE ITEMS

Category Name	Yugoslavia χ^2	r^a	Thailand χ^2	r^a
1. Voice and Speech Qualities	.04	—.57	3.76	.99
2. Relevance and Emphasis	10.46 *	—.19	7.60	.79
3. Coverage	3.43	.98	9.86 *	.52
4. Achievement of Aims	5.73	.04	.81	.78
5. Gesture and Movement	.33	.54	5.20	.64
6. Use of Visual Aids	7.71	—.53	9.36 *	.51
7. Organization and Planning	24.85 **	.95	2.88	.88
8. Knowledge of Material	7.23	.72	12.87 **	.86
9. Level of Speech or Vocabulary	10.57 *	.69	3.92	.93
10A. Sense of Humor	8.40 *	—.45	25.73 **	—.17
B. Enthusiasm, Vitality, Energy, etc.	3.47	—.70	22.80 **	.25
C. Interest and Involvement in the Topic	3.00	—.20	24.00 **	.27
D. Confidence, Poise, etc.	6.07	—.44	11.33 **	—.20
E. Friendliness, Warmth, Casual Manner, etc.	3.88	—.48	17.00 **	—.14
11. Interesting	2.25	—.56	10.42 *	.78
12. Rate of Delivery	1.56	—.31	.00	.00
13. Use of Outline	28.66 **	.97	7.16	.26
14. Use of Examples and Illustrations	.50	—.38	2.33	—.79
15. Good Introduction	10.57 *	.41	.25	—.03
16. Good Conclusion	3.33	.60	3.80	.70
17. Unclassified	2.86	.37	2.21	.94

* $p < .05$ ** $p < .01$
^{a} $N = 4$ teacher-lessons

TABLE 9.8

CHI-SQUARE TESTS OF SIGNIFICANCE AND PEARSON PRODUCT-MOMENT
CORRELATION COEFFICIENTS FOR NEGATIVE FREE-RESPONSE ITEMS

Category Name	Yugoslavia		Thailand	
	χ^2	r [a]	χ^2	r [a]
1. Voice and Speech Qualities	2.89	—.19	3.45	—.41
2. Relevance and Emphasis	1.31	—.74	3.73	—.67
3. Coverage	.00	.00	6.44	—.45
4. Achievement of Aims	5.00	.09	10.00 *	—.64
5. Gesture and Movement	.78	.81	7.45	.68
6. Use of Visual Aids	5.87	—.93	6.00	.31
7. Organization and Planning	14.15 **	—.82	12.68 **	—.89
8. Knowledge of Material	25.24 **	—.93	19.66 **	—.88
9. Level of Speech or Vocabulary	15.02 **	—.40	2.57	.89
10A. Lacks Sense of Humor	2.00	.75	+	.28
B. Lacks Enthusiasm, Vitality, Energy, etc.	5.66	—.06	9.73 *	—.75
C. Lacks Interest and Involvement in the Topic	7.54	.82	2.20	—.68
D. Lacks Confidence, Poise, etc.	10.48 *	—.98	11.94 **	.66
E. Lack of Friendliness, Warmth, Casual Manner, etc.	3.88	.08	5.00	—.71
11. Uninteresting, Boring	11.00 *	.42	33.23 **	—.83
12. Rate of Delivery	.38	.31	12.40 **	.08
13. Use of Outline	+	—.73	+	—.03
14. Use of Examples and Illustrations	+	.00	+	.00
15. Poor Introduction	+	.54	+	.00
16. Poor Conclusion	+	.80	6.80	—.86
17. Too Many "Uh"s	3.60	—.68	+	—.79
18. Unclassified	3.14	—.52	1.06	—.35

* $p < .05$ ** $p < .01$

NOTE: Where the number of responses to an item was less than two, no χ^2 difference could be determined. This is indicated in the table by a plus sign $(+)$.

[a] $N = 4$ teacher-lessons.

r's between the frequency of rater responses and the actual teacher scores, also presented in these tables. In view of the exploratory nature of this study, it was decided that a category would be accepted as having discriminatory value if the chi-square test showed differences in frequency of a free-response category significant at the .05 level, and if the correlation between free-response frequencies and actual teacher scores was above ± .40.

Using these bases for choosing categories for discussion, and looking at the Yugoslavia and Thailand responses separately, one can discern the following general picture. The positive free responses of student raters in the Yugoslavia group portray the good teacher as one who:

1. was organized and had planned well,
2. spoke at an appropriate cognitive level,
3. was serious and did not openly display a sense of humor,
4. had and used an outline effectively, and
5. had a good introduction in the sense that he stated objectives clearly and provided adequate background information.

Positive Categories 3, 5, 7, 8, 9, and 16, although not all of them discriminated among the four teacher-lessons on the basis of the chi-square tests, and therefore not all of them fully met the requirements for validity stated above, nevertheless correlated highly with the criterion scores across both teacher-lesson samples and may have some value in discriminating between good and poor lecturers.

Taken as a whole, the *consistent* results for the free-response categories suggest several conclusions which may be useful in further teacher effectiveness studies. First, as far as these judges are concerned, the most important aspects of good teaching appear to involve teacher activities related primarily to preparation and presentation. Thus they rate highest those teachers who plan well, are well organized and prepared, speak at an appropriate cognitive level, use an outline— which may be related to planning—and cover the material well. These teacher activities are basically cognitive in nature. That is, they involve mainly matters which describe the teachers' pre-planning and application of strategies aimed at structuring lesson materials so as to make the subject matter meaningful. Even the references to poise and self-confidence, though not consistently related to good teaching in this study, can be construed as a sign that the teacher is sure of his material and presentation. It may be, of course, that many of the responses made by the raters are based on the appearance of the teacher—that is, he may not really be better prepared or organized, but he appears to be sure and presents his material in a businesslike and efficient manner.

Second, items relating to personality variables and vocal quality do not discriminate consistently in this context. According to the positive free responses made by the Yugoslavia raters to Category 10A, the better teacher is serious rather than humorous. The only other reference to what may be non-cognitive aspects of the presentation are the references to enthusiasm and vitality (Category 10B of the Thailand group), and the references to Negative Category 11, which describes the good teachers as boring in the Yugoslavia sample and the poor teachers as boring in the Thailand sample. This reversal is difficult to explain. It may be that this factor does not discriminate between good and poor teachers, or it may result from the raters' viewing a businesslike presentation as boring but still giving a high general rating to the teacher because of other positive characteristics.

The check list study. In this phase of the study, the judges were exposed once more to each of the lessons for a six-minute period and were asked to rate each teacher on a series of 27 seven-point bipolar scales consisting of adjectives and phrases selected from the research literature because of their presumed relevance to teacher effectiveness.

An analysis of variance was carried out for each of the 27 scales. Pearson *r*'s between scale ratings and actual teacher scores were also computed.

The results of these analyses appear in Tables 9.9 and 9.10 and indicate that the descriptions of good and poor explainers, by means of these scales, agreed in general with those provided by the raters' free responses. Scales judged consistently valid by the procedures described above for both teacher-lesson samples indicated that the good teachers were skillful in presenting the material, made the content of the lesson clear, knew the subject matter well, and had apparently done a good job of planning the lesson. The opposite was true of the poor teachers.

Again, these findings suggest that the good teacher is seen by these raters as the one who is verbally and cognitively in control of the situation. No relationships consistent across content groups were found between non-cognitive variables and the achievement criterion.

Implications

The findings of this study suggest ideas and questions on which to base further research.

1. The results of this study indicated that the AV protocol was the best source of cues for rating the teacher's effectiveness in explaining when such effectiveness was measured on the basis of student achievement. One reason for this finding may have been that the AV presentation was the one most similar to the type of classroom presentation with which the judges were familiar and therefore capable of evaluating. This finding suggests that in studies where ratings of teacher effectiveness are to be made, AV records should be used in preference to other records of behavior, such as audio tape recordings and typewritten transcripts. Yet it should be noted that the ratings made were over-all effectiveness ratings; and the researcher, in deciding which record of behavior to use, would need to decide whether the variables

TABLE 9.9

F-RATIOS AND LEVELS OF SIGNIFICANCE FOR 27 SEVEN-ITEM SCALES
FOR FOUR YUGOSLAVIA AND FOUR THAILAND TEACHER-LESSONS

Scale No.	Scale Description	Yugoslavia F-ratio	Thailand F-ratio
1.	businesslike *vs.* slipshod	12.87 **	25.99 **
2.	clear *vs.* obscure, vague	7.97 **	14.13 **
3.	dynamic *vs.* phlegmatic	12.63 **	2.87 *
4.	emphatic *vs.* unemphatic	12.28 **	1.93
5.	enthusiastic *vs.* unenthusiastic	17.97 **	6.25 **
6.	energetic *vs.* lethargic	30.08 **	10.57 **
7.	friendly *vs.* unfriendly, aloof	27.13 **	6.50 **
8.	fluent in expression *vs.* halting in expression	3.49 *	8.39 **
9.	humorous *vs.* dull	31.97 **	4.94 **
10.	interesting *vs.* boring	13.02 **	6.12 **
11.	imaginative *vs.* unimaginative	18.43 **	2.53
12.	interested *vs.* uninterested	12.21 **	2.35
13.	poised *vs.* awkward	1.29	11.33 **
14.	positive attitude *vs.* negative attitude	6.35 **	1.59
15.	stimulating *vs.* dull, unstimulating	10.38 **	2.56
16.	skillful *vs.* inept, unskillful	15.78 **	11.88 **
17.	warm *vs.* cold	13.75 **	4.68 **
18.	knows and understands subject *vs.* does not know and understand subject	10.56 **	13.42 **
19.	lesson is well planned *vs.* lesson is not well planned	11.11 **	14.45 **
20.	English expression good *vs.* English expression not good	.61	14.74 **
21.	states objectives of lesson clearly *vs.* does not state objectives of lesson clearly	2.06	7.45 **
22.	makes relationships clear *vs.* does not make relationships clear	3.70 *	4.09 *
23.	clearly indicates when moving from one topic to another *vs.* does not clearly indicate when moving from one topic to another	2.75 *	3.64 *
24.	makes effective use of voice *vs.* does not make effective use of voice	9.03 **	2.34
25.	points out clearly what should be learned *vs.* does not point out clearly what should be learned	4.03 **	2.98 *
26.	gives adequate amount of detail *vs.* does not give adequate amount of detail	1.46	2.07
27.	summarizes and reviews frequently *vs.* does not summarize and review frequently	1.47	2.37

* $p < .05$ ** $p < .01$

with which he is concerned could best be measured via such a record. In other words, which protocol is best may depend on the variable being investigated.

2. The curriculum materials used in this study were more or less typical of the social studies; research is needed to determine whether the characteristics which discriminated among good and poor teachers

TABLE 9.10

PEARSON PRODUCT-MOMENT CORRELATION COEFFICIENTS AND ESTIMATES
OF MONOTONIC RELATIONSHIPS FOR FOUR YUGOSLAVIA AND FOUR
THAILAND TEACHER-LESSONS

Scale No.	Scale Description	Yugoslavia ($N = 38$)		Thailand ($N = 38$)	
		r	Mon.[a]	r	Mon.[a]
1.	businesslike *vs.* slipshod	.20	+	.55 **	+
2.	clear *vs.* obscure, vague	.35 *	+	.45 **	+
3.	dynamic *vs.* phlegmatic	.32 *	+	−.18	−
4.	emphatic *vs.* unemphatic	.32 *	+	−.15	−
5.	enthusiastic *vs.* unenthusiastic	.35 *	+	−.33 *	−
6.	energetic *vs.* lethargic	.42 **	+	−.35 *	−
7.	friendly *vs.* unfriendly, aloof	.07	−	−.28	−
8.	fluent in expression *vs.* halting in expression	.14	+	.39 *	+
9.	humorous *vs.* dull	.05	−	−.20	−
10.	interesting *vs.* boring	.29	+	.02	−
11.	imaginative *vs.* unimaginative	.22	−	.03	−
12.	interested *vs.* uninterested	.27	+	−.16	−
13.	poised *vs.* awkward	−.03	−	.43 **	+
14.	positive attitude *vs.* negative attitude	.21	+	.05	−
15.	stimulating *vs.* dull, unstimulating	.24	+	−.02	−
16.	skillful *vs.* inept, unskillful	.40 **	+	.43 **	+
17.	warm *vs.* cold	.04	−	−.19	−
18.	knows and understands subject *vs.* does not know and understand it	.28	+	.44 **	+
19.	lesson is well planned *vs.* lesson is not well planned	.26	+	.49 **	+
20.	English expression good *vs.* English expression not good	.05	+	.47 **	+
21.	states objectives of lesson clearly *vs.* does not state objectives clearly	.06	+	.35 *	+
22.	makes relationships clear *vs.* does not make relationship clear	.21	+	.25	+
23.	clearly indicates when moving from one topic to another *vs.* does not clearly indicate	−.02	−	.23	+
24.	makes effective use of voice *vs.* does not make effective use of voice	.32 *	+	−.02	−
25.	points out clearly what should be learned *vs.* does not point out clearly what should be learned	.02	+	.21	+
26.	gives adequate amount of detail *vs.* does not give adequate detail	.09	+	.16	+
27.	summarizes and reviews frequently *vs.* does not summarize and review frequently	.05	−	.01	−
		Multiple $R = .69$		Multiple $R = .74$	

* $p < .05$ ** $p < .01$

[a] Monotonic relationship as described above is indicated here by a plus sign
(+). A minus sign (−) indicates that such a relationship was not found with
reference to the means of the rater-assigned scores.

in this study would also hold for other subject matters. Similarly, research at different grade levels is needed. The effects of various teacher characteristics may interact with subject matter and grade level.

3. The dependent variable against which significant characteristics of explaining behavior were reflected in this study was the adjusted mean achievement scores of the classes of the teachers in each sample. While this was probably a satisfactory first approximation for establishing a criterion, further studies might do well to test this criterion more extensively. One approach might be to play the video-taped lessons of a group of teachers to a number of groups of pupils assigned at random to each teacher-lesson. Pupils, especially at the higher grade levels, may be able to adjust to certain aspects of their own teacher's behavior. But playbacks to pupils who had never before been exposed to the teacher would help to control for such accommodation and thus enhance the validity of the criterion measure.

4. Further research might also be directed at refining the dependent variable used in this study. "Explaining," used here as a "microcriterion of effectiveness," is still a broad criterion. It may be desirable to break down the explaining process into smaller units and to measure the effectiveness of teachers in handling these smaller aspects of the task.

5. The perceived characteristics of teachers shown in this study to be related to explaining effectiveness are similarly broad in nature. These characteristics should be defined operationally in behavioral terms and then revalidated.

Study III. Objectively Measured Behavioral Predictors of Effectiveness in Explaining

BARAK ROSENSHINE

This investigation was aimed at determining objectively measured teacher behaviors that discriminate between more and less successful explanations of social studies material.

The variables investigated were the stimuli received by the pupils, that is, the verbal and non-verbal behaviors of teachers while they lectured. For some aspects of the lectures, a grammar of objective terms already existed which could be used to categorize the characteristics of the lectures. For example, a number of existing grammars can be used to categorize the length and type of individual words or independent clauses. But, for most of the aspects of the lectures, it was necessary to construct an analytic grammar by selecting significant variables which had been developed in other kinds of investigations and adapting them to the process of teaching and giving explanations by lecture.

The variables were developed from 27 categories derived from the research in four areas: linguistics, instructional set, experimental studies of instruction, and multivariate studies of the behavioral correlates of teaching effectiveness.

Thirty lectures were selected for investigation. Five high-scoring and five low-scoring lectures, as measured by the students' residual mean achievement scores on the Yugoslavia test, comprised a "hypothesis group." Another five high-scoring and five low-scoring lectures on Yugoslavia comprised a "validation group." The five most and the five least effective teachers in explaining the material on Thailand were used as a "cross-validation group." The frequency of occurrence of each variable was first tabulated using the lectures in the hypothesis group. Those variables that discriminated at the .15 level between the high-scoring and low-scoring lectures in the hypothesis group were then counted in the remaining two groups. The significance of the discrimination was tested by means of a two-way analysis of variance in which the hypothesis, validation, and cross-validation groups formed the columns, and the high-scoring and low-scoring lectures formed the rows.

Results

Linguistic categories. The linguistic categories were developed primarily from the research on readability. The most frequently consulted references were the summaries of research by Chall (1958) and Klare (1963) and the factor analytic studies by Brinton and Danielson (1958) and Stolurow and Newman (1959).

The 43 variables investigated in this area were developed from nine categories: (1) *word length;* (2) *total number of relevant words;* (3) *length and structure of independent clause units;* (4) *prepositional phrases;* (5) *readability estimate*—the readability of the lectures as determined by the multiple-regression formula developed by Flesch; (6) *personal references*—counts of first and second person pronouns; (7) *negative sentences*—counts of sentences containing "not" modifying the verb, "not" modifying a noun, and/or "not only" or an equivalent phrase; (8) *passive verbs*—counts of independent and/or dependent clauses containing passive verbs; and (9) *awkward and fragmented sentences*—counts of sentences which depart from usual sentence construction and/or phrases which lack a subject or a verb but which add information (e.g., "Now to foreign affairs").

Variables in four of these nine categories discriminated between high-scoring and low-scoring lectures in the hypothesis group, but none of the differences in frequencies was significant across the three groups. For the hypothesis group *only*, the high-scoring lectures contained fewer syllables per word, independent clause units with more words and clauses, and more prepositional phrases. They also contained more words rated as directly or indirectly relevant to the criterion questions.

Instructional set. The next two categories were developed from the experimental research on the influence of pre-instructional procedures, or instructional set, upon the effects of subsequent presentations. The most frequently consulted references were the research of Ausubel (1963), Hovland, Lumsdaine, and Sheffield (1949), May and Lumsdaine (1958), Allen (1955), and Rothkopf (1966).

Thirty-seven variables in two categories were investigated. One category, (10) *structuring sets,* contained variables which might resemble "discriminating advance organizers," that is, words or phrases which indicate that the speaker is attempting to clarify distinctions between new and previously learned material. The other category, (11) *focusing or arousing sets,* contained variables which might identify phrases designed to arouse or focus attention. None of the variables in these two categories discriminated between the high and low lectures in the hypothesis group.

Presentational categories. Nine "presentational" categories were developed from a broad class of experimentally tested variables which might be related to explaining ability. The most frequently consulted references were reviews by Travers *et al.* (1964), Lumsdaine (1963), and Petrie (1963). These were the nine categories: (12) *use of rule-and-example pattern,* (13) *number of examples,* (14) *organization of topics,* (15) *use of enumeration,* (16) *movement and gesture,* (17) *breaks in speech,* (18) *use of maps and chalkboard,* (19) *rate of speech,* and (20) *repetition and redundancy.*

Variables in three of these categories discriminated between the high and low lectures in the hypothesis group, but not across the three groups. In the hypothesis group only, the high-scoring teachers spoke faster, used fewer pauses and verbalized breaks, used the chalkboard less frequently, and used maps more often. They also appeared to use more between-sentence repetition, but this category was dropped because it was impossible to develop a reliable coding system for repetition or review.

Variables in two categories—rule-and-example pattern, and movement and gesture—discriminated between the high and low lectures across the three groups. These findings will be discussed below.

Multivariate studies of teaching behaviors. The categories studied in this fourth area were developed from research on the relationship between specific teaching behaviors and measures of adjusted student gain. Representative studies are those by Medley and Mitzel (1959), Flanders (1965), Spaulding (1963), Bellack *et al.* (1966), and Soar (1966).

Five categories based upon the significant findings of these investigators were selected for investigation, but variables in none of these categories appeared in sufficient frequency to be counted. The categories were: (21) *verbal hostility*, (22) *non-verbal affect*, (23) *reference to pupil's interests*, (24) *expansion of pupils' ideas*, and (25) *ratio of acceptance and praise to criticism*.

The frequency of occurrence of variables in two additional categories was counted: (26) *conditional words* and (27) *explaining links*. The frequency of conditional words such as "but," "however," and "although" did not discriminate between the high and low lectures in the hypothesis group. The frequency of explaining links was significant across the three groups and will be discussed below.

Discussion

Variables in 21 of the 27 categories occurred with sufficient frequency to merit counting and could be reliably counted. Variables in ten of these categories discriminated between the high and low lectures in the hypothesis group, and variables in three of these ten categories discriminated across all three groups. The latter three, consistently discriminating, categories, as shown in Table 9.11, were rule-and-example pattern, explaining links, and gesture and movement.

Gesture and movement. Gesture was defined as movement of the arms, head, or trunk, and movement was defined as lateral (left and right) movement of the teacher from one fixed place to another. When the unit of measure was per lecture, the high groups had more gestures, seconds of gesture, movements, and seconds of movement than the low groups ($p < .05$). Three of these variables were significant or nearly significant when the unit was per minute, and one (movement) was nearly significant ($p < .06$) when the unit of measure was per hundred words.

UNIVERSITÉ DE MONCTON

À:

DE:

RE:

DATE:

MEMO

COMMUNICATION INTERNE

TABLE 9.11

THE DISCRIMINATING POWER OF VARIABLES WITHIN 21 CATEGORIES

Area	Category
Linguistic Categories	* 1. Word length
	* 2. Word relevance
	* 3. Independent clause length and structure
	* 4. Prepositional phrases
	5. Readability estimate
	6. Personal references
	7. Negative sentences
	8. Passive verbs
	9. Awkward and fragmented sentences
Instructional Set	10. Structuring sets
	11. Focusing or arousing sets
Presentational Categories	** 12. Rule-and-example pattern
	13. Number of examples
	14. Organization of topics
	15. Use of enumeration
	** 16. Gesture and movement
	* 17. Breaks in speech
	* 18. Use of map and chalkboard
	* 19. Rate of speech
	20. Repetition and redundancy
Multivariate Studies	21. Verbal hostility
	22. Non-verbal affect
	23. Reference to pupils' interests
	24. Expansion of pupils' ideas
	25. Ratio of acceptance and praise to criticism
	** 26. Explaining links
	27. Conditional words

* Variables in this category discriminated between high and low lectures in the hypothesis group, but *not* across the three groups.
** Variables in this category discriminated between the high and low lectures across the three groups.

These gestures and movements may have the effect of arousing or focusing attention. However, verbal variables taken singly and in combination which might have been classified as attention-arousing variables did not discriminate between the high and low lectures in the hypothesis group. These verbal variables included phrases stating the importance of material or recalling material, cognitive reversal, and references to problems and conflict.

Rule-example-rule pattern of discourse. The term *rule* refers to the use of a summary statement before or after a series of examples. The high lectures contained a higher frequency ($p < .01$) and percentage ($p < .01$) of patterns which contained two rules, one before *and* one after a series of examples. The low lectures had a higher frequency ($p < .01$) and percentage ($p < .01$) of patterns with a single rule only before the examples; the low lectures also had a significantly higher frequency ($p < .01$) and percentage ($p < .01$) of sequences with a single rule given either before *or* after the examples.

These results may indicate that a pattern of explanation which opens with a structuring statement, follows it with details, and concludes by restating the structuring statement is more effective than other patterns. But it is difficult to generalize this finding to the analysis of written or spoken prose because it is difficult to distinguish between examples and statements of fact. In this study, we were able to identify examples only by referring to the original *Atlantic* articles and selecting as examples those statements of fact which were preceded or followed by an organizing principle. If we had not had the original articles as references, the results of coding might well have been much less consistent.

An extension of this idea might be the proposition that a paragraph would be more effective if it began and ended with a topic sentence. But we were unable to identify topic sentences in the lectures studied in this investigation.

Explaining links. The concept of a cognitive process labeled *explaining* was developed from the research of Bellack and his associates (1966), who developed their work in this area from the research of B. O. Smith. The explaining process was defined by Bellack as consisting of statements describing relations between objects, events, or principles, or statements reporting either cause and effect or comparison and contrast. Words such as "because" and questions containing "why" were cited as indicators of explanation.

In this investigation the frequency of explanation was assessed by counting explaining links, that is, prepositions and conjunctions which indicated the cause, result, means, or purposes of an event or idea. Words and phrases such as "because," "in order to," "if . . . then," "therefore," and "consequently" were counted, as well as specified instances of words and phrase such as "since," "by," and "through." The high lectures contained more of these words ($p < .01$) in each of three units of measure: per lecture, per minute, and per hundred words.

Words such as these explaining links may function to link phrases either within or between sentences so that a phrase or clause containing an explaining link elaborates and expands upon another phrase or clause. This special linkage may be illustrated by the following three sentences, which are almost identical:

The Chinese dominate Bangkok's economy, *and* they are a threat.
The Chinese dominate Bangkok's economy, *but* they are a threat.
The Chinese dominate Bangkok's economy; *therefore* they are a threat.

The third sentence may be the easiest to comprehend because it contains the explaining link "therefore" instead of "and" or "but." Different types of explaining links also seem to be interchangeable, as in the following three examples:

The Chinese dominate Bangkok's economy; *therefore*, they are a threat. (Statement of consequence)
The Chinese are a threat *because* they dominate Bangkok's economy. (Statement of cause)
By dominating Bangkok's economy, the Chinese are a threat. (Statement of means)

It should be noted that the explaining links counted in this study were only a convenience for identifying "explaining sentences." There is no claim that the words selected represented all words which could be selected. This category should be investigated more closely, eliminating words which are not true explaining links and determining whether certain nouns and verbs can be included in this category.

Semantic subordination. The notion that an explaining link introduces a clause which adds to or elaborates upon another clause is close to the grammarian's definition of subordination. But in this investigation, common measures of subordination such as dependent clauses and prepositional phrases *did not* discriminate between the high and low lectures. The words chosen as explaining links included subordinating and coordinating conjunctions, as well as certain adverbs and prepositions. Although these words are grammatically dissimilar, they are semantically similar; they introduce a clause or phrase which states a means, reason, or consequence for the main clause. It might be productive in future studies to analyze teachers' statements by this semantic method rather than by traditional sentence structure.

There are many other phrases or words which are grammatically dissimilar but perform the same semantic function. The prepositional phrase "in general" does not appear to be semantically different from the adverb "generally"; the prepositional phrase "at the present time" seems similar in function to the noun "today"; the dependent clause "if a person were to visit Thailand" is similar to the phrase "a person visiting Thailand."

The converse may also be true. Some forms of speech are grammatically similar but perform different semantic functions. For example, prepositional phrases can introduce a major topic or minor topic, a definition, or a summary; and they can be used for sequencing, emphasizing, or elaborating. Dependent clauses and participial phrases can also perform these functions. Because of this variety in function, an indiscriminate increase or decrease in the proportion of certain grammatical structures, such as prepositional phrases or gerunds, in a communication cannot be expected to affect comprehension.

The results from the coding of explaining links suggest that only some of the functions of subordinate clauses and phrases are effective in increasing the comprehensibility of communications. For this reason, attempts to discriminate between effective and ineffective lectures by counting different parts of speech may have limited promise. More significant results may be obtained when subordination is investigated by distinguishing certain subordinate clauses and phrases from others according to the way in which they function in a sentence. The present investigation of explaining links may have identified one type of functional subordination.

Recommendations for Experimental Studies

There is as yet no firm basis for translating any of these findings into recommendations for teaching because the investigation was not an experimental study. A *post hoc* study such as this one can only suggest potential correlates of teaching effectiveness. Experimental research will be necessary before we can claim that any of the presently significant variables represent causal factors.

One such experiment could proceed by selecting teachers whose performance was low as measured both by the adjusted achievement scores of their students and by the frequency of their use of movement and gesture, the rule-example-rule pattern, and explaining links. Some of these teachers would then be trained to use these behaviors more frequently. These teachers would then teach new material to new classes, and their effectiveness in explaining would be compared with that of a similar group of untrained teachers.

A second experiment could test whether the verbal and non-verbal findings are independent of each other. Some students would *read* the transcripts of the high-scoring lectures and other students would read the low-scoring lectures. The ranking of these students' achievement scores could be compared with those of the students in the original study. Using transcripts alone would eliminate the effects of non-verbal variables such as movement, gesture, and rate. Such procedures might also control for factors such as quality of voice and teacher personality.

Another way of studying the effects of the use of explaining links and the rule-example-rule pattern would be to add or eliminate instances of these behaviors from the lectures. Several transcripts from this investigation could be used, some high-scoring and some low-scoring. The high-scoring lectures could be altered so that the explaining links and the second statement of the rule are removed, and the low-scoring lectures could be altered by adding explaining links and a second statement of a rule to the original material. There would then be four lectures, an original and an altered version for both the high and the low lectures. Experiments could test hypotheses that the manipulations decrease the effectiveness of the high-scoring lecture and increase the effectiveness of the low-scoring lecture.

If the significant findings concerning explaining links and the rule-example-rule pattern are replicated through the use of transcripts alone, then these variables may be considered useful additions to the correlates of readability. Consideration of these variables may explain some of the inconsistent findings in studies of instructional set. The use of instructional sets may decrease in relative effectiveness as the number of explaining links in the instructional material is increased. If so, explaining links may provide the same sort of linkage and organization within the lecture as the instructional set gives in the introduction to the lecture.

Study IV. Computer Analysis
of Teachers' Explanations

DARYL DELL | JACK H. HILLER

Reliability is always a problem in content analysis studies when human judges are used for such boring or complex tasks as counting word length, sentence length, the frequency of occurrence of different words, and words used in various functions. This study represents an initial attempt to apply computer programs developed in connection with other problems to the analysis of teacher explaining behavior and to the discovery of variables whose frequency of occurrence might correlate with effectiveness in explaining.

Page (1966) has demonstrated that the computer can be used with high scoring reliability and high objectivity to tally items such as average sentence length, average word length, number of commas, standard deviation of sentence and word length, word frequency, and word ratios. The report on the authorship of the Federalist papers

(Mosteller & Wallace, 1964) presents many notable examples of this technique. Other investigators have developed computer programs which go beyond the counting of word length or word frequency. For example, the *General Inquirer* (Stone *et al.*, 1966) includes a dictionary look-up system which counts the frequencies of different types of words. Systems such as these include the use of a "dictionary" of words classified as to type, affect loading, or any other dimension chosen by the investigator. The computer then is given textual material, and it uses the dictionary to report on the frequencies of designated words in this material. The dictionaries can be changed to meet the needs and growing knowledge of the investigators, and the original data can be rerun against the new hypotheses which were used to develop the new dictionaries.

Procedures of the Study

Transcripts of selected lectures of the teachers in this study were keypunched on IBM cards, and were used as the material to be analyzed. The first approach to analysis was to use the computer programs developed by Page and his staff to count items such as average sentence length, average word length, number of commas, and the standard deviation of sentence and word length. The scores of the lectures on these variables did not correlate significantly with the mean adjusted achievement scores for the lectures. One of the difficulties may have been the questionable reliability of inserting commas and periods in transcribed spoken prose. At any rate, because of these difficulties and because the results appeared to confirm those reported by Rosenshine in Study III of this chapter, this approach was discontinued.

The *General Inquirer* could not be used to count the frequencies of certain types of words because the program was not usable with the computer equipment available. But the use of a dictionary to count the frequency of words classified according to semantic and affective categories seemed promising, and this approach was used in the study. Three existing dictionaries were used, and three additional dictionaries were created to fit our purposes.

The first existing dictionary was the Stanford Political Dictionary developed by Holsti (1966). This dictionary contains over 3,000 words that have been evaluated on the semantic differential scales developed by Osgood, Suci, and Tannenbaum (1957). These scales consist of three bipolar dimensions yielding the following six categories: *good* or *bad, active* or *passive,* and *strong* or *weak.* Within each of the six categories the words in the dictionary are rated on a three-point continuum. Each of the 3,000 words in the dictionary was rated only on the scales that were judged to be appropriate to it. The program as developed by Holsti and his group required the use of specially coded data, and evaluated the data in terms of perceptual viewpoint.

Two additional existing dictionaries were used. These were the 83 categories of the Harvard Third Psychosociological Dictionary (Stone *et al.*, 1966) and the Dale list of the 3,000 most commonly used words (1948).

Three additional dictionaries were developed specifically for this project. Hiller developed a *vagueness* dictionary of words considered to indicate that the speaker is not certain about the material in his presentation. Examples of such words are "almost," "generally," "may be," "many," and "most." We hypothesized that teachers with a high proportion of vagueness words would be ineffective lecturers, that is, that there would be a negative correlation between the proportion of vagueness words and lecturing effectiveness. The following is an excerpt taken from a lecture with a high vagueness count:

—and the young author's name, although this is not too important thing to remember is that it was a young author who wrote this. I will put his name up on the board anyway. It is really not very important at all. MIHAJOV—that is the way you pronounce that word—Uh, Mihajlov wrote those articles. And someone, he has done something that is fine someone very similar had done and there was another author whose name, uh, uh, let us just remember there is another author. That one has spelling problems too. Two authors, two authors. One we know is Mihajlov, the other one wrote earlier in nineteen sixty-two. Both of them complained about conditions, especially in Russia. And this one was in prison because he wrote a book about conversations with Stalin and, I do not know if you have ever heard of the book. And this one also just recently has also been in prison.

Hiller also developed an *adherence-to-detail* dictionary consisting of all proper nouns and place designations in the original articles, and a *problem-issue* dictionary consisting of words such as "conflict," "divergent," and "issue," which might be used by teachers to highlight certain problems and issues.

In addition, a dictionary was made of *explaining links* as defined by Rosenshine, although our dictionary is not identical to the one developed by Rosenshine because we included words, *regardless of their context*, that might serve as explaining links. For example, in our dictionary we included *all* instances of words such as "to" and "since," as well as such words as "therefore" and "because." Although the coders in Rosenshine's study counted all instances of such words as "therefore" and "because," they relied upon context to decide which instances of words such as "to" and "since" should be counted.

The total list of words used in all the dictionaries was approximately 7,000. But many of these words appeared in more than one dictionary.

Results

To test the usefulness of computer analysis, a random sample of 15 was drawn from the group of 35 lectures on Yugoslavia, and a second sample of 15 on Thailand was drawn at random from the lectures of teachers not represented in the Yugoslavia sample. In other words, two groups of 15 lectures each were drawn, with no teacher represented in both groups.

The computer referred to the dictionaries to count the frequency and proportion of words in each category, and then correlated this proportion with the teacher's effectiveness score. Some of the correlations of interest are presented in Table 9.12. (For $N = 15$, an r of .514 is significant at the .05 level.)

The first nine categories listed in Table 9.12 came from the Harvard Third Psychosociological Dictionary. In Categories 6, *medical*, and 8, *sex theme*, the mean scores on these items were so low that undue chance factors may have been involved; no plausible explanation relating sex themes or medical terms to the effectiveness criterion suggested itself. The results for the other "Harvard Psy III" categories suggested the speculation that successful explanations are communications involving task orientation for the pupils (Categories 5, *academic*), place orientation (Categories 1, *space reference*, and 2, *social place*), and relationships between elements (Categories 3, *avoid*; 4, *get*; 7, *sign reject*; and 9, *danger theme*). In general, the correlations of these categories were low enough to make such speculation dubious.

The results in Table 9.12 also bear upon the promise of the categories in the semantic differential approach of Holsti's Stanford Political Dictionary. In general, these categories (10 and 11) had little value in accounting for variance in effectiveness in explaining.

Categories, 14, *explaining links* 2, and 15, *explaining links total*, are related to the explaining links described above in the section on procedures. Here, as already noted, the measures of this variable were reduced to a count of words without regard to context. Consequently, although the resulting correlations remain high ($r =$ about .4), they have dropped below the level of significance found in Study III.

The results for Category 12, *problem-issue*, indicated that the more effective teachers used a higher proportion of words such as "conflict," "divergent," and "issue." Such words may have served to arouse attending behavior or to focus pupil attention on critical points.

The results for Category 16, *adherence to detail,* indicated that the more effective teachers in both groups used a greater proportion of proper nouns and place designations. This finding is difficult to interpret without further detailed study of the original transcripts. One possibility is that the less effective teachers used a greater number of pronouns in place of the proper nouns, and that such pronoun references detracted from the clarity achieved by using proper nouns.

The initial research in the use of the computer to count instances of *vagueness* (Category 13) was expanded in a subsequent study by Hiller, Fisher, and Kaess (1968). In that investigation, Fisher developed a new computer program, SCORTXT, which is capable of counting instances of selected phrases in addition to single words. As a result of the new computer capability, a new vagueness dictionary was developed, consisting of 233 entries in several subdivisions. The subdivisions and examples of the new vagueness words and phrases are presented in Table 9.13. The validity of this new dictionary was tested on 32 lectures on Yugoslavia and 23 lectures on Thailand. In this study, the correlation between the proportion of vagueness words and phrases and the effectiveness-in-explaining criterion was —.59 for the Yugoslavia groups, and —.48 for the Thailand group; both r's are significant beyond the .02 level.

Discussion

This research has demonstrated that computer techniques can be developed to count certain aspects of classroom discourse. The development of computer programs which can count phrases appears to be a significant step beyond the first programs, which were limited to counting specific words. Such a new program has led, for example, to the discovery that the proportion of certain words and phrases classified as indicating "vagueness" is a significant negative correlate of effectiveness in explaining. This initial finding appears promising and warrants future research. Particular subcategories of the vagueness words should be validated to determine which of the nine subcategories should be retained or dropped in future research. In addition, the computer can be used to validate the words and phrases that had been included in the subcategories on an *a priori* basis.

In short, much replicational and cross-validational work remains to be done on the categories of words and phrases studied thus far. Future work on these and other dictionaries that might show promise will be necessary to strengthen or discredit their significance as predictors of teacher effectiveness in explaining. The major limitation of the computer as an aid to analysis lies in the inability of the computer

TABLE 9.12
Frequencies of Words in Various Categories: Their Mean Frequencies and Correlations with Effectiveness in Explaining

Item No.	Category	Source and Definition	Word Sample	Yugoslavia (N = 15) Correlation	Yugoslavia (N = 15) Mean Frequency	Thailand (N = 15) Correlation	Thailand (N = 15) Mean Frequency
1.	Space Reference	Harvard Psy. III Reference to spatial dimensions	about, ahead, back	.509	75.9	.337	67.7
2.	Social Place	Harvard Psy. III Political, social, economic locations	America, bedroom, cabin	.371	27.4	.350	29.0
3.	Avoid	Harvard Psy. III Movement away from	abandon, absent	.405	8.7	.541	11.5
4.	Get	Harvard Psy. III Achieving action	afford, attain, beg	.454	16.7	.316	11.6
5.	Academic	Harvard Psy. III	assignment, correct, teach	.394	30.6	.324	26.1
6.	Medical	Harvard Psy. III	therapy, treatment, injury	−.560	1.1	−.347	.2
7.	Sign Reject	Harvard Psy. III Words implying rejection	anger, betray, sulk	.319	33.3	.373	29.7
8.	Sex Theme	Harvard Psy. III Reference to sex act	engagement, attentive, embrace	.749	4.5	.368	4.5

9. Danger Theme	Harvard Psy. III Connoting concern for danger	blast, warn, deviant	.342	9.4	.524	4.9
10. Affective–2 (proportional)	Holsti Words with middle rating on affective negative scale	complain, embarrass, slander	–.336	26.1	–.368	23.5
11. Strong	Holsti Weighted	competent, shatter, leader	–.032	393.1	.230	387.9
12. Problem-Issue	Words used by teachers in presenting issues	conflict, divergent, issue	.290	9.7	.551	11.0
13. Vagueness (proportional)	Indicating lack of precision	almost, generally, many	–.375	42.6	.249	49.9
14. Explaining Links 2	Rosenshine (Study III above)	Contains only the words: if, then, to	.407	55.3	.407	56.2
15. Explaining Links Total	Rosenshine (Study III above)	All of Explaining Links 2 above, plus 15 other words, such as: consequently, because, since	.384	119.4	.372	112.5
16. Adherence to detail	All proper nouns and place designations in original article	Thailand, Tito, Hitler	.321	121.4	.476	111.6

TABLE 9.13
ILLUSTRATED VAGUENESS CATEGORIES AND STATISTICS

Category	Example	Number of Items	Mean Number Occurring
Ambiguous designation		39	4.7
	all of this and things somewhere other people		
Negated intensifiers		48	1.2
	not all not many not very		
Approximation		25	2.3
	about as almost pretty much		
"Bluffing" and recovery		27	8.3
	a long story short anyway as you all know of course		
Error admission		14	1.3
	excuse me not sure maybe I made an error		
Indeterminate quantification		18	10.3
	a bunch a couple few some		
Multiplicity		26	7.8
	aspects factors sorts kinds		
Possibility		17	8.0
	may might chances are could be		
Probability		19	2.0
	probably sometimes ordinarily often frequently		
	Totals	233	45.9

to determine context. Thus, although a human rater can distinguish between the use of the word "since" to indicate "because" and its use to indicate "after," a computer is unable to perform this task at present. Such a limitation may be only temporary, however, and may be overcome by imaginative and resourceful investigators.

Comments

JOHN B. CARROLL

I can't say too strongly that I want to commend Gage and his colleagues for undertaking this program of research. It's a kind of research that we have waited for for a long time, *too long* in fact, for it goes right to the center of the teaching process conceived as the communication of knowledge. Some critics, of course, would be tempted to argue that lecturing is not a central element in teaching, or, even if it is, that it should not be. I would defend Gage and his colleagues against this argument on two grounds: (1) lecturing is here to stay whether it's desirable or not, and actually there's not a great deal of convincing evidence against lecturing; and (2) even if straight monologue exposition by teachers is not or should not be a customary practice in teaching, there is certainly an element of verbal exposition in almost any live teacher-pupil interaction, whether or not it is a part of a dialogue between teacher and pupils that includes questions and answers or other repartee.

Therefore, verbal exposition merits study, and one way to study it is to look at it in concentrated doses, that is, in teachers' lectures. Just why there should be so much reaction by some people to the idea of lecturing, I fail to understand. Telling people things—telling stories, explaining things—is a characteristic activity of the human species. Apparently, what we don't like about lectures is the peculiar form of verbal behavior that sometimes occurs when people get up on platforms. I assume that Gage and his colleagues' teachers were not lecturing from platforms.

I suppose a discussant is expected to do two kinds of things—(1) criticize and (2) offer suggestions. If I criticize, I shall try to do so constructively, and thus achieve both ends. However, if I am expected to offer suggestions about new interpretations of the research reported here, or new directions for it to follow, I am somewhat at a loss, for I am as puzzled by the findings as the researchers appear to be. It is evident that even after these brave efforts we are a long way from understanding what makes teachers' explaining effective.

Rosenshine's study, in which attempts were made to find protocol elements that were associated with the effectiveness of explaining, was one of the most interesting and yet puzzling in this series. There is an air of desperation in this story of initial success that proved illusory, followed by dismal failures and then tantalizing half-successes again. One cannot fault the study for not trying everything that could be thought of. Perhaps basic limitations in the data handicapped the effort. Nevertheless, one can accept with reasonable confidence the significance of the three categories he isolated as being related to explanation effectiveness. And they make sense: the rule-example-rule pattern, the "explaining links," and gesture and movement. All three may be concomitants or indicators of preparation and organization as well as of attention-eliciting devices. Yet, the "explaining links" measures had disappointingly low validity in the second study!

Because of the necessary brevity of the report, it is not clear exactly how certain variables were coded. For example, among the linguistic categories we find Category 9, "awkward and fragmented sentences—counts of sentences which depart from usual sentence construction and/or phrases which lack a subject or a verb but which add information (e.g., Now to foreign affairs)." From a linguistic viewpoint, this category is a mixed bag. It might include broken-off sentences which might be confusing to the student, but it might also include semi-sentences that could be actually quite enlightening, like the cited phrase, "Now to foreign affairs." I would recommend that Gage and his colleagues look into the work of Walter Loban (1963) and R. C. O'Donnell (1967), who have done a lot of careful development of techniques for isolating "mazes" or "garbles" in speech. Certainly the protocol reproduced on page 211 is a fine example of a text containing many "mazes" or broken-off and restarted sentences. The coding must be done by hand rather than by computer, but a measure of grammatical disconnectedness might offer a highly valid variable.

Another thing that Rosenshine might have tried is some measure of "fact density" to try to ascertain how many facts or ideas were actually presented in the lectures. We cannot rely much on the high school students' ratings of "coverage" obtained in the final study; yet I would think there could be fairly reliable and valid measures of actual coverage. The students presumably could not do the tests well if they were not presented with the basic facts and ideas.

The study by Dell and Hiller is almost as fascinating as Rosenshine's. It addresses itself to the problem of what a computer might do in identifying and isolating elements of explanation effectiveness. As in the first study, just about anything and everything was tried, but this time within the limitations of computer coding. Again there was a story of partial successes and failures. The course of research does not run smooth. I think, however, more should be done with the "vagueness" variable, perhaps with an item analysis technique. Some kinds of vagueness are necessary, when they betoken justified caution; others betoken merely ignorance. Again I refer to Loban's work with the language of school children: he found that children with high verbal ability were more likely to use expressions of caution—"maybe," "I don't know," "It could be . . . ," and the like.

To take up the study by Belgard, Rosenshine, and Gage: I am a little worried about the concern for obtaining generality of a "trait" of effective explaining behavior. In the first place, we know people are highly variable in complex behaviors; most of us teach well one day and poorly the next. If there is any generality in the ability to explain, it is probably weak at best. It may be a trait rather analogous to ability in written composition. All the research on the evaluation of quality in written composition suggests that you get reliability only by compiling results from a variety of writing sessions on different topics rated by a multitude of raters. In this study, the authors attempted to find generality over just *two* performances on the part of the teachers. Admittedly, they realized that a multitude of "raters" (i.e., students taking the comprehension tests) were necessary to obtain any decent reliability in the measures. In the second place, and more important, I think that progress in understanding the effectiveness of explanations will come through the isolation of elements in particular performances that make them effective. In fact, studying effective and ineffective teaching performances of single teachers would have some advantages since it would control certain possibly extraneous elements such as sex, appearance, characteristic gestures, and the like. Most of the researchers reporting here recognize this when they use the teacher-*lesson* as the unit of study rather than the teacher.

A serious methodological problem in this particular study is the fact that the same teachers were used in the two lessons and that, moreover, these teachers were teaching their regular classes. Any results reported may have been influenced by actions of teachers that occurred before the experiment began. Note, for example, that student-reported "attention" during the lectures was one of the significant variables associated with effectiveness; but the student's degree of attention, which itself had good generality over the two lectures, may have been a function of teaching-pupil relationships that had been built up before the Stanford group intervened with its experiment. The suggestion is made (and I would concur with it) that data should be obtained with teachers confronting fresh classes. We have to hold in mind this possible limitation before jumping to the conclusion that these results would also hold for teachers put in front of unfamiliar classes.

There is another serious methodological problem latent in this first experiment, and that is the use of the *taped* lecture results as the control. I assume this was an audio tape, not a video tape: we are not told. Nor are we told anything that would lead us to think that the taping was optimal from the point of view of delivery or anything else. In fact, the mean scores on the taped Israel selection were lower than those for the live lectures. Furthermore, there is a suggestion in Unruh's study that students are not able to respond as well to an audio-taped lecture as they are to an audiovisual presentation. Why wasn't the control lecture video-taped by a teacher selected for good appearances and delivery? At least we would know that the pupil responses were to the same order of thing as in the live lectures.

The one result that strikes me in this first study is that effectiveness was associated with the amount of attention students reported paying to the lectures. So we should ask the question: What elicits the students' attention? Perhaps a kind of time-and-motion study would indicate the points in the live lectures that elicited the most attention.

Let me move on to Unruh's study. I would point out the discouragingly small *N*'s used here. Almost every coefficient reported is based on an *N* of four teacher-lessons. I am not persuaded that the *AV* (audiovisual) presentation was clearly better than other modes of presentation such as typewritten transcript or audio record. Nor do I think one can put much reliance, at this stage, on the results in those portions of the study that attempted to find correlates of lecture effectiveness. I would be very conservative in interpreting the study: to me, the only results that are probably significant are those for the categories "organization and planning" and "knowledge of material," and even those held up better on the negative side (Table 9.8) than on the positive (Table 9.7). Well, if planning and knowledge of one's subject are important, as would seem reasonable, there ought to be some way of extracting a measure of planning and of knowledge in the protocols. This, apparently, was not attempted by Rosenshine or Dell and Hiller.

To sum up, I commend this group for exciting and promising work, but so far it must be considered exploratory. With larger *N*'s, better measurements, and better experimental designs they should be able to make a couple or more breakthroughs in this business of explaining teachers' explaining behavior, and breakthroughs we need badly.

Comments

ROBERT GLASER

Surprisingly enough, only a small proportion of the work in the psychological and educational literature on verbal learning addresses itself to the question of how a student learns from a lecture or a verbal explanation. In the light of this, it is particularly fascinating to see a group of investigators attacking this problem. Since teacher explanations are an important part of instruction, it is necessary that explicit investigation be carried out on the conditions under which verbal explanation is effective so that we know how to employ it, how to modify it, and when to substitute other procedures for it. With this in mind, I should like to comment on some of the details of this subject.

In the first paper, by Belgard, Rosenshine, and Gage, there is the search for the generality of the teacher's effectiveness in explaining over a number of instances. It was concluded that generality is indicated by a correlation coefficient of .47 between the mean comprehension scores on one lesson and those on another. For experimental work, a correlation that accounts for approximately 22 per cent of the variance seems too low to investigate explaining behavior with confidence, and it may be necessary to develop experimental situations in which it is more reliable.

The conclusions based on correlational evidence in this first paper are interesting to examine. Student ratings of dimensions of the teacher's performance correlated with how much the students learned; in addition, students' self-reported attention to the lesson also correlated with what they learned. What immediately comes to mind as a result of these data is the possibility of artifactual or superstitious behavior on the part of the student. What may be happening is that the student observes certain activities in the teacher that alert the student to paying careful attention to what is being said. It may be that such alerting or attention-producing stimuli are significant variables in causing the student to learn—perhaps even more significant than the form and content factors of the presentation which are supposedly related to good explanatory exposition. This might be suggested by the pattern of correlations which showed that "clarity of aims" and "clarity of presentation" correlate fairly well with mean comprehension scores but that "pacing the lesson" and "teacher-pupil rapport" correlated lowest with comprehension scores. The former aspects may alert the student to the fact that this teacher is well prepared, while pacing and rapport may be closer to being instructional aspects of presentation. I shall try to see how this hypothesis fares as I proceed in my comments.

In Unruh's paper it is to be noted, in the study of the relative effectiveness of different kinds of protocols, that the audio plus video record had the highest correlation coefficient between actual teacher ranks and later assigned ranks. Either the student raters judged as most effective what was most like the typical classroom situation, or else certain mannerisms of the teacher, perhaps reflecting enthusiasm and seriousness, were easily detected by the students and interpreted as signs for them to pay attention.

A conclusion in Unruh's paper was that as far as the student raters were concerned, the most important aspects of good teaching appeared to involve teacher activities related primarily to preparation and presentation. This might involve a more shallow variable than would be implied. The student might be thinking, "The teacher seems to know what he is doing, therefore I will learn it," although these aspects may be related to content, style of exposition, and instructional strategies which structure the lesson material so as to make it more meaningful. In the check list study, the findings suggested that a good teacher is one who is interpreted as being verbally and cognitively in control of the situation; but the mediating factors that result in learning must be analyzed.

In the paper by Rosenshine I must applaud the detailed search for categories and variables which predict effectiveness in explaining. Examination of these categories shows that the linguistic variables that might be related to comprehension were generally not related to effectiveness. Instructional set variables were not related; this may be so because these variables that have to do with pre-instructional procedures have to be set up and explicitly built into lesson materials. Of the presentational variables, two categories—"rule-and-example pattern" and "movement and gesture"—discriminated between high and low teachers across the three samples. Gestures and movements may have the effect of arousing attention, which may be a point for my notion about alerting variables.

With respect to rule-and-example pattern, studies on concept learning would lead to the comment that it depends on what is being tested and the nature of the rule being taught. Is one testing the recall of the rule, or application of the rule to new examples? Different rule-example combinations might be better for teaching one kind of behavior than the other. The nature of the subject matter is also influential; I would suggest that when a rule defining a concept is clear-cut and can be explicitly stated, then it might best be taught by stating the rule so the student remembers it and then giving him examples to work. On the other hand, if the rule is less precise, as it is for concepts like "freedom" and "justice," then one builds up a rule on the basis of a history of experiences with different instances.

In the analysis of presentational variables, I find the notion of "explaining links" very appealing. The use of explaining links, as the author points out, may serve to provide some organizational structure for a verbal explanation, and the possibility that this may be the case is very interesting. At the present time in psychological research on verbal behavior much attention is being paid to the nature of organizational factors which lead to kinds of coding, subordinating, and grouping which facilitate the memory and understanding of verbal material.

In suggestions for future research, the problem of the "unit of study" is discussed; this is indeed an interesting factor. I would suggest that the optimum unit takes on different characteristics depending upon the behavior involved. In working through a passage to comprehend it, short-term memory is involved, which may depend upon repetition, coding practices, primacy effects, and so forth. In using the comprehension attained over a longer period of time for transfer to new situations, perhaps more schematic organizational structures would be involved.

In the paper by Dell and Hiller, the authors recognize that their analyses are concerned primarily with isolated words and phrases, they are quick to recognize the importance of organizational characteristics, and they point out that they are not as yet prepared to deal with this complexity. As I have indicated, organizational characteristics, both those which a learner brings to impose on a verbal production and those inherent in the verbal production itself, appear to be powerful variables.

The discussion in the Dell and Hiller paper emphasizes the strong influence of the "vagueness" factor, and the authors indicate that the measure of vagueness serves as a cue for other behaviors. This can be made into a point in the case for the alerting behavior hypothesis; the authors suggest that a causal interpretation for the strengths of the fluency and vagueness correlations with effectiveness is that students will interpret high vagueness and low fluency as an indication that the teacher does not know the material and has little interest in it; in such circumstances, students are less likely to attend closely.

Some general notions can now be discussed. One way to get more precision in studying the teacher's explaining behavior is to consider working with individual students and to examine the way in which they adapt to various explanatory materials. A student's organizational capabilities before learning might be measured and this entering behavior related to materials with different organizational structures.

Perhaps a better experimental approach is to have the student in some way manipulate a verbal presentation so that he can get the most sense out of it. The general principle here is to get the student's behavior as overt and as explicit as possible by designing experimental situations in which he has to show how he organizes a presentation in order to learn. Another experimental approach is suggested by the work of Rothkopf (1966) where various kinds of test-like events are inserted into written material in order to investigate how well learners attend to the material and how well they comprehend it.

Finally, the papers on this project have said very little about just what is measured by the tests of students' comprehension. It is useful to provide some detailed analysis of the dependent variable under consideration. It is highly likely that the nature of what is measured as learning outcomes greatly influences the interesting results reported.

PART

IV

Conclusion

TEN

Problems and Prospects

IAN WESTBURY

It seems necessary now to attempt to review, and perhaps assess, the suggestions that have been made in this volume, through all the chapters, about next steps in research into classroom processes. The logical starting point for such a review has to be a backward look, and in context the obvious reference point is the 1962 Teachers College conference reported in *Theory and Research in Teaching* (Bellack, 1963). The concern of that conference—to draw together for the first time workers who were using systematic observations of classroom activities as a method for focusing attention on the "verbal and nonverbal behavior of teachers and students . . . with special reference to the roles, functions, and activities of teachers"—carried through to the 1967 OISE seminar. A review of the contrasts and shifts in emphasis in these two set of papers, those of the 1962 conference and those in this volume, should make possible the beginnings of an appraisal of what six years have brought to the problems and questions of the tradition and of where we might be now.

Some of the issues implied by this suggestion have, of course, been dealt with in this book. The chapter by Rosenshine, when read alongside the comprehensive reviews of Boyd and DeVault (1966), Biddle (1967), Meux (1967), Campbell (1968), and Nuthall (1968), makes any further remarks about techniques or substantive conclusions redundant. However, there is still a place for an attempt to highlight some of the methodological and theoretical issues raised explicitly in Part I of this book and implicit in all of the papers both here and in *Theory and Research* (as I shall call the earlier volume hereafter). Three such sets of issues will be the foci for these comments: (1) the concern lying behind statements advocating the need for *theories of teaching* as distinct from *theories of teaching and learning;* (2) the research goals embodied in prescriptions for such theories; and (3) the adequacy of the explanation structures and the questions asked of classroom phenomena in the research reported here.

Theories of Teaching and Theories of Teaching and Learning

The Problem

In the opening essay of *Theory and Research,* B. O. Smith outlined very briefly an argument he had made earlier, suggesting a need for an autonomous theory of teaching which "recognized teaching as a distinctive phenomenon general enough to embrace normative definitions as well as special cases" (1961, p. 90). This argument was a protest against views of teaching which assimilate the teacher's act into a unitary teaching-learning construction so as to permit principles of teaching to be derived, inferentially or logically, from theories of learning or education.

Smith's own view, that "teaching is one thing and learning quite another," is, as he points out, clearly significant for pedagogical research:

It enables us to analyze the concept of teaching without becoming entangled in a web of argument about the processes and conditions of learning; in short, to carry on investigations of teaching in its own right (B. O. Smith, 1961, p. 90).

In consequence, the questions "What is teaching?" and "How can it be described?" become meaningful and valid.

The proposition that there is a clear distinction to be made between teaching and learning, as objects of enquiry, has been widely accepted. It has produced this book. The distinction has defined a subject matter for investigation and has justified, heuristically at least, much of the recent interest in teaching as an activity worth empirical study for its own sake. To the extent that this direction was contained in Smith's argument and has led to meaningful conclusions, the fruits of his analysis cannot be questioned.

Recently, however, Smith's formal distinction between teaching and learning has been meeting heavy weather amongst some educational philosophers. Komisar (1968), for example, has accused Smith of being responsible for a dogma that is not defensible analytically. He has argued that Smith's distinction is meaningless: to say "I am teaching somebody something" implies an intention that somebody will learn something and also implies that the intention is being translated into some reality through appropriate methods. To claim less, Komisar would say, is to deny the very nature of teaching. Scheffler (1960) has made a similar claim: ". . . teaching, as normally understood, is an activity requiring effort and allowing for the exercise and development of proficiency and oriented toward a goal that may lie beyond any segment of it" (p. 63). This goal is learning conceived of in some way.

Some practical implications of these arguments are picked up by McClellan in this book. In both his paper and in the discussion of his paper, McClellan insists that, to discuss teaching fully, many more issues than Smith's distinction allows must be entertained as researchers attempt to come to terms with what they are going to look *at* in the classroom. The most important of these issues for the discussion here center around the necessity, posited indirectly by McClellan, of seeing teaching and learning as so totally related that teaching can *only* be defined within the terms of the relationship. For McClellan, teaching must be characterized as a more or less conscious set of means directed either toward ends external to the teaching situation or toward ends-in-view embedded within the act itself. The analytical structure used to describe teaching must, as a consequence, address both means and end *pari passu*.

However, while an argument of this kind leaves us with an attitude toward what classroom research is about that is different from that suggested by Smith, it does not necessarily deny the significance of Smith's programmatic distinction between teaching and learning. McClellan also views teaching acts as *means* that exist as phenomena in their own right. Yet he argues that to the extent that a researcher wishes to investigate teaching, ends need to be invoked as a way of stabilizing what it is that should be counted as a *teaching* act. The invocation of ends in any argument of this kind is thus artifactual; it is part of a search for terms that permit complex phenomena to be *interpreted* before being entered into a scientific discussion.

McClellan (MacMillan & McClellan, 1968, pp. 147–48) sets out this problem forcefully in another paper:

In any concrete instance, an action-consequence relation is an abstraction from a much more complex situation containing all sorts of objects and events having all sorts of different relations. If reasoning about the total situation concentrates too exclusively on a particular action-consequence relation taken as means to ends, it may err in different ways: (i) It may so concentrate on the desirable feature of the chosen end that the undesirable aspects of the total situation are ignored. . . . (ii) It may so concentrate on the action's intended consequence that it ignores the longer term and unintended consequences of the same action. . . .

It is clearly prudential to avoid both of these errors. . . . But we submit that these prudential considerations do not preclude the use of means-ends reasoning; they rather establish the conditions for using it wisely. A teacher should be able to distinguish what he's doing to help youngsters learn to read, e.g., teaching the ITA, flashing word object combinations on the board, from what else is happening in the same situation, e.g., children held passive, isolated and protected from novel words and objects. . . . In sum, it is prudential to recognize and take account of the existential situation from which any actual means-ends reasoning is abstracted. But that is not to stop doing means-ends thinking.

The existential context of teaching acts can itself only be interpreted in means-ends terms. A range of teaching acts must be distinguished from non-teaching acts performed within the classroom in ways that, at least tacitly, invoke notions about the ends of the classroom setting. To take one trivial example: for most observers the act of a teacher blowing his nose would be unambiguously regarded as a non-teaching act. However, for an observer who regards the learning of mannered social conventions as a central function of the school, the way in which a teacher blows his nose might be of sufficient pedagogic importance to be acknowledged—and even, perhaps, evaluated. Such a decision, with the implication that nose-blowing is a teaching action, would be made and be meaningful in the light of ends and purposes. Such ends and purposes must be reified sufficiently *for the purposes of discussion* to permit the action-consequence flux in the classroom to be stabilized and made to stand still long enough for observation and analysis.

Implications

My treatment of McClellan's argument has implied that the philosophical arguments between, say, Smith and Komisar, Sheffler, and McClellan are consequential for classroom researchers attempting to assess what their work is about. My problem in the balance of this paper is to offer a rationalization for this assumption and to show the ways in which the resolution of a philosophical argument affects empirical research. I will address two general questions: Do conceptual questions of the kind I have been discussing matter for research? Do the solutions to problems of this kind, arrived at after philosophical analysis, matter sufficiently to affect in significant or potentially significant ways the kinds of research an empirical tradition might undertake and the results a tradition might yield?

The emphases of B. O. Smith's chapter in *Theory and Research* suggest that he did not consider these questions and their resolution central to his immediate concerns, inasmuch as he did not attempt a full development of his own previously argued position.[1] In fact, the assertiveness with which he made his point in *Theory and Research* seems to belie the complexity and subtlety of his earlier stipulation (1961).[2] McClellan, on the other hand, raised all of these questions in this book with his proposition that, if classroom research is concerned with a process, and "if a process is not the sort of thing that can be looked at, we have to decide what it is we are going to look *at* before deciding what to look *for*." The consequences for McClellan's argument of this proposition have already been outlined and will be attended to again in the last pages of this paper. For the discussion here I take his argument as a disagreement with the burden of Smith's position as it affects the bounding of a set of research concerns: McClellan would require classroom research to incorporate near its center a relatively sophisticated treatment of learning and values. For the balance of this section I want to develop the implications of McClellan's position and to make a case for the limited utility of the distinction which implies that there can be separate theories of teaching and teaching and learning.

The postulate of all studies of social and psychological phenomena is that sense can be made of interesting aspects of human behavior. This postulate is a reflection of the "rationality" that is the end-in-view of all science; all scientific constructs and explanations have their origins in a quest for meaningful understanding of the real-world phenomena and events that are their subject matters. There are, however, differences between the different forms of science—between, say, the natural sciences and the social sciences—in the ways in which their conclusions and methods are accountable to the complexity (of the kind that common sense can reveal) of the ordinary phenomena that they claim to address. The phenomena of the human sciences have a real existence within an unambiguous and real social milieu which is prior, in a very immediate sense, to the theorizing that is the science. Any discipline or tradition which ignores this fundamental reality invalidates its phenomena in the most serious of ways.[3]

An example far from the problems of this book (and borrowed from Winch, 1958, p. 51) will illustrate this problem: If one is concerned in some way with "voting," it must be presumed that it is voting and not something else that is being studied. Voting is a meaningful social act, and the term can only be applied to acts which conform to the expectations we have about things and their names. Thus, if subjects are to be observed voting or are to be asked to vote in some experimental situation, it has to be presumed that there is some choice and some true awareness of the symbolic relationship between the action at a ballot box and what might happen afterwards as a consequence of a vote. Otherwise no observer, and no reader later, can believe that a vote, in any sense of the word, has taken place. The continuing debates about the meaning and meaningfulness of the plebiscite provisions of the Geneva Accords make this point clear. Without some fairly precise presumption about the kinds of act a voter is engaged in, both language and our presumptions about acts are tortured beyond the limits of common sense. If "voting" does not mean voting, words no longer have meaning.

To generalize this example: All social actions are meaningful to the participants and meaningful (i.e., understandable) to an observer to the extent that they are in accord with, or are perceived to be in accord with, sets of rules which define an act as an act of a certain kind, make actions out of specific acts, and connect the particular to the more general. These rules set out, to both the actor and the observer, the roles that others will have and how they can be expected to react.

Teaching is just such a rule-governed characterization of certain actions of certain people; the concept, with all the attendant limits of appropriateness both of the action ("Teachers learn to think like children") and of the label, exists within a real social milieu. It is not a conception that can be imposed by outsiders at will and in accord with *their* rules for identifying and naming phenomena. Teaching is not something that can be stipulated out of a concern for one's theoretical needs, but is a phenomenon that must be accounted for and understood in its own terms as a previously existing and known set of actions. If the connections that are drawn out of any teacher's action are real connections, they already exist in the actions themselves prior to any theory about those actions. In a real sense the end of any science of teaching is to draw out and point to that which is already present, although perhaps not known; the test of the usefulness of any scientific statement is the amount of assistance it gives us in extracting from real experience.

The demand made by this complex relationship between the scientist and his already existing phenomena has not been adequately handled in methodological prescriptions for social science. Kaplan (1964) refers to it as the problem of *interpretation*. He distinguishes *act meaning,* the significance of acts to an actor or to those with whom he is interacting and the consequent conventional assignment of *acts* to *actions* (e.g., the act of hitting to the action of a baseball game), from *action meaning,* the significance of actions to the theoretical constructs of a scientist.

> . . . an interpretation is the assignment of either an act meaning or an action meaning. . . . An interpretation construes an act as a certain action, then offers an explanation of the action. But these two processes are easily confused with one another. It is often tacitly assumed that as soon as we understand the act, we have thereby arrived at an understanding of the action. The first interpretation is usually easy to come by . . . But it is a very different matter to arrive at an understanding of the action, a scientific explanation on the basis of suitable laws or theories of behavior, or of some comprehensive pattern into which the action can be fitted (Kaplan, 1964, pp. 359–60).

Interpretation is then fundamental, but the difficulties of interpretation of *act meanings* are writ large in the discussion reported here of Mc-Clellan's and Travers' papers. It is not clear how a research tradition should go about assigning and creating a working consensus even about *act meaning;* yet, as Kaplan makes clear, this is a basic task.

Weber's concept of *Verstehen,* for example, points to this problem without answering it. It is only a truism to say that by means of an intuition (i.e., *Verstehen*), we gain insight into the meaning that acts have for subjects. It is not explicitly helpful to say that, through this understanding, the subjective meaning the acts have for the actors is drawn into the consciousness of the investigator, and from there into his theorizing and conjecture. Some intuition of this kind must, of course, be implicit in all of the papers in these two collections. We all share the conviction that research studies should not be undertaken simply because some problem is practicable methodologically. Yet, despite this conviction, there is a near-total uncertainty about what agreement about the role of intuition means, both generally and specifically. For example, how, apart from intuition and introspection, do we gain access to phenomena as such? What is obvious to one person's intuition or common sense, the ways one person answers the validity question, is not the way another necessarily sees the issues. It is clear that within education there are almost as many meanings of learning as there are investigators (and few which accord with a teacher's understanding), or, in the context of this book, as many meanings for teaching as there are studies. Some objective process for elucidating these meanings is required.[4]

It is in the context of this problem of interpretation that the *analysis* of the concept of "teaching" that Smith omitted from his *Theory and Research* paper suggests a strategy that classroom research might explore again. This approach was only mentioned briefly in this volume (by McClellan: see pages 12–13), but it is the dominating method in a series of important papers on teaching by Komisar (1966; 1967; 1968). These papers raise enough methodological and empirical questions for it to be worth attempting to spell out the assumptions of such analysis and to raise, at the same time, the possibility that the conclusions of such analysis, and its method, might be brought again within the boundaries of research into the messy phenomena of teaching and learning.

Much recent philosophy has been written within a tradition in which the careful and systematic analysis of simple declarative propositions is the dominating characteristic. Philosophers of this ilk seek understanding of the concepts which they assume are the apparatus of our thinking through a careful and systematic exploration of the behavior of words in common speech. Speech, one exponent of the approach has written,

[is] subjected to the severest of all tests of efficiency, as a medium for the expression and communication of our thoughts—the test of constant use, with the potentially useful result that one can come to understand philosophically puzzling concepts by carefully and accurately noting the ways in which the related linguistic expressions are actually used in discourse (Strawson, 1956, p. 336).

Inasmuch as words control and embody our thought, this kind of analysis can offer, on the one hand, a way to look for distortions which language, or the false use of language, can bring to our understanding of the world,[5] and, on the other, a way of constructing true maps and schemes of relatively unknown parts of the world. Obviously there are other ways to theory- or construct-building (see, for example, Glaser & Strauss, 1967, ch. 7),[6] yet it is tantalizing to see the under-utilization in this book of one powerful technique that is, in a sense, indigenous to research on teaching. I shall pick this theme up again in the last pages of these comments.

The Forms of Theories of Teaching

The most convincing test for the necessity of raising the general questions I have been suggesting is the empirical pay-off secured from the concepts that are being entered into research studies. When intention and purpose are used as criteria against which results achieved are measured we must ask whether or not classroom research is yielding anything significant about the kinds of things that interest us. Rosenshine's review suggests that this should be an important question. The OISE conference began an appraisal along these lines. Solution or resolution of some of the conceptual questions implied in this questioning might liberate our research for a further, and fresher, attack.

The concrete questions that a research tradition attends to are as much a function of assumptions about the forms of the principles brought to concepts describing phenomena as they are functions of phenomena in and of themselves. An approach to these problems of principles is however much less direct than is a discussion of the nature of our "true" phenomena as subject-matter datum. This issue was joined in both conferences, and there is in fact the beginning of a marked shift in the ways in which the problem can be seen. This part of these comments will pick up this theme.

Predictive Theory

In *Theory and Research*, Smith, Flanders, and Medley and Mitzel all address themselves in one way or another to the problem of the form of a theory of teaching, teacher effectiveness, or instruction. Smith's conception of a theory of teaching has already been outlined above. Flanders sets out a prolegomenon for a theory of instruction which "would be quite apart from the various subjects taught and would be concerned with the effects of the teacher's behavior on motivation and attitude formation" with the intention of specifying the conditions under which learning is maximized (p. 37). Flanders' understanding of the form of such a theory is indicated by his suggestions that such a theory should be tested in terms of the adequacy of its specifications of the "effects of integrative or dominative contacts for different types of situations that occur frequently in the classroom" (p. 42). Medley and Mitzel make a broadly similar prescription. They ask for rules or principles of teaching that can be given to beginning teachers and that compare in adequacy with the "rigorous quantitative sets of laws" which form the substance of training for achitecture or engineering (pp. 81–82).

The behaviors of teachers while they teach and pupils while they learn are beginning to become objectively quantifiable. Better measures of at least some of the changes in pupil behavior which represent the effects of teacher behavior than have ever been available before are provided by several achievement batteries developed in the forties and fifties. The potentialities which inhere in modern statistical methods for teasing out relationships between behaviors and effects, despite the many irrelevant factors which tend to mask them, are beginning to be realized and exploited; this is, of course, greatly facilitated by modern high-speed computers. Are we on the verge of a major breakthrough in the science of teacher behavior? (Medley & Mitzel, 1963b, p. 90).

The bracketing of these suggestions by Smith, Flanders, and Medley and Mitzel in one place is not meant to imply a necessary unity of purpose and intention between these three points of view. There is, however, enough resemblance between Flanders and Medley and Mitzel (and less certainly between Flanders and Smith) for it to be a reasonable inference that the "theory" being projected is perceived of as a series of law-like statements connecting sets of antecedent conditions with consequent effects. In this book, Ginther describes a series of experiments that conforms in large part to these expectations; and Rosenshine's review, Birkin's paper, and the work of the Stanford group show a movement to the antecedent-consequent model through correlational studies.

Paradoxically, however, just as the prescriptions for "scientific" theory are being elaborated and partially fulfilled (at least methodologically) the once-united demand for theory-building of this form is beginning to break. Gump, for example, raises the specter that laboratory-type or experimental studies of the kind that Travers (for one) sees as essential cannot, *in principle*, produce the forms of understanding implied by a demand that we should seek to understand "teaching" as a potentially meaningful real-world act (see above, pp. 155–56; also Gump & Kounin, 1960). Gump's criticisms are not so much directed at the form of a conceivable theory as at the meaningfulness and validity of the ways in which theory might be developed; his objection does, if taken, limit the ways in which "theory" might be seen as representative of phenomena.

To some extent Gump's specter is a qualification of the ways in which the prescription for theory should be taken. L. M. Smith, on the other hand, in his castigation of dust-bowl empiricism that yields only trivial conclusions and taxonomies of events that go nowhere, is explicitly demanding that attention be given to new kinds of concerns. He asks us to attend explicitly to the conceptualization of the "latent" variables of the classroom; the thrust to such a conceptualization, hinted at in his paper here and richly illustrated in *The Complexities of an Urban Classroom* (1958) and "*Go, Bug, Go*" (1970), is quite different in character from that being urged by Travers, Medley and Mitzel, and Flanders. The world of Smith's classroom is less homogeneous in texture, with many strands and many actions. Viewing Smith's work from the perspective of *Theory and Research* and Rosenshine's review, we have the problem of the least rigorous and least systematic investigation being the most intriguing.

Some of the force of this contrast in forms of research fades, of course, when results are looked at in detail. L. M. Smith's conclusions and his suggestions about "Where next?" although at this point uncertain, are couched in the antecedent-consequent frame suggested by Medley and Mitzel and by Flanders; his theory of *personalized interaction* is perfectly amenable to the form of the classical paradigms exemplified in Medley and Mitzel's prescription and in the Stanford work. In common with this form, his results draw attention to regularity, without necessarily offering explanation. His language, although not his microethnographic method, is that of verification rather than invention or theory development.[7] Nevertheless there are thrusts not yet fully developed, to new research genres, in the methods of Smith and Gump.

Explanatory Theory

Yet, despite these differences, the emphasis upon the term "theory" in all of these papers must be seen as parts of an attempt to make a common case for constructs and theories which order and explain real-world phenomena. Such theories and constructs should offer a frame within which the events of the classroom might be rationally understood; out of this understanding the range of possibilities for *action* on the part of participants in similar settings should be increased. The orientation to theory in these papers implies a commitment to this kind of endeavour; the classificatory efforts of B. O. Smith, Meux, Aschner, and Adams, the experimental work of Ginther, and the correlational studies of Birkin and the Stanford group are directed, in their long-term thrust, at the development of languages and forms of law which might be entered into different kinds of explanation structures. The articulation of this thrust and the recognition of its importance should serve as a corrective to the jejune classification that is beginning to be the hallmark of research into teaching (Westbury, 1969).

Obviously, however, a thrust to theory development, in any sense that this might be taken, does not entail an inevitable achievement. Perhaps not surprisingly, no general theory of teaching or instruction is in the offing and, as Travers argues so persuasively, no theories of teaching exist at present. There are no immediate grounds in this situation for pessimism, but given the poverty of so many other fields of educational research there does seem some place for a Cassandra figure to raise a specter of doom. Four possible explanations might be suggested: failure might be a result of the limited time that research into teaching has been at theory development; it might be a function of our collective poverty of invention; it might be the consequence of a failure to develop the means of organizational mobilization and accumulation of energy and resources; or it might be a fruit of the forms in which enquiry is couched. Let me attempt to deal with the last of these suggestions.

As I have already suggested, the least "theoretical" of the work reported in these two books, that of L. M. Smith, is some of the most arresting being attempted.[8] It is this feeling which raises some questions about the forms being advocated for theory development. Has an unconscious truncation of the conception of explanation entered research into teaching (and much of educational research besides) through the failure to recognize the character of the decision-making that is teaching and through the assimilation, under one head, of the logically distinct concepts of *explanation, theory, law-like theory,* and *understanding?*

"Explanation" in the ordinary sense of the term resolves a puzzlement caused by some collection of circumstances to someone who is not familiar with a situation in question. Scientific puzzlement, in its broadest and most generic sense, is simply a transformation of this very ordinary and common form. A satisfactory resolution of puzzlement depends simply on what we know and what we want to know. A satisfactory reduction of puzzlement, or in other words a satisfactory explanation, has no *a priori* association with any particular logical form, whether definition, classification, interpretation, instruction for using, or reduction to a common general law, and the like (Passmore, 1965, pp. 19–20). The scientific assimilation of all forms of explanation into a few logical forms (e.g., subsumption under a general law) is a restriction of the ordinary sense of explanation; as such, a restriction of the ordinary form is, at best, a scientific assumption—that explanation always consists in using a general law as a means for explaining the behavior of particular cases or kinds of cases. It is not necessary for all logically acceptable explanations to conform to this assumption, or (depending on how one defines "science") for all scientifically acceptable explanations to follow this pattern. The use of antecedent-consequent connections as an explanatory device does not exhaust (and might not even meet) the range of scientifically acceptable forms of explanation available, although it might well be a practically useful way of ordering a body of data.

History, to take one study that does not conform to these explanatory forms, uses in a highly disciplined way structures of explanation that are very close to those of everyday life, and, from the viewpoint of the historian, scientific explanation is a peculiar and unacceptable form (Passmore, 1965, p. 33). Yet history lives happily with ordinary forms because it is not attempting to develop a body of law-like theory, but to show how particular courses of events, in all their complexity, occurred and are patterned. Applied social sciences conceivably share more with history than they are accustomed to recognize:

What is sometimes termed "applied" science . . . is directly concerned with . . . instrumentalities at work in effecting modifications of existence in behalf of conclusions that are reflectively preferred. . . . "Application" is a hard word for many to accept. It suggests some extraneous tool ready-made and complete which is then put to uses that are external to its nature. But . . . application of "science" means application *in,* not application *to.* Application *in* something signifies a more extensive interaction of natural events with one another, an elimination of distance and obstacles; provision of opportunities for interactions that reveal potentialities previously hidden and that bring into existence new histories with new initiations and endings. Engineering, medicine, social arts realize relationships that were unrealized in actual existence. Surely in their new context the latter are understood or known as they are not in isolation (Dewey, 1925, pp. 161–62).

Informed decision-making toward some desired end-in-view, the aim of the applied sciences, can come from the interaction of experience and understanding in application to real situations, with all their complexity. This twofold demand, for understanding of a range of ways in which situations can be seen, with the implication that these will offer some foresight about what might happen *and* with the presumption that these ways will conform in their nature to the demands of decision-making in a variety of ever-different situations, implies a range of general concepts which can be applied, with judgment, to the revision of methods and tactics by an involved actor. To achieve this end, a potentially useful theory must fit the substantive area of presumed application, it must be understandable to the actors concerned, and it must be sufficiently general to be appropriate to the number of contexts and situations that the domain of application implies (Glaser & Strauss, 1967, p. 237). The reality of the actor's world and his perceptions of its meaningfulness are the ultimate criteria of verification.

A point of view of this kind explains some of the appeal of L. M. Smith's work. Forms of explanation, and therefore forms of research and forms of theory, must be appropriate to the complexity of a subject matter and to the ends implicit in application of any understanding to that subject matter. The relevance of any particular form of explanation or theory is intrinsic to its area of application and is *not* a function of some externally imposed conception of what *should* be fitting. Theories of teaching should, as Gump suggests, reflect the reality of both the domain of phenomena that teachers work on and the needs of teachers for certain kinds of understanding. Perhaps, therefore, the best theory is the one that gives the most complete understanding rather than the one which offers the greatest number of reliable predictions and the greatest deference to canons of reliability.

It is not appropriate for this essay to attempt to exhaust this point in its application to the specific area of research into teaching and learning. However, two points do stand out and are worth asserting.

If no particular form of explanation, and in consequence no particular form of theory, is *a priori* preferable, there is no need to feel constrained to undertake any particular kind of research or seek any particular kind of end. L. M. Smith's cautious hesitancy about the form of his research is therefore quite unjustified. It might well be that grounded theory development along the lines suggested by Smith is immediately the most practical work that we might do, in that it should provide, in its thrust and conclusions, the context for all other theorizing.

The second point comes out of a reading of Glaser and Strauss's (1967) emphasis on invention as opposed to verification and quantification. As they argue, "the one canon for judging the usefulness of a theory is how it is generated" (p. 5). Good theory is the fruit of methods of theory development rather than of such external standards as reliability, methods of data collection, and certain expressions of logical adequacy. Attention to real phenomena, to the need for appropriate theory, and then to the ways in which explanation might be offered and verified seems to be the way that offers the most direct hope for useful and meaningful theory. An ordering of our tasks and priorities in this way should put the forms of theory and explanation into their proper relationship to needs, imply the standards of proof or verification that are required, and demand, at the same time, that our work has something to say.

Forms of Enquiry in Research into Teaching

"What Do Scientists Do?"

To this point, I have been arguing the importance of a number of methodological considerations without demonstrating in more than a passing way the necessary relevance of problems of this kind to the actual research that is being reported in the papers I have been discussing. I now want to attempt to tie these considerations down and show that they do bear on practical problems. I shall pick up the two themes I have been discussing, the phenomena we are addressing and the forms of theory-building, by using a framework suggested by Schwab's "What Do Scientists Do?" (1960). By applying Schwab's terms and relationships to the papers in *Theory and Research* and in this book, it should be possible to explore, in a specific way, what it is that research into teaching is doing.

Schwab's purpose in "What Do Scientists Do?" is to spell out, within a structure of a set of "decision-points," the finite number of methodological considerations and issues which control the initiation and development of all working scientific research. His starting point is the one I have argued from in the first parts of this essay: a working science is the result of an interaction between phenomena (a "subject-matter-in-fact") and the particular ways in which phenomena are seen ("principles of enquiry"). The results of this interaction are the data of a science (a "subject-matter-under-enquiry").

A subject-matter-under-enquiry is, in this view, the only thing that can be really accessible; phenomena are created out of a world by the imposition of broadly philosophical frames on things that exist only in the sense that they can refute, not form, the ways in which they are seen. The two problems for research into teaching, then, are how we can know what teaching and learning are, and, once we have them, what we can make of them. My presumption is that it is impossible to talk in any fruitful way about a research into teaching without addressing these problems.

Schwab's frame, organized as a set of six *decision-points*, permits the full range of methodological issues involved in the resolution of these problems to be pulled into a common structure. He argues that to pursue an enquiry, a scientist has to:

1. Invent or select a form of principle that will create a subject matter;
2. Make a judgment of the proposed principle in terms of its application to a concrete investigation of some presumed phenomenon;
3. Select among alternative sets of specific terms a particular language that gives some optimal validity and reliability;
4. Select a "stable" or a "fluid" mode of enquiry;
5. Select one phase of enquiry for repeated endeavor;
6. Make a personal decision in terms of consensus within a field about viable problems, in terms of existing technologies of enquiry, and in terms of feelings about personal virtuosity.

All of the decision-points and the problems they entail are relevant to a full investigation of our field; here I want only to explore points 1, 2, and 3.

The framework of assumptions about the nature of research that is the origin of these six decision-points is set out in Figure 10.1. A *subject-matter-in-fact* is a presumption about the nature of the world. A *subject-matter-under-enquiry* is a tightly organized and bounded thing representing an interaction between the results of the *phenomenal analysis* that produces any understanding we might have of a subject-matter-in-fact and the instruments of methodological analysis that are *principles of enquiry*. Principles—Schwab suggests six types (reductive, holistic, anti-principled, primitive, rational, and classificatory)—are reconstructions of the organizing frameworks that all scientists tend to use in their attempts to explain how things become the way they are.

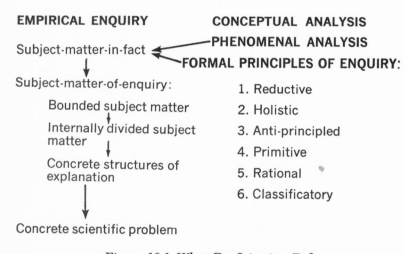

Figure 10.1 What Do Scientists Do?

A subject-matter-in-fact cannot, therefore, be explored through subject-matter-under-enquiry which is totally impregnated with both principles and presumptions about how things become the way they are. Distinct and separate methods of analysis, instruments of *phenomenal analysis*, are required to explore the full scope of any subject-matter-in-fact. As I have suggested, this function has been usefully served in much recent classroom research by philosophical analysis.

To be useful in the analysis of a specific research tradition, this structure of headings must be filled in. In theory a complete set of such headings should make possible an analysis of the full scope of a research tradition; such a map then becomes the basis for an analysis of what a research tradition is doing and for discussion of the theoretical possibilities remaining for investigation. It is not, except in the most formal sense, a substitute for invention or intensive empirical research.

Let us now turn to what seem to be the specific sets of issues that should concern research into teaching. One set will come under the heading of *phenomenal analysis,* the other under *methodological analysis* (principles of enquiry).

Phenomenal analysis. Most attempts within research in teaching to use techniques for phenomenal analysis are incomplete in an absolute sense, although complete enough in context inasmuch as they are intended to clear ground for a particular study. The relative success of the philosophical and other methods that have been used suggests that it might be useful to follow up the fuller sets of distinctions developed by philosophers and advocates of common sense for this problem area. There are more than enough such distinctions available to suggest that something approaching completeness might be possible.

Four general categories seem to emerge: (1) teaching actions, (2) forms of learning, (3) kinds of teaching acts, and (4) contexts of teaching acts. The first two of these categories, reflecting the concept of teaching as intentional and learning as end-in-view, are fundamental; but they need to be supplemented by the third and fourth categories, defining the pedagogic influences a teacher has at his command to effect his teaching intentions and the contexts in which teaching functions are exercised. The outline that follows briefly characterizes these categories and summarizes some ways of viewing their specifics.

1. *Teaching actions:* A number of attempts have been made to produce lists of the generic kinds of teaching actions. (See, e.g., Komisar, 1968; Jackson, 1964; Peters, 1957.) The simplest yet most serviceable categorization reflecting the kinds of intention brought to his task by the teacher is suggested by Komisar (1968, p. 180) and paraphrased here.

    a) The actions of a teacher directed to the production of intellectual acts within the classroom. The teacher may produce such acts by talking himself, or by causing his students to talk, or by causing other instruments, e.g., books or other technologies, to produce such acts.

b) The actions of a teacher directed at making his students "learningable." He moves to arouse interest, to motivate his students, to "reach" his students, to control them both supportively and punitively. In general, these are the actions of a teacher directed at the creation of both an environment and a state of mind which permits and supports learning.

c) The actions of a teacher which are intended to contribute directly to the student's learning. This class of actions is strictly pedagogic in intention and is directed at the fixing of learning or the practice of learned materials or techniques, rather than at processes of the type categorized as "intellectual acts." Drilling, revising, testing, and the like characterize this class of actions.

2. *Forms of learning:* A view of the role of learning within a study of teaching has been set out very generally in the first part of this essay. In the simplest terms it is necessary to answer the question "What is the teacher's intention?" to distinguish teaching from non-teaching acts and to distinguish different kinds of teaching acts themselves. "Learning" is therefore a necessary complement to "teaching" in the study of classroom process. Komisar (1966, 1967) and Beck (1968) suggest that the common distinctions within the concepts of learning and knowing, relative to teaching, fall into the following five classes:

a) Learning implying the acquisition and mastery of information in such a form that it can reasonably be said that a student knows something, that his knowledge is relatively permanent, and that in the course of some test of the knowledge a student can show that he has "got the idea."

b) Learning implying the acquisition of skills or behaviors; a student can perform on demand correctly or use behaviors to achieve the ends the behaviors are subordinated to.

c) Learning implying not only the correctness of the knowledge but some understanding of the conditions for use, the rules of appropriateness, and inclination to use knowledge in the appropriate way at the appropriate time.

d) Learning implying the self-conscious acceptance of knowledge and acts and a responsibility for them. The learner is committed to performing as well as he can, knows why he should perform, and is conscious both of the reasons for performance and the consequences of his failure to perform.

e) Learning in the sense that a student is moving to mastery or is concerned to learn ("learningability") without a presumption that any full command of the knowledge has been attained.

3. *Kinds of teaching acts:* Views of teaching differ in the emphasis they put on the ways in which the teacher uses himself and his talents to effect learning. Three such resources seem important (see Herbert, 1967; Hedegard, 1967):

a) Giving lessons.

b) Creating an environment.

c) Presentation of the teacher as a model.

4. *Contexts of teaching functions:* Again, views of teaching and learning differ in their perception of where, in time and physical location, the teacher exercises his instructional function. Three distinctions seem important;

a) Teaching is conducted within the time and space limits set by the formal designation of a lesson.

b) Teaching consists in all actions that a teacher might undertake within the classroom without the necessity of a lesson of any kind being in progress.

c) Teaching is conducted whenever a student and a teacher (or artifact) interact within the environment of the school.

Methodological analysis: principles of enquiry. Schwab's term "principle of enquiry" highlights the habitual assumptions and frames, implicit in all sciences, which transform naively perceived phenomena and naive questions into scientific problems. Thus, in the terms of one of Schwab's examples, the biologist who asks which of the virus strains causes distemper is implicitly deriving his notion of "cause," his ideas about the taxonomy of microorganisms, his conceptions of the relation of invaders to a body's health, and his conception of disease from his principles of enquiry. A principle *bounds* and *analyzes* a subject matter; it determines what elements of subject matter might be investigated and orders questions in an expectation of meaningful answers. Of course, the assertion that there are principles is an assumption, while the identification of any given array of principles is a reconstruction of the themes and strategies which *seem* to underlie both doctrinaire and habitual investigations of subject matters. Principles as such do not pervade actual thoughts about hypotheses or specific studies; but, once identified, they can be used to give insights that might tighten actual investigations or an investigator's feeling for the theoretical frameworks in which the fruits of research might be placed.

Any given principle can, of course, manifest itself in a number of guises according to the demands of a subject-matter-in-fact and the methodological traditions of a particular field. Skinner's behaviorism, for example, is a form of reductionism insofar as it searches for explanation in terms of the irreducible minimum under investigation; [9] but as applied in a specific research tradition, such an approach has to find its own appropriate terms. Thus, in classroom research, behaviorism manifests itself as a demand for investigation of the specific stimulus-response connections that need to be established by the teacher as instruments of instruction, or in terms of an analysis of the stimulus environment which the teacher does in fact present to his classes (see Skinner, 1968; Jahnke, 1967; Krasner & Ullman, 1965).

Schwab analyzes *principles of enquiry* in terms of six general classes,[10] which may be briefly characterized as follows:

1. *Reductive:* These principles rest on the assumption that things are as they are because of the basic elements that make them up. A scientific enquiry is, therefore, an investigation of these elements, and explanation is sought in their behavior. The *molecular reduction* characteristic of the social sciences sees these elements as the irreducible minimum of the subject matter under investigation, not as components of a different, i.e. *atomic,* order of phenomena.

2. *Holistic:* These principles rest on an assumption that a subject matter must be explained in terms of the combination of constituents that sets a particular subject matter apart from all others. Parts of the phenomena are sought but they are defined and seen to exist as analytic elements of the whole, not as elements which assembled make the whole.

3. *Anti-principled:* These principles rest on a rejection of "metaphysical" interpretations of phenomena and seek explanation in terms of simple and invariant relations between whole phenomena or consistent parts of the phenomena. The approach is illustrated most clearly in the classical antecedent-consequent view of causation in which explanation is defined in terms of stable antecedent-consequent connections and when there is no requirement of further meaningfulness of the laws established.

4. *Primitive:* These principles rest on a rejection of more formal and ideological approaches and emphasize, by implication, the simple *ad hoc* investigations of queries that flow from practical problems. As such, primitive principles are characteristic both of immature sciences and of all sciences at times when continuing acceptance of long-standing explanatory schemes seems of little use.

5. *Rational:* These principles rest on an assumption that explanation of phenomena is to be sought in terms of some larger determinative whole or in terms of some *ratio* (rationale) imposed from without. These external determinative structures may be either idealized forms such as mathematics or theoretical entities, such as Marxist social classes, which are seen as totally pervading the phenomena in question.

6. *Classificatory:* Classification and taxonomy do not represent principles as such, although in use they may become quasi principles. Methodologically, however, they must be seen as indispensable prerequisites to all more formally principled approaches.

What Is Classroom Research Doing?

These two sets of terms—for phenomenal and methodological analysis—should cover the topics and approaches to research on teaching. Theoretically, at least, the sets should offer a total map that points to the clusters of problems that a complete theory of teaching and learning might address itself to, and a set of the ways in which a theory or theories might present themselves. Obviously, however (and this qualification must be made in the same breath as these assertions), these categories are both second-level hypotheses and formal idealizations. They idealize a set of pure topics and forms that *might* be useful for categorizing and methodological theorizing without pointing to the particular forms of theory or terms that might be used in an actual investigation or theory.

These qualifications obviously affect the ways in which the uses of topics and forms of principle should be taken. The simplicity of the ideal model should not be expected, and the application of the categories to actual studies should be expected to be messy. Nevertheless, I will attempt to show that the application of these coordinates to the research reported here and in *Theory and Research* does make it possible to illuminate both what the work reported here has achieved and something of what remains to be done.

The simplest way to approach this task is to outline how the studies reported in the two sets of papers fall out in the schematic model after the most liberal reading of the thrusts seemingly implicit in each paper. I will present my reading and categorization first and comment later. In the outline, the two sets of papers are identified by the publication dates of the books: 1971 for this one; 1963 for *Theory and Research*.

Phenomenal Analysis:

1. Teaching Actions
   a) Acts directed to the production of intellectual phenomena:
      1971: ———
      1963: B. O. Smith, Meux, Aschner-Gallagher, Aschner-Wise, Shapiro
   b) Acts directed at making students "learningable":
      1971: Birkin, L. M. Smith, Gump, Adams
      1963: Hughes, Kohn, Leacock
   c) Acts directed pointedly at ensuring student learning:
      1971: Stanford studies, Ginther
      1963: Hughes, Aschner-Gallagher, Leacock

2. Forms of Learning
   a) Acquisition and mastery of information:
      1971: Birkin, Stanford studies, Ginther
      1963: Shapiro, Leacock
   b) Acquisition of social and intellectual skills and behaviors:
      1971: Ginther, L. M. Smith, Birkin
      1963: B. O. Smith, Leacock
   c) Acquisition of conditions of use:
      1971: ———
      1963: B. O. Smith
   d) Acquisition of self-conscious habits and a sense of responsibility:
      1971: ———
      1963: ———
   e) Movement to mastery and learningability:
      1971: Adams, L. M. Smith
      1963: Shapiro, Leacock
   Not classified: Meux, Aschner-Gallagher, Aschner-Wise, Kohn, Gump

3. Kinds of teaching acts
   a) Giving lessons:
      1971: Birkin, Adams, Stanford studies, Ginther
      1963: B. O. Smith, Meux, Hughes, Aschner-Wise, Shapiro
   b) Creating an environment:
      1971: L. M. Smith, Adams, Gump
      1963: Kohn, Leacock
   c) Presentation of the teacher as model:
      1971: ———
      1963: ———

4. Contexts of teaching acts
   a) Lesson:
      1971: Birkin, Stanford studies, Ginther
      1963: B. O. Smith, Meux, Hughes, Aschner-Gallagher, Aschner-Wise, Shapiro
   b) Classroom behavior:
      1971: L. M. Smith, Adams, Gump
      1963: Leacock

c) Within a school:
       1971: L. M. Smith (?)
       1963: ―――――

Principles of Enquiry (Methodological Analysis):

1. Reductive:
       1971: ―――――
       1963: ―――――
2. Holistic:
       1971: Gump
       1963: B. O. Smith, Meux, Aschner-Gallagher
3. Anti-principled:
       1971: Birkin, L. M. Smith, Stanford studies, Ginther
       1963: Hughes, Flanders, Medley & Mitzel
4. Primitive:
       1971: Adams
       1963: Aschner-Wise, Shapiro, Kohn, Leacock
5. Rational:
       1971: Gump (?)
       1963: ―――――
6. Classificatory:
       1971: Adams; less centrally: Stanford studies, Gump
       1963: B. O. Smith, Meux, Hughes, Aschner-Gallagher, Shapiro, Kohn

The multiplicity of interests and principles characteristic of the social sciences in general is evident in this schematization. More of the categories would, of course, be filled if a wider selection of studies were used for classification; Gump, for example, worked on the school as a community before turning to the classroom (Barker & Gump, 1964). However, some of the omissions (unfilled categories) are interesting and perhaps significant.

No studies in these collections address themselves to the form of learning we have called "acquisition of self-conscious habits and a sense of responsibility"; only B. O. Smith raises the possibility of exploring the learning of the "conditions of use" of the information and skills that are the predominant concern. Only L. M. Smith considers explicitly the school as a factor in classroom learning, and none of the studies of secondary classrooms look at the effects of the constant regrouping of students as they meet different teachers for different subjects. Perhaps more surprising, given the traditions of educational psychology and the vigorous parallel field of behavior modification [11] (of which teaching research should be seen as a possible subfield), none of these studies has attempted to apply reductive principles of enquiry.

All of these omissions are explicable, but one wonders whether they represent a kind of misunderstanding about what the phenomena of education are and the unwitting failure (so characteristic of educational research) to use parallel research modes. However, such considerations applied to what we are *not* doing are perhaps not helpful.

The shifts in emphasis between the Teachers College and OISE conferences are, conceivably, less interesting absolutely but more important in an appraisal of a research tradition.

One internal shift is quite marked: the OISE conference shows a developing emphasis on experimental and correlational studies couched within an anti-principled frame and a lessening emphasis on the kinds of descriptive and classificatory, holistic studies that were beginning to characterize classroom research.

At the same time there has been a shift away from studies of those teacher acts which are directed at the production of intellectual phenomena and a sharpening focus on teacher acts pointedly directed at the production of learning. Only hindsight would make a judgment about the meaning of this shift possible, although perhaps it is already possible to speculate on the implications of the deliberate retreat away from explanation that the anti-principled frame implies. A reading of Rosenshine's review can be, within the context of the argument I have attempted to develop in the second part of this chapter, less than satisfying. There is, however, another issue here which might make interpretation of this shifting emphasis possible. It might be worth while to attempt such an interpretation, albeit a pessimistic one, in the hope that I might be proven wrong.

Ginther reports the only truly experimental work in these two collections. He is interested in the effectiveness of two specific modes of teaching, both as teaching methods in the general sense and in terms of differential effects on students of certain kinds (ch. 6 above; see also Rippey, 1969). Thus he is searching for explanation both through the interaction of students as personality types with the teaching mode that is, indirectly, the fruit of the teacher, and also through a number of specific and immediate suggestions about the effectiveness of immediate procedures. He is not concerned with the reduction of all his phenomena to one formal set of terms or with any movement or manifestation of an ultimate end. His scientific principle is almost classically antecedent-consequent, as that approach is described by Schwab (1960, p. 10):

The world is seen as a web of partial uniformities whose separate strands— of invariant antecedent-consequent relations—are the only proper objects of enquiry. The webbing, itself, the frequent or invariant recurrence of N antecedent-consequent strands to constitute, e.g., a man or a swan, is treated as a locus of problems but not *as* a problem for enquiry.

Ginther goes after his scientific problem by an analogical extension of programmed instruction modes to classroom teaching; he constructs his two teacher modalities, "errorless" and "dialectical," which become, not teaching methods in a real world, but theoretically constructed, almost pure, forms of method, recognizable in the world but not of it. In this there is one of the best of the few examples within instructional research of the *theory-impregnated* experimentation that is characteristic of most sciences. In any long run Ginther's work would have the explanatory power of the theoretical structure at its center; hypotheses are truly predictable, and, if refuted, offer meaningful and theoretically interpretable results. Experiments are truly replicable and controllable. The analogical extension implicit in his whole thrust permits him to claim that his work is a true and meaningful extension of other related and parallel work.

However, this breakthrough is achieved at a certain potential cost. The confusion implicit in the earlier studies between the intellectual acts of the classroom and those acts which have a very specific pedagogical end is clarified, but at the expense of a study of intellectual acts. Feasibility and immediate scientific meaningfulness and precision are enhanced, but perhaps at the expense of an ultimate validity. Scientific verification becomes possible, but perhaps at the expense of invention.

These concerns are not, of course, directed at Ginther's work as such, but at a potential that is represented in the tradition that he is applying so skillfully and creatively to research into teaching. In an extreme form the problem is that suggested by the third of Schwab's decision-points: the potentially competing claims of reliability and validity as alternative formulations of idealized criteria of "success" in an enquiry.

For Schwab, *reliability* stands for concerns such as the extent to which the terms of a research program are free of ambiguity and vagueness, can be manipulated with precision and rigour, and can be replicated with uniform consequences. *Validity* stands for the extent to which the terms of a science approximate the presumed richness of phenomena and reflect meaningfully the range of primitive, but real, issues in the world that is a subject-matter-in-fact. Clearly, reliability and validity are not poles to one of which sole allegiance must be given; both concerns must be reflected in every enquiry. My emphasis in this paper has been exclusively directed toward an articulation of some of the components of validity insofar as it affects research into teaching; I would argue, of course, that an appropriate understanding of reliability is dependent on an acknowledgment of the issues posed by an understanding of validity. Yet I recognize that I have not solved, even rhetorically, the problems posed by the recognition of these two quite different issues. This lack of resolution is, in context, inevitable and conceivably appropriate. The danger lies in the resolution of this tension by the adoption of one or other of these absolute standards as *the* standard against which research must be tested. A preoccupation with reliability leads to one form of threat to a meaningful enquiry:

A subject-matter simplified in the interest of reliability is not simplified merely in thought. It is a genuine article, an artifact of the laboratory or field, created by controlling the conditions of enquiry. The facts ignored in conception are suppressed or held constant in fact. Otherwise, the reduction in validity would have no consequent increase in reliability.

Since this relatively invalid subject of enquiry does exist in those places where the scientist spends most of his time, it is easy for him to become habituated to thinking about his named subject ("learning," "society," "culture") only in the restricted terms of his research. It is almost as easy for him to come to believe in all sincerity that factors omitted in his created version of the subject but claimed by others to exist are products of those others' fancy or gullibility (Schwab, 1960, p. 19).

A parallel and equally distorted preoccupation with validity can lead to either vague or data-free theorizing or to rejection of the possibilities of even a relatively rigorous science as a way to understanding of the world.

These specters are not threatened by Ginther's paper, but by one reading, perhaps inappropriate, of the kind of research his work can represent. Gump makes this same point in the introduction to his paper before reporting his own quite different reliablist research. Obviously, too, classification and taxonomy offer no greater promise, and they pose the graver short-run and implict problem of exhaustion before anything is achieved because of the complexity of the end-in-view that is contained in the holistic premise. Reliability is a virtue well-argued in Travers' paper; simple and relatively valid enquiries offer success and data that later investigations of more complex phenomena can organize. Schwab makes this same point. However, we do need to defer at the same time to the problems posed by the criterion of validity and undertake analysis of our subject matter that is appropriate for our long run. The theorizing about teaching that is our task merely has to steer a middle course between the obstacles I have been attempting to raise; the intellectual problem is one of maintaining a sense of perspective.

Notes

Chapter One

MCCLELLAN

1. There are two obvious questions which I must try to avoid: I. Just how closely must a research situation approximate an ordinary class session if it is to fall within the boundaries of CR? II. What are the strengths and limitations of CR as contrasted with other forms of research? Concerning I: It seems clear that the "microteaching" situations established by Gage (1966) do fall comfortably within the boundaries of CR. On the other hand, an effort to measure the effect, say, of a one minute commercial on isolated viewers would not qualify for CR. The line lies somewhere between the two. Concerning II: I am totally skeptical of any claim to the effect that research or theory or models or scientific method can make "education" a profession, or schools interested in learning. Hence I am totally skeptical when I see such claims advanced for CR (McDonald, 1965). But there are two justifications for CR: Generally, any increase in knowledge, whatever its value or lack of it, is a good, worth pursuing until it overly conflicts with other goods. Specifically, since many of the practitioners of CR seem to be the type who, were they not pursuing CR, would be educational administrators or worse, CR can stand on the grounds of negative utilitarianism (Biddle, 1964).

2. I do not even mention the use of action-at-a-distance to *explain* what's going on, for it is unclear to me what explanatory principles are or could be appealed to in CR.

3. Grunbaum's discussion concludes with a statement which would seem to have implications for CR: "It is because no relations of absolute simultaneity *exist* to be measured that measurement cannot disclose them; it is not the mere failure of measurement to disclose them that con-

stitutes their nonexistence, much as [i.e., even though] that failure is *evidence* for their nonexistence."

4. I'm tempted to digress on the parallel between Aristotle's treatment of the moral problem of slavery and certain contemporary treatments of the moral problem of teaching: neither Aristotle nor, say, James Bryant Conant recognizes that the moral problem lies in *institutional* structure and not in individual conscience. But I resist that temptation.

5. One naturally thinks of Jean-Jacques Rousseau as advocating such a doctrine of individuality. Actually, I can find no evidence that Rousseau held that view; it seems closer to say that his theories assumed a single, unitary concept of *man* which all education ought to try to actualize. Perhaps the English Public School educators who were forced to distinguish the boys who could be flogged into righteousness from those who couldn't were on the trail of the doctrine of individuality (Bamford, 1960, pp. 108–113). Perhaps the clearest way to think about the doctrine of individuality is the analogy offered by Dr. Robert W. Fuller of the Battello Memorial Institute of Seattle. Fuller points out that in planning to optimize physical growth, one may consider diet variables independently (or almost so) of genetic variables: that is to say, an optimum diet does not have to treat each genetic variation as a unique problem. But when we talk of "actualizing," the unique potentialities of each should be fed; we have to speak of the individual nature of each child and what education can make of *that*. I'm still curious about the history of this revolutionary idea.

6. A very closely related field in which it became necessary (and, finally, possible) to distinguish form from frequency is transformational linguistics. For the argument, see Chomsky (1957, ch. 2, p. 17). An effort to treat cognitive rationality in teaching as a personality variable is found in Sprinthall, Whitely, and Mosher (1956).

7. Incidentally, this study brilliantly confirms some of the hypotheses about the "culture of the classroom" which B. O. Smith (1956) had formulated a decade earlier.

Chapter Four

ADAMS

1. The term "noninvolved" carries no overtones of censure or judgment. Operationally, noninvolved virtually meant manifested behavior which could legitimately be interpreted as not attending to the prevailing communication.

Chapter Six

GINTHER

1. My assumption here is that if you stopped a lecturer at any point and asked him what he expected from students, he would say, "To remember what I am telling them."

2. "Errorless" instruction by teachers, with overt responses required from pupils, has recently become popular in studies of learning in culturally depressed areas of U. S. cities.

3. Analyses of more than 100 studies were done by several students engaged by the Center for the Cooperative Study of Instruction during the time I was Director. A summary of these analyses, entitled "Fitting Research on Instruction into the Conceptual Model" (Rippey, 1965a), was presented by Robert M. Rippey as part of my symposium at the APA meeting in Chicago, September, 1965.

Chapter Eight

SMITH

1. The reference here is to conceptual definitions. For research purposes all concepts obviously require valid operational definitions. Although of obvious necessity, obtaining valid operations is an exceedingly difficult issue in methodology.

2. On an observational schedule our tentative operational definition of this concept involves a minimal two-step sequence: (1) teacher comment to an individual pupil, and (2) pupil perception or response indicating awareness.

3. This proposition has been elaborated more intensively to illustrate the additional complexities introduced by taking advantage of Jackson's (1960) conception of the structure of norms.

Chapter Ten

WESTBURY

1. This relegation of a question to a periphery of concern is not, of course, scientifically reprehensible and my assumptions about the focus and the margins of Smith's empirical interests are not meant to imply that I regard any such relegation as *a priori* significant or worth comment. It is an issue methodologically only when such bounding assumptions affect specific conclusions in such a way that they become subject to the possibilities of significant error, or become, by virtue of the considerations that are excluded, potentially trivial. I am, of course, by raising this point suggesting that this may be the case.

2. "The word 'teacher' is a dispositional term in the sense that under specifiable conditions—classroom, pupils, and so forth—the individual referred to as a teacher tends to behave in characteristic ways. He may explain something with the expectation that what he says will be remembered by the pupil; he may draw a diagram and point out certain features of it, emphasizing that these are to be remembered; or he may read from a book and ask the pupil to interpret the passage. When the teacher behaves in these and many other ways, we say he is teaching. To repeat, teaching thus conceived may be defined as a system of actions

directed to pupils. These actions are varied in form and content and they are related to the behavior of pupils, whose actions in turn are related to those of the teacher. From the execution of these actions and the interactions of teacher and pupil, learning occurs. . . . The theoretical conception of teaching we propose to present will include all the actions of teachers necessary to explain and predict the behavior of pupils and the occurrence of learning, though such explaining and predicting cannot be made from these actions alone" (B. O. Smith, 1961, pp. 90–91).

3. For a discussion of this notion see Schutz (1963), Winch (1958), and Grene (1966).

4. There is no obvious treatment of the methodological aspects of this problem. It is not raised explicitly, for example, in Natanson's (1963) important reader in the philosophy of the social sciences.

5. "Words are not (except in their own little corner) facts or things; we need, therefore, to prize them off the world, to hold them apart from and against it, so that we can realize their inadequacies and arbitrariness, and can relook at the world without blinkers" (Austin, 1961, p. 130).

6. Again Bruyn (1966) is most provocative.

7. The important and, for our field, critical emphasis of Glaser and Strauss (1967) on the *discovery* of grounded theory is not as yet one of our intuitive modes of thought. "Most writing on sociological method has been concerned with how accurate facts can be obtained and how theory can thereby be more rigorously tested. In this book we address ourselves to the equally important enterprise of *how the discovery of theory from data—systematically obtained and analyzed in social research—can be furthered.* We believe that the discovery of theory from data—which we call *grounded theory*—is a major task confronting sociology today, for, as we shall try to show, such a theory fits empirical situations, and is understandable to sociologists and laymen alike. Most important, it works—provides us with relevant predictions, explanations, interpretations, and applications" (p. 1).

8. Gump's work is as interesting in this sense as L. M. Smith's; it is often seen as atheoretical and bracketed with Smith's in thrust. I do not believe that this is so and would want to argue that it reflects both a right kind of theory and an explicit concern with invention. See Westbury (1969).

9. "It is presumably not possible to show that behavior as a whole is a function of the stimulating environment as a whole. A relation between terms as complex as these does not easily submit to analysis and may perhaps never be demonstrated. The environment enters into a description of behavior when it can be shown that a given part of behavior may be induced at will by a modification in part of the forces affecting the organism. Such a part of the environment . . . is traditionally called a *stimulus* and the correlated part of the behavior a *response*. Neither

term may be defined as to its essential properties without the other. For the observed relation between them, I shall use the term *reflex*. . . . So defined a reflex is not, of course, a theory. It is a fact. It is an analytical unit, which makes an investigation of behavior possible" (B. F. Skinner, quoted in Schwab, 1960, p. 5).

10. See Schwab (1960), pp. 2–13, for a complete discussion of these principles and a discussion of the subclasses of principle.

11. I.e., in the most generic sense. Krasner and Ullman (1966) illustrate the range of this field.

References

Ackerman, W. I. Teacher competence and pupil change. *Harvard educ. Rev.*, 1954, 24, 273–289.

Aiken, H. D. The aesthetic relevance of artists' intentions. In W. E. Kennick (Ed.), *Art and philosophy; Readings in aesthetics*. New York: St. Martin's, 1964. Pp. 403–412.

Allen, W. H. Research on film use: Class preparation. *A-V Comm. Rev.*, 1955, 3, 183–196.

Amidon, E. J., & Flanders, N. A. *The role of the teacher in the classroom*. Minneapolis: Association for Productive Teaching, 1967.

Amidon, E. J., & Hough, J. B. (Eds.). *Interaction analysis: Theory, research, and application*. Reading, Mass.: Addison-Wesley, 1967.

Amidon, E. J., & Simon, A. Teacher-pupil interaction. *Rev. educ. Res.*, 1965, 25, 130–139.

Anderson, H. H. The measurement of domination and of socially integrative behavior in teachers' contacts with children. *Child Developm.*, 1939, 10, 73–89.

Anscombe, G. E. M. *Intention*. (2nd ed.) Ithaca, N.Y.: Cornell Univ. Press, 1957.

Aschner, M. J. M. The analysis of verbal interaction in the classroom. In A. A. Bellack (Ed.), *Theory and research in teaching*. New York: Teachers College Press, 1963. Pp. 53–78.

Atkinson, J. W., & Litwin, G. H. Achievement motive and test anxiety as motive to approach success and motive to avoid failure. *J. abnorm. soc. Psychol.*, 1960, 60, 52–63.

Austin, J. L. A plea for excuses. In J. L. Austin, *Philosophical papers*. Oxford: Clarendon Press, 1961. Pp. 123–152.

Ausubel, D. P. *The psychology of meaningful verbal learning: An introduction to school learning*. New York: Grune & Stratton, 1963.

Axelrod, J., *et al. Teaching by discussion in the college program*. Chicago: The College, Univ. of Chicago, 1949.

Bales, R. F. *Interaction process analysis: A method for the study of small groups.* Cambridge, Mass.: Addison-Wesley, 1950.

Bamford, T. W. *Thomas Arnold.* London: Cresset Press, 1960.

Barker, R. G. (Ed.). *The stream of behavior: Explorations of its structure and content.* New York: Appleton-Century-Crofts, 1963.

Barker, R. G. Explorations in ecological psychology. *Amer. Psychologist,* 1965, 20, 1–14.

Barker, R. G. *Ecological psychology.* Stanford, Calif.: Stanford Univ. Press, 1968.

Barker, R. G., & Gump, P. V. (Eds.) *Big school, small school.* Stanford, Calif.: Stanford Univ. Press, 1964.

Barker, R. G., & Wright, H. F. *Midwest and its children: The psychological ecology of an American town.* Evanston, Ill.: Row, Peterson, 1954.

Beck, C. Knowing that, knowing how to, knowing to and knowing how. Unpublished paper, Ontario Institute for Studies in Education, 1968.

Bellack, A. A. (Ed.) *Theory and research in teaching.* New York: Teachers College Press, 1963.

Bellack, A. A., et al. *The language of the classroom: Meanings communicated in high school teaching.* New York: Institute of Psychological Research, Teachers Coll., Columbia Univ., 1965.

Bellack, A. A., et al. *The language of the classroom.* New York: Teachers College Press, 1966.

Bereiter, C. Multivariate analyses of the behavior and structure of groups and organizations. In R. B. Cattell (Ed.), *Handbook of multivariate experimental psychology.* Chicago: Rand McNally, 1966. Pp. 753–768.

Berlin, B. M. The relation of the learning experiences of students to certain structured learning situations. Unpublished doctoral dissertation, Univ. of Chicago, 1965.

Bernard, V. W.; Ottenberg, P.; & Redl, F. Dehumanization: A composite psychological defense in relation to modern war. In M. Schwebel (Ed.), *Behavioral science and human survival.* Palo Alto, Calif.: Science & Behavior Books, 1965. Pp. 64–82.

Bhushan, V. A study of the effectiveness of two methods of teaching elementary matrix algebra. Unpublished paper, Center for the Co-operative Study of Instruction, Univ. of Chicago, 1965.

Biddle, B. J. The integration of teacher effectiveness research. In B. J. Biddle & W. J. Ellena (Eds.), *Contemporary research on teacher effectiveness.* New York: Holt, Rinehart & Winston, 1964. Pp. 1–40.

Biddle, B. J. Methods and concepts in classroom research. *Rev. educ. Res.,* 1967, 37, 337–357.

Biddle, B. J., & Adams, R. S. *The analysis of classroom activities.* Columbia, Mo.: Univ. of Missouri, 1967.

Biddle, B. J.; Fraser, G. S.; & Jellison, J. M. (Eds.) Teacher role: Conceptions and behavior. In B. J. Biddle et al. (Eds.), *Essays on the social systems of education.* (Final Report, Proj. No. 5–0892, U. S. Office of Education.) Columbia, Mo.: Univ. of Missouri, 1965. Pp. 238–369.

Bormuth, J. R. Readability: A new approach. *Read. Res. Quart.*, 1966, 1, 79–132.

Boyd, R. D., & DeVault, M. V. The observation and recording of behavior. *Rev. educ. Res.*, 1966, 36, 529–551.

Brinton, J. E., & Danielson, W. A. A factor analysis of language elements affecting readability. *Journ. Quart.*, 1958, 35, 420–426.

Bruyn, S. T. H. *The human perspective in sociology: The methodology of participant observation.* Englewood Cliffs, N. J.: Prentice-Hall, 1966.

Buchler, J. *Nature and judgment.* New York: Columbia Univ. Press, 1955.

Campbell, W. J. Classroom practices. *New Zealand J. educ. Studies,* 1968, 3, 97–124.

Cattell, R. B. *Personality and motivation: Structure and measurement.* Yonkers-on-Hudson, N.Y.: World Book, 1957.

Cattell, R. B. (Ed.) *Handbook of multivariate experimental psychology.* Chicago: Rand McNally, 1966 (a).

Cattell, R. B. Multivariate behavioral research and the integrative challenge. *Multivariate behav. Res.*, 1966 (b), 1, 4–23.

Cattell, R. B., & Stice, G. F. Four formulae for selecting leaders on the basis of personality. *Human Relations,* 1954, 7, 493–507.

Chall, J. S. *Readability: An appraisal of research and applications.* Bureau of Educational Research Monographs, No. 34. Columbus: Ohio State Univ., 1958.

Chall, J. S., & Feldmann, S. C. *A study in depth of first grade reading: An analysis of the interactions of professed methods, teacher implementation, and child background.* (Coop. Res. Proj. No. 2728, U. S. Office of Education.) New York: The City College of the City Univ. of New York, 1966.

Chomsky, N. *Syntactic structures.* 's-Gravenhage: Mouton, 1957.

Coats, W. D. *Investigation and simulation of the relationships among selected classroom variables.* (Res. Proj. No. 6–8330, U. S. Office of Education.) Ann Arbor: Univ. of Michigan, 1966.

Cogan, M. L. Theory and design of a study of teacher-pupil interaction. *Harvard educ. Rev.*, 1956, 26, 315–42.

Cogan, M. L. The behavior of teachers and the productive behavior of their pupils: 1, "perception" analysis and 2, "trait" analysis. *J. exp. Educ.*, 1958, 27, 89–124.

Cogan, M. L. Research on the behavior of teachers: A new phase. *J. Tchr. Educ.*, 1963, 14, 238–243.

Combs, N. W. *The professional education of teachers: A perceptual view of teacher preparation.* Boston: Allyn & Bacon, 1965.

Committee of College and University Examiners. *Taxonomy of educational objectives. Handbook I: Cognitive domain.* B. S. Bloom (Ed.). New York: David McKay, 1956.

Committee of College and University Examiners. *Taxonomy of educational objectives. Handbook II: Affective domain.* D. R. Krathwohl, B. S. Bloom, & B. B. Masia (Eds.). New York: David McKay, 1964.

Conners, C. K., & Eisenberg, L. *The effect of teacher behavior on verbal intelligence in Operation Head Start children.* (Head Start Contract No. 510, U. S. Office of Economic Opportunity.) Baltimore: School of Medicine, Johns Hopkins Univ., 1966.

Cook, W. W.; Leeds, C. H.; & Callis, R. *Manual for the Minnesota Teacher Attitude Inventory.* New York: The Psychological Corp., 1951.

Cooley, W. W., & Lohnes, P. R. *Multivariate procedures for the behavioral sciences.* New York: Wiley, 1962.

Cronbach, L. J. The logic of experiments on discovery. In L. S. Shulman & E. R. Keislar (Eds.), *Learning by discovery: A critical analysis.* Chicago: Rand McNally, 1966. Pp. 77–92.

Crowder, N. A. Automatic tutoring by means of instrinsic programming. In E. Galanter (Ed.), *Automatic teaching: The state of the art.* New York: Wiley, 1959. Pp. 109–116.

Dahllöf, U. S., & Lundgren, U. P. *A project concerning macro-models for the curriculum process: A short presentation.* Project Compass 12, Göteborg, Sweden. The Institute of Education, Univ. of Göteborg, 1969.

Dale, E. A formula for predicting readability. *Educ. Res. Bull.,* 1948, 27, 37–54.

Dewey, J. *Experience and nature.* Chicago: Open Court, 1925.

Dewey, J. *How we think.* Boston: D. C. Heath, 1933.

Dollard, J., & Miller, N. E. *Personality and psychotherapy: An analysis in terms of learning, thinking, and culture.* New York: McGraw-Hill, 1950.

Eigen, L. The implications for research methodology of some behavioral studies in programmed instruction. Paper read at Conference on Programmed Instruction and Teaching Machines, Berlin, Germany, 1963.

Ennis, R. H. Operational definitions. *Amer. Educ. Res. J.,* 1964, 1, 183–201.

Fieldhouse, A. E. *A.C.E.R. silent reading tests.* Wellington: New Zealand Council for Educational Research, 1954.

Flanders, N. A. Teacher influence in the classroom. In A. A. Bellack (Ed.), *Theory and research in teaching.* New York: Teachers College Press, 1963. Pp. 37–52.

Flanders, N. A. Some relationships among teacher influence, pupil attitudes, and achievement. In B. J. Biddle & W. J. Ellena (Eds.), *Contemporary research on teacher effectiveness.* New York: Holt, Rinehart & Winston, 1964. Pp. 196–231.

Flanders, N. A. *Teacher influence, pupil attitudes, and achievement.* Cooperative Research Monograph No. 12. Washington, D. C.: U. S. Dept. of Health, Education and Welfare, Office of Education, 1965.

Flanders, N. A., *Analyzing classroom behavior.* Reading, Mass.: Addison-Wesley, 1970.

Flanders, N. A., & Simon, A., Teacher effectiveness. In R. L. Ebel (Ed.), *Encyclopedia of educational research.* (4th ed.) New York: Macmillan, 1969. Pp. 1423–1437.

Flesch, R. A new readability yardstick. *J. appl. Psychol.,* 1948, 32, 221–233.

Fortune, J. C. *The generality of presenting behaviors in teaching preschool children.* Unpublished paper, 1966.

Fortune, J. C. *A study of the generalities of presenting behaviors in teaching.* (Proj. No. 6–8468, U. S. Office of Education.) Memphis: Memphis State Univ., 1967.

Fortune, J. C.; Gage, N. L.; & Shutes, R. E. Generality of the ability to explain. Paper read at American Educational Research Assn., Chicago, February, 1966.

Fowler, B. D. Relations of teacher personality characteristics and attitudes to teacher-pupil rapport and emotional climate in the elementary classroom. Unpublished doctoral dissertation, Univ. of South Carolina, 1962.

Furst, N. F. The multiple languages of the classroom. Paper read at American Educational Research Assn., New York, 1967.

Gage, N. L. Explorations in teachers' perceptions of pupils. *J. Tchr. Educ.,* 1958, 9, 97–101.

Gage, N. L. Paradigms for research on teaching. In N. L. Gage (Ed.) *Handbook of research on teaching.* Chicago: Rand McNally, 1963. Pp. 94–141.

Gage, N. L. Research on cognitive aspects of teaching. In Association for Supervision and Curriculum Development, Seminar on Teaching, *The way teaching is.* Washington: National Education Assn., 1966. Pp. 29–44.

Gage, N. L. An analytical approach to research on instructional methods. Research Memorandum No. 2, Stanford Center for Research and Development in Teaching, Stanford Univ., 1967.

Gage, N. L. Teaching methods. Research Memorandum No. 33, Stanford Center for Research and Development in Teaching, Stanford Univ., 1968.

Gage, N. L., & Unruh, W. R. Theoretical formulations for research on teaching. *Rev. educ. Res.,* 1967, 37, 358–370.

Gallagher, J. J., & Aschner, M. J. A preliminary report on analyses of classroom interaction. *Merrill-Palmer Quart.* 1963, 9, 183–194.

Getzels, J. W., & Jackson, P. W. The teacher's personality and characteristics. In N. L. Gage (Ed.), *Handbook of research on teaching.* Chicago: Rand McNally, 1963. Pp. 506–582.

Ginther, J. R. Pedagogy rears its ugly head. *Elem. Sch. J.,* 1962, 62, 233–242.

Ginther, J. R. A conceptual model for analyzing instruction. In J. P. Lysaught (Ed.), *Programmed instruction in medical education.* Rochester, N. Y.: Rochester Clearinghouse, Univ. of Rochester, 1965. Pp. 43–54.

Glaser, B. G., & Strauss, A. L. *The discovery of grounded theory: Strategies for qualitative research.* Chicago: Aldine, 1967.

Gnagey, W. J. Effects on classmates of a deviant student's power and response to teacher-exerted control techniques. *J. educ. Psychol.,* 1960, 51, 1–8.

Grene, M. *The knower and the known.* New York: Basic Books, 1966.

Grunbaum, A. *Philosophical problems of space and time.* New York: Knopf, 1963.

Guilford, J. P. *Psychometric methods.* (2nd ed.) New York: McGraw-Hill, 1954.

Guilford, J. P. *The nature of human intelligence.* New York: McGraw-Hill, 1967.

Gump, P. V. *The classroom behavior setting: Its nature and relations to student behavior.* (Proj. No. 5–0334, U. S. Office of Education.) Oskaloosa, Kans.: Mid-West Psychological Field Station, Univ. of Kansas, 1967.

Gump, P. V., & Kounin, J. S. Issues raised by ecological and "classical" research efforts. *Merrill-Palmer Quart.*, 1960, 6, 145–152.

Harris, A. J., *et al. A continuation of the CRAFT project: Comparing reading approaches with disadvantaged urban Negro children in primary grades.* (Proj. No. 5–0570–2–12–1, U. S. Office of Education.) New York: Division of Teacher Education of the City Univ. of New York, 1968.

Harris, A. J., & Serwer, B. *Comparison of reading approaches in first grade teaching with disadvantaged children: The CRAFT project.* (Coop. Res. Proj. No. 2677, U. S. Office of Education.) New York: Research Foundation of the City Univ. of New York, 1966.

Hedegard, J. M. An overview of historical formulations. In L. Siegel (Ed.), *Instruction: Some contemporary viewpoints.* San Francisco: Chandler, 1967. Pp. 3–23.

Herbert, J. *A system for analyzing lessons.* New York: Teachers College Press, 1967.

Hiller, J. E.; Fisher, G.; & Kaess, W. A computer investigation of the characteristics of teacher lecturing behavior. Paper read at American Educational Research Assn., Chicago, February, 1968.

Holsti, O. R. Content analysis research in the social sciences. Paper read at I.B.M.–Texas A. and M. Conference on Computers in Humanistic Research, College Station, Texas, November, 1966.

Homans, G. C. *The human group.* New York: Harcourt, Brace, 1950.

Hovland, C. I., Lumsdaine, A. A., & Sheffield, F. D. *Experiments on mass communication.* Princeton, N. J.: Princeton Univ. Press, 1949.

Hughes, M. M. *Development of the means for the assessment of the quality of teaching in the elementary schools.* (Coop. Res. Proj. No. 353, U. S. Office of Education.) Salt Lake City: Univ. of Utah, 1959.

Hughes, M. M. Utah study of the assessment of teaching. In A. A. Bellack (Ed.), *Theory and research in teaching.* New York: Teachers College Press, 1963. Pp. 25–36.

Hull, C. L. Quantitative aspects of the evolution of concepts. *Psychol. Monogr.*, 1920, 28, No. I (Whole No. 123).

Hull, C. L. *Principles of behavior: An introduction to behavior theory.* New York: Appleton-Century, 1943.

Hutchinson, W. L. Creative and productive thinking in the classroom. Unpublished doctoral dissertation, Univ. of Utah, 1963.

Jackson, J. M. Structural characteristics of norms. In N. B. Henry (Ed.), *The dynamics of instructional groups.* 59th Yearb. of Nat. Soc. Stud. Educ. Chicago: Univ. of Chicago Press, 1960.

Jackson, P. W. The conceptualization of teaching. *Psychol. in the Schs.,* 1964, 1, 232–243.

Jackson, P. W. The way teaching is. In Association for Supervision and Curriculum Development, Seminar on Teaching, *The way teaching is.* Washington: National Education Assn., 1966. Pp. 7–27.

Jackson, P. W., & Belford, E. Educational objectives and the joys of teaching. *Sch. Rev.,* 1965, 73, 267–291.

Jahnke, J. C. A behavioral analysis of instruction. In L. Siegel (Ed.), *Instruction: Some contemporary viewpoints.* San Francisco: Chandler, 1967. Pp. 181–206.

Jayne, C. D. A study of the relationship between teaching procedures and educational outcomes. *J. exp. Educ.,* 1945, 14, 101–134.

Kaplan, A. *The conduct of inquiry.* San Francisco: Chandler, 1964.

Kaya, E., *et al.* Developing a theory of educational practice for the elementary school. Norwalk, Conn.: Board of Education, 1967.

Klare, G. R. *The measurement of readability.* Ames, Iowa: Iowa State Univ. Press, 1963.

Kliebard, H. M. The observation of classroom behavior. In Association for Supervision and Curriculum Development, Seminar on Teaching, *The way teaching is.* Washington: National Education Assn., 1966. Pp. 45–76.

Kohn, M. Analysis of two kindergarten settings. In A. A. Bellack (Ed.), *Theory and research in teaching.* New York: Teachers College Press, 1963. Pp. 102–111.

Komisar, B. P. The non-science of learning. *Sch. Rev.,* 1966, 74, 249–264.

Komisar, B. P. More on the concept of learning. In B. P. Komisar & C. B. J. Macmillan (Eds.), *Psychological concepts in education.* Chicago: Rand McNally, 1967. Pp. 211–223.

Komisar, B. P. Teaching: Act and enterprise. *Stud. Phil. & Educ.,* 1968, 6, 168–193.

Kounin, J. S.; Friesen, W. V.; & Norton, A. E. Managing emotionally disturbed children in regular classrooms. *J. educ. Psychol.,* 1966, 57, 1–13.

Kounin, J. S., & Gump, P. V. The "Ripple" effect in discipline. *Elem. Sch. J.,* 1958, 59, 158–162.

Kowatrakul, S. Some behaviors of elementary school children related to classroom activities and subject areas. *J. educ. Psychol.,* 1959, 50, 121–128.

Krasner, L., & Ullman, L. P. *Research in behavior modification.* New York: Holt, Rinehart & Winston, 1965.

LaShier, W. S. An analysis of certain aspects of the verbal behavior of student teachers of eighth grade students participating in a BSCS laboratory block. Paper read at National Science Teachers Assn., New York, April, 1966.

Leacock, E. Classroom processes study. In A. A. Bellack (Ed.), *Theory and research in teaching.* New York: Teachers College Press, 1963. Pp. 112–117.

Lewin, K.; Lippitt, R.; & White, R. Patterns of aggressive behavior in experimentally created "social climates." *J. Soc. Psychol.*, 1939, 10, 271–299.

Loban, W. *The language of elementary school children: A study of the use and control of language and the relationships among speaking, reading, writing and listening.* Champaign, Ill.: National Council of Teachers of English, 1963.

Lorge, I., & Solomon, H. Group and individual behavior in free-recall verbal learning. In J. H. Criswell, H. Solomon, & P. Suppes (Eds.), *Mathematical methods in small group processes.* Stanford: Stanford Univ. Press, 1962. Pp. 221–231.

Lumsdaine, A. A. Instruments and media of instruction. In N. L. Gage (Ed.), *Handbook of research on teaching.* Chicago: Rand McNally, 1963. Pp. 583–682.

MacMillan, C. J. B., & McClellan, J. E. Can and should means-ends reasoning be used in teaching? In C. J. B. MacMillan & T. W. Nelson (Eds.), *Concepts of teaching: Philosophical essays.* Chicago: Rand McNally, 1968. Pp. 119–150.

May, M. A., & Lumsdaine, A. A. *Learning from films.* New Haven, Conn.: Yale Univ. Press, 1958.

McCall, W. A.; Herring, J. P.; & Loftus, J. J. Measuring achievement in activity and control schools in New York City. *Teachers Coll. Rec.*, 1937–1938, 39, 423–432.

McDonald, F. J. The influence of learning theories on education: 1900–1950. In E. R. Hilgard (Ed.), *Theories of learning and instruction.* 63rd Yearb. of Nat. Soc. Stud. Educ. Chicago: Univ. of Chicago Press, 1964.

McDonald, F. J. Research on learning in school settings. Paper read at Midwest and Western Regional Conference on Educational Research, San Francisco, January, 1965.

Medley, D. M.; Impellitteri, J. T.; & Smith, L. H. *Coding teachers' verbal behavior in the classroom: A manual for users of OScAR 4v.* Report of the Office of Research and Evaluation. New York: Division of Teacher Education of the City Univ. of New York, n. d.

Medley, D. M., & Mitzel, H. E. A technique for measuring classroom behavior. *J. educ. Psychol.*, 1958, 49, 86–92.

Medley, D. M., & Mitzel, H. E. Some behavioral correlates of teacher effectiveness. *J. educ. Psychol.*, 1959, 50, 239–246.

Medley, D. M., & Mitzel, H. E. Measuring classroom behavior by systematic observation. In N. L. Gage (Ed.), *Handbook of research on teaching.* Chicago: Rand McNally, 1963 (a). Pp. 247–328.

Medley, D. M., & Mitzel, H. E. The scientific study of teacher behavior. In A. A. Bellack (Ed.), *Theory and research in teaching.* New York: Teachers College Press, 1963(b). Pp. 79–90.

Merton, R. K. *Social theory and social structure.* (Rev. ed.) Glencoe, Ill.: Free Press, 1957.

Meux, M. The evaluating operation in the classroom. In A. A. Bellack (Ed.), *Theory and research in teaching*. New York: Teachers College Press, 1963. Pp. 11–24.

Meux, M. O. Studies of learning in the school setting. *Rev. educ. Res.*, 1967, 37, 539–562.

Meux, M., & Smith, B. O. Logical dimensions of teaching behavior. In B. J. Biddle & W. J. Ellena (Eds.), *Contemporary research on teacher effectiveness*. New York: Holt, Rinehart & Winston, 1964. Pp. 127–164.

Miles, M. B. (Ed.) *Innovation in education*. New York: Teachers College Press, 1964.

Miller, G. L. An investigation of teaching behavior and pupil thinking. Unpublished doctoral dissertation, Univ. of Utah, 1964.

Miller, G. L. Collaborative teaching and pupil thinking. *J. Tchr. Educ.*, 1966, 17, 337–358.

Miller, N. E., & Dollard, J. *Social learning and imitation*. New Haven, Conn.: Yale Univ. Press, 1941.

Morrison, B. M. The reactions of internal and external children to patterns of teaching behavior. Unpublished doctoral dissertation, Univ. of Michigan, 1966.

Morsh, J. E. *Systematic observation of instructor behavior*. USAF Pers. Train. Res. Cent. Development Report, 1956, No. AFPTRC–TR–56–32.

Morsh, J. E., & Wilder, E. W. *Identifying the effective instructor: A review of the quantitative studies, 1900–1952*. USAF Pers. Train. Res. Cent. Res. Bull., 1954, No. AFPTRC–TR–54–44.

Mosteller, F., & Wallace, D. L. *Inference and disputed authorship: The Federalist*. Reading, Mass.: Addison-Wesley, 1964.

Natanson, M. (Ed.) *Philosophy of the social sciences*. New York: Random House, 1963.

Nuthall, G. A. Types of research on teaching. *New Zealand J. ed. Studies*, 1968, 3, 125–147.

Nuthall, G. A., & Lawrence, P. J. *Thinking in the classroom*. Wellington: New Zealand Council for Educational Research, 1966.

O'Donnell, R. C.; Griffin, W. J.; & Norris, R. C. *Syntax of kindergarten and elementary school children: A transformational analysis*. Champaign, Ill.: National Council of Teachers of English, 1967.

O'Leary, K. D., & Becker, W. C. Behavior modification of an adjustment class: A token reinforcement program. *Except. Child.*, 1967, 33, 637–642.

Orme, M. E. J., & Purnell, R. F. *Behavior modification and transfer in an out-of-control classroom*. Monograph No. 5. Cambridge: Center for Research and Development on Educational Differences, Harvard Univ., 1968.

Osgood, C. E.; Suci, G. J.; & Tannenbaum, P. H. *The measurement of meaning*. Urbana: Univ. of Illinois Press, 1957.

Overing, R. L. R., & Travers, R. M. W. Effect upon transfer of variations in training conditions. *J. educ. Psychol.*, 1966, 57, 179–188.

Overing, R. L. R., & Travers, R. M. W. Variation in the amount of irrelevant cues in training and test conditions and the effect upon transfer. *J. educ. Psychol.*, 1967, 58, 62–68.

Page, E. B. Grading essays by computer. *Phi Delta Kappan*, 1966, 47, 238–243.

Passmore, J. Explanation in everyday life, in science, and in history. In G. H. Nadel (Ed.), *Studies in the philosophy of history*. New York: Harper & Row, 1965.

Paton, J. M. Teaching people to think: Unresolved dilemma and instructional challenge. *J. educ. Thought*, 1967, 1, 15–30.

Perkins, H. V. The effect of climate and curriculum on group learning. *J. educ. Res.*, 1950, 44, 269–286.

Perkins, H. V. Teachers' and peers' perceptions of children's self-concepts. *Child develop.*, 1958, 29, 203–220.

Perkins, H. V. A procedure for assessing the classroom behavior of students and teachers. *Amer. educ. Res. J.*, 1964, 1, 249–260.

Perkins, H. V. Classroom behavior and under-achievement. *Amer. educ. Res. J.*, 1965, 2, 1–12.

Peters, R. S. What is an educational process? In R. S. Peters (Ed.), *The concept of education*. London: Routledge & Kegan Paul, 1967. Pp. 1–23.

Petrie, C. R., Jr. Informative speaking: A summary and bibliography of related research. *Speech Mon.*, 1963, 30, 79–92.

Porter, R. B., & Cattell, R. B. *Handbook for the IPAT children's personality questionnaire, "the CPQ."* Champaign, Ill.: Institute for Personality and Ability Testing, 1959.

Powell, E. R. Teacher behavior and pupil achievement. Paper read at American Educational Research Assn., Chicago, February, 1968.

Reichenberg-Hackett, W. Practices, attitudes and values in nursery group education. *Psychol. Rep.*, 1962, 10, 151–172.

Rippey, R. M. Fitting research on instruction into the conceptual model. Unpublished paper, Center for the Co-operative Study of Instruction, Univ. of Chicago, 1965 (a).

Rippey, R. M. A study of differences in achievement due to personality differences in four classroom environments. *Sch. Rev.*, 1965 (b), 73, 375–383.

Rippey, R. M. A contrast between the teacher and materials. *Sch. Rev.*, 1966, 74, 283–291.

Rippey, R. M. The Ginther model: Four dimensions of research on instruction. *Elem. Sch. J.*, 1969, 4, 215–223.

Rosenshine, B. Objectively measured behavioral predictors of teacher effectiveness in explaining. Unpublished doctoral dissertation, Stanford Univ., 1968.

Rothkopf, E. Z. Learning from written instructive materials: An exploration of the control of inspection behavior by test-like events. *Amer. educ. Res. J.*, 1966, 3, 241–249.

Ryans, D. G. *Characteristics of teachers*. Washington, D. C.: American Council on Education, 1960.

Ryans, D. G. *An information-system approach to theory of instruction with special reference to the teacher.* Santa Monica, Calif.: Systems Development Corp., 1963.

Schantz, B. M. B. An experimental study comparing the effects of verbal recall by children in direct and indirect teaching methods as a tool of measurement. Unpublished doctoral dissertation, Pennsylvania State Univ., 1963.

Scheffler, I. *The language of education.* Springfield, Ill.: Charles C Thomas, 1960.

Schutz, A. Common-sense and scientific interpretation of human action. In M. Natanson (Ed.), *Philosophy of the social sciences.* New York: Random House, 1963. Pp. 302–346.

Schwab, J. J. What do scientists do? *Behav. Sci.,* 1960, 5, 1–27.

Sears, P. S. *The effect of classroom conditions on the strength of achievement motive and work output of elementary school children.* (Coop. Res. Proj. No. OE 873, U. S. Office of Education.) Palo Alto, Calif.: Stanford Univ., 1963.

Shapiro, E. Study of children through observation of classroom behavior. In A. A. Bellack (Ed.), *Theory and research in teaching.* New York: Teachers College Press, 1963. Pp. 91–101.

Sheehan, T. J. The relationships between student's degree of freedom and success in higher mental process learning. Unpublished doctoral dissertation, Univ. of Chicago, 1965.

Siegel, L., *et al.* Student's thoughts during class: A criterion for educational research. *J. educ. Psychol.,* 1963, 54, 45–51.

Simon, A., & Boyer, G. E. (Eds.) *Mirrors for behavior: An anthology of classroom observation instruments.* Philadelphia: Research for Better Schools, Inc., 1967.

Skinner, B. F. Are theories of learning necessary? *Psychol. Rev.,* 1950, 57, 193–216.

Skinner, B. F. *The technology of teaching.* New York: Appleton-Century-Crofts, 1968.

Smith, B. O. On the anatomy of teaching. *J. Tchr. Educ.,* 1956, 7, 339–346.

Smith, B. O. A concept of teaching. *Teachers Coll. Rec.,* 1960, 61, 229–252.

Smith, B. O. A concept of teaching. In B. O. Smith & R. H. Ennis (Eds.), *Language and concepts in education.* Chicago: Rand McNally, 1961. Pp. 86–101.

Smith, B. O. Toward a theory of teaching. In A. A. Bellack (Ed.), *Theory and research in teaching.* New York: Teachers College Press, 1963 (a). Pp. 1–10.

Smith, B. O., *et al. A study of the logic of teaching.* (Coop. Res. Proj. No. 258, U. S. Office of Education.) Urbana: Bureau of Educational Research, Univ. of Illinois, 1963 (b).

Smith, L. M., & Brock, J. A. M. *"Go, Bug, Go!": Methodological issues in classroom observational research.* CEMREL Occasional Paper Series. No. 5. St. Ann, Mo.: Central Midwestern Regional Educational Laboratory, 1970.

Smith, L. M., & Geoffrey, W. *Teacher decision-making in an urban classroom.* (Coop. Res. Report No. S–048, U. S. Office of Education.) St. Louis: Graduate Institute of Education, Washington Univ., 1965.

Smith, L. M., & Geoffrey, W. *The complexities of an urban classroom.* New York: Holt, Rinehart & Winston, 1968.

Smith, L. M., & Hudgins, B. B. *Educational psychology: An application of social and behavioral theory.* New York: Knopf, 1964.

Snider, R. M. A project to study the nature of effective physics teaching. Unpublished doctoral dissertation, Cornell Univ., 1966.

Soar, R. S. *An integrative approach to classroom learning.* (Final Report, Public Health Service Grant No. 5–R11–MH 01096 & National Institute of Mental Health Grant No. 7–R11–MH 02045.) Philadelphia: Temple Univ., 1966.

Soar, R. S. Optimum teacher-pupil interaction for pupil growth. Paper read at American Educational Research Assn., Chicago, February, 1968.

Solomon, D.; Bezdek, W. E.; & Rosenberg, L. *Teaching styles and learning.* Chicago: Center for the Study of Liberal Education for Adults, 1963.

Solomon, D.; Bezdek, W. E.; & Rosenberg, L. Dimensions of teacher behavior. *J. exp. Educ.* 1964 (a), 33, 23–40.

Solomon, D.; Rosenberg, L.; & Bezdek, W. E. Teacher behavior and student learning. *J. educ. Psychol.,* 1964(b), 55, 23–30.

Spaulding, R. L. *Achievement, creativity, and self-concept correlates of teacher-pupil transactions in elementary school classrooms.* (Coop. Res. Proj. No. 1352, U. S. Office of Education.) Urbana: Univ. of Illinois, 1963.

Spearman, C. E. *The nature of "intelligence" and the principles of cognition.* London: Macmillan, 1923.

Sprinthall, N. A.; Whiteley, J. M.; & Mosher, R. L. A study of teacher effectiveness. *J. Tchr. Educ.,* 1966, 17, 93–106.

Stern, G. G., *et al. Methods in personality assessment.* Glencoe, Ill.: Free Press, 1956.

Stolurow, L. M., & Newman, J. R. A factoral analysis of objective features of printed language presumably related to reading difficulty. *J. educ. Res.,* 1959, 52, 243–251.

Stone, P. J., *et al. The general inquirer: A computer approach to content analysis.* Cambridge, Mass.: M.I.T. Press, 1966.

Strawson, P. F. On referring. *Mind,* 1950, 59, 320–344.

Swift, L. F. Explanation. In B. O. Smith & R. H. Ennis (Eds.), *Language and concepts in education.* Chicago: Rand McNally, 1961. Pp. 179–194.

Taba, H., & Elzey, F. F. Teaching strategies and thought processes. *Teachers Coll. Rec.,* 1964, 65, 524–534.

Taba, H.; Levine, S.; & Elzey, F. F. *Thinking in elementary school children.* (Coop. Res. Proj. No. 1574, U. S. Office of Education.) San Francisco: San Francisco State Coll., 1964.

Taylor, F. Human engineering and psychology. In S. Koch (Ed.), *Psychology: A study of a science.* Vol. 5. New York: McGraw-Hill, 1963. Pp. 831–907.

Thompson, G. R., & Bowers, N. C. Fourth grade achievement as related to creativity, intelligence, and teaching style. Paper read at American Educational Research Assn., Chicago, February, 1968.

Thyne, J. M. *The psychology of learning and techniques of teaching.* London: Univ. of London Press, 1963.

Torrance, E. P. *Preliminary manual for personal-social motivation inventory.* Research memorandum BER–63–3. Minneapolis: Bureau of Educational Research, Univ. of Minnesota, 1963.

Travers, R. M. W. Towards taking the fun out of building a theory of instruction. *Teachers Coll. Rec.,* 1966, 68, 49–59.

Travers, R. M. W. *Essentials of learning: An overview for students of education.* (2nd ed.) New York: Macmillan, 1967.

Travers, R. M. W., *et al. Research and theory related to audiovisual information transmission.* (Interim Report, Project No. 3–20–003, U. S. Office of Education.) Salt Lake City: Bureau of Educational Research, Univ. of Utah, 1964.

Tyler, R. W. *Constructing achievement tests.* Columbus, Ohio: Ohio State Univ., 1934.

Ulrich, R.; Stachnik, T.; & Mabry, J. *Control of human behavior.* Glenview, Ill.: Scott, Foresman, 1966.

Unruh, W. R. The modality and validity of cues to lecture effectiveness. Unpublished doctoral dissertation, Stanford Univ., 1967.

Videbeck, R. On the learning of norms in the classroom. In B. J. Biddle et al. (Eds.), *Essays on the social systems of education.* (Final Report, Proj. No. 5–0892, U. S. Office of Education.) Columbia, Mo.: Univ. of Missouri, 1965. Pp. 370–410.

Waimon, M. D., & Hermanowicz, H. J. A conceptual system for prospective teachers to study teaching behavior. Paper read at American Educational Research Assn., Chicago, February, 1965.

Wallen, N. E. *Relationships between teacher characteristics and student behavior: Part 3.* (Coop. Res. Proj. No. 2628, U. S. Office of Education.) Salt Lake City: Univ. of Utah, 1966.

Wallen, N. E., & Travers, R. M. W. Analysis and investigation of teaching methods. In N. L. Gage (Ed.), *Handbook of research on teaching.* Chicago: Rand McNally, 1963. Pp. 448–506.

Wallen, N. E., & Wodtke, K. H. *Relationships between teacher characteristics and student behavior: Part 1.* (Coop. Res. Proj. No. 1217, U. S. Office of Education.) Salt Lake City: Univ. of Utah, 1963.

Warburton, F. W.; Butcher, H. J.; & Forrest, G. M. Predicting student performance in a university department of education. *British J. educ. Psychol.,* 1963, 33, 68–79.

Wasik, B. H., *et al. Behavior modification with culturally deprived school children: Two case studies.* Durham, N. C.: Education Improvement Program, Duke Univ., 1968.

Weick, K. E. Systematic observational methods. In G. Lindzey & E. Aronson (Eds.), *Handbook of social psychology,* Vol. 2. Reading, Mass.: Addison-Wesley, 1968. Pp. 357–451.

Westbury, I. The reliability of measures of classroom behavior. *Ont. J. educ. Res.*, 1967, 10, 125–138.

Westbury, I. An investigation of some aspects of classroom communication. Unpublished doctoral dissertation, Univ. of Alberta, 1968.

Westbury, I. Essay-review of John Herbert, *A system for analyzing lessons. Sch. Rev.*, 1969, 77, 157–163.

White, M. G. *Toward reunion in philosophy.* Cambridge, Mass.: Harvard Univ. Press, 1956.

Winch, P. *The idea of a social science and its relation to philosophy.* London: Routledge & Kegan Paul, 1965.

Withall, J. Research tools: Observing and recording behavior. *Rev. educ. Res.*, 1960, 30, 496–512.

Zetterberg, H. L. *On theory and verification in sociology.* (3rd ed.) New York: Bedminster Press, 1965.

Author Index

References to tables and figures are printed in boldface type.

Subject Index

275